Conor C

An Argument Defending the Right of the Kingdom of Ireland (1645)

First Publication in English

with

Conor O'Mahony, the 1641 Rebellion and the Independence of Ireland

by

John Minahane

Aubane Historical Society
Aubane
Millstreet
Co. Cork

Also by John Minahane:

The Christian Druids:
on the filid or philosopher-poets of Ireland
Repr. Howth Free Press, Dublin 2008. 245 pages
(1st publication 1994) ISBN 0 9553163 0 8

The Contention of the Poets.
An Essay in Irish Intellectual History
Sanas Press, Dublin/Bratislava 2000. 71 pages
ISBN 0 9522582 4 2

Ladislav Novomesky: Slovak Spring
First English translation of poems and essays
by a leading 20th century Slovak poet
Belfast Historical and Educational Society, Belfast 2004. 166 pages
ISBN 1 872078 10 9

The Poems of Geoffrey O'Donoghue/
Dánta Shéafraidh Uí Dhonnchadha an Ghleanna
Aubane Historical Society, Aubane 2008. 304 pages
ISBN 9 781 903497 49 4

An Argument Defending the
Right of the Kingdom of Ireland
Conor O'Mahony
John Minahane
2010
ISBN **978-1-903497-63-0**
Aubane Historical Society

ORDERS: **jacklaneaubane@hotmail.com**

CONTENTS

INTRODUCTION

Conor O'Mahony's *Argument Defending the Right of the Kingdom of Ireland*, translated here from the Latin original, was the first book written in favour of Irish independence. It made a spectacular appearance in the great Irish political crisis of the 1640s. The author, a native of Muskerry, was a member of the Jesuit Order who had been educated in Spain and afterwards spent over 20 years in Portugal and the Azores.

O'Mahony was a scholastic theologian, an academic with many years' teaching experience, but his book about Ireland was much more than an academic exercise. To say that it caused controversy would be an understatement. How many other Irish books can we name which were banned in two countries, created an international scandal, and became a major issue in our domestic political conflicts? O'Mahony's *Argument* (in the original Latin *Disputatio Apologetica de Iure Regni Hiberniae*) achieved all that in the course of a few months in 1647, when it became publicly known in Portugal and Ireland.

The *Argument* is part of our buried political literature. It is one of a number of neglected books that shed light on the most extraordinary decade of Irish history, the 1640s. Not the least extraordinary thing about that time was the volume, intensity and variety of political argument that went on in three languages. There has never been anything like it before or since.

One would hardly suspect as much from what is being written currently. Not that 17th century Ireland is ignored. In fact, at the moment there's something of a boom in the production of academic books about Ireland in the 16th and 17th centuries, the most influential coming from the university presses of the neighbouring island, especially Oxford's. And in some of those books one can hear a distinct ring of confidence. The confidence of Nicholas Canny's *Making Ireland British*, published in Oxford in 2001, can perhaps be compared with the confidence of Richard Cox's *Hibernia Anglicana* ('English Ireland'), published in London in 1689. There's a sense that the troublesome western island is at long last ready for intellectual conquest.

We are assured that this is going to be done even-handedly. Professor S. J. Connolly, author of *Contested Island: Ireland 1460-1630* (published by Oxford University Press) deplores *"the tired and inaccurate gibe that history is written from the standpoint of the winners."* In his own work we are guaranteed *"deliberate changes of focus, with successive sections written from the perspectives of different social groups."* It is encouraging to be told that we won't be seeing everything through Oxford eyes. (I say "Oxford eyes" figuratively, because I think it will be acknowledged that for centuries Oxford was one of the power centres of England, although now it is anxious to see things from everybody's points of view.)

Professor Connolly must be given credit for his good intentions, and perhaps it is understandable if he isn't quite able to put them into practice. Although I have strained my reader's eye trying to find his different perspectives, I cannot detect them. Possibly the fault is mine. I do find changes of focus, but even Lord Macaulay managed some of those: there are moments, after all, in his *History of England* when he turns to the Gaels and condescends to describe how they viewed their bleak condition and prospects.

In every page of Professor Connolly's book I cannot help seeing a governing perspective which is not exposed to disturbance: the perspective of a 21st century Oxford-approved British Isles professor of history. But let's admit that this business of seeing things through other people's eyes is tricky. You can get in deep – and who wants to go too deep into the minds of the Gaels? Do that often enough, and your professional colleagues may start feeling that you aren't quite as reliable as they had supposed...

There's a reasonable limit to playing about with perspectives. It's a bit like time travel – what if you couldn't come back? And what if, while you're doing your cubist history of Ireland, those Gaelic perspectives somehow got mixed with and stuck onto your own?

But even making every allowance, one has to say that Irish history as it is currently written is in some ways a little bit strange. It seems odd, in this day and age, that anyone should write accounts of a great rebellion while ignoring extant records of what the rebels, using their own language, actually said. But this is what the general body of historians of the Irish rebellion of the 1640s do! (Breandán Ó Buachalla was a partial exception, but he proved the rule.)

The first-hand evidence of what the rebels said to one another is mainly in the form of poetry. This presents special difficulties, and our scholars are quick to admit defeat (complaining that the poems are "stylised", or whatever). But in other countries poetry of this kind would be carefully collected, edited, translated and commented on minutely, and historians writing about the period would draw upon it as a matter of course. The historians of other countries do not feel they can safely ignore the historical materials written in the language of the major population group. Most especially when that was the language of those who gave the decisive push to events.

In Ireland, for mysterious reasons, the case is different. Historians of the Irish rebellion appear to have special exemption from consulting historical records in the rebels' language. A historian can perfectly well specialise in the Irish rebellion without coming across Diarmaid Óg Ó Murchadha and his "Burn Cork" poem, or Gofraidh Óg Mac an Bhaird explaining that "the rule of the English bandits is at an end" (*Deireadh flaithis ag féin Gall*). Is it not just a tiny bit peculiar?

If anyone is seeking some sort of sketch of the poetry of the great rebellion, I can only recommend my own essay "Ireland's War Poets 1641-53" in *The Poems of Geoffrey O'Donoghue*. This is seriously incomplete: I have discovered other materials since, in particular two tremendous poems of incitement by Gofraidh Óg Mac an Bhaird. But that book will do for want of better. Two of the early agitational poems are printed there with translations and selections are given from two others. Readers will find them of interest if, indulging an idle curiosity, they would like to know what those involved in the Irish rebellion may have said to one another in their own language. For practitioners of the currently very curious trade of writing Irish history, possibly this will not be relevant...

*** ***

Ireland's political literature in Latin is not as badly neglected as Ireland's political literature in Irish. A Government-funded translation of the very valuable *Rinuccinian Commentary* is said to be appearing soon. And I gather there are scholars in Cork University who intend, in the course of the next few decades and depending on funding, to produce rounded editions of some of the important Latin books of Ireland. My blessings on their enterprise! About a dozen years ago they were seeking funding for a translation of Philip O'Sullivan Beare's *Compendium of the History of Catholic Ireland*. Sadly, they don't seem to have succeeded. They should try again.

One should mention too that Four Courts Press and others have produced a fair number of books on the Irish in 16th/17th/18th century

Europe. The outstanding work to date is Benjamin Hazard's biography of 'Hugh O'Neill's Archbishop' (who influenced many, Conor O'Mahony among them): *Faith and Patronage. The Political Career of Flaithrí Ó Maolchonaire*. This many-sided man's diplomatic, political and military activities in Europe are covered extremely well. On the other hand, his continuing, complex involvement with the order of professional poets (to which he belonged until about the age of thirty) is ignored. This is a serious fault, and the result is that Flaithrí Ó Maolchonaire still cannot be seen clearly and the part he played in the fates of Ireland has not been described properly. And yet, when one sees how much Hazard has managed to do in such an unfavourable historical culture, it would be churlish not to say that his book is admirable.

Even UCD isn't totally idle. We believe that somebody there is busy on this very book of O'Mahony's! And the best of luck to her! There is room for more than one edition of this challenging work, where the author is calling on all the powers of a well-trained, strong and audacious mind.

Conor O'Mahony's first language was Irish. But it was natural for him to write his book in Latin, the learned language of Europe and (for him more importantly) the medium of all Catholic priests. O'Mahony set out to change the course of events, to raise the stakes and push the Catholic political movement beyond its conservative aim of Catholic emancipation. When writing about contemporary Catholic politics he is anxious to be positive and enthusiastic, and his negative thoughts are expressed generally. But one senses that he feels the rebellion is in danger of losing its way. It needs new energy and a new clarity of purpose. And it needs to take that one last liberating step: to break the connection with England.

His political model was Portugal, which had rebelled in 1640, shaking off the rule of Spain and restoring its own national monarchy. The Irish rebellion of 1641 was not as clearcut as that. In the introductory essay I present a few thoughts on this complicated subject. But I should emphasise here that I think it was a real rebellion, and I don't believe that at any time it was a blind, uncontrolled, undisciplined, purely spontaneous outburst. There were excesses, but the movement did not go out of control. It was deliberately spread throughout the country; it was argued for and justified. There is evidence at all times of intelligent control and direction.

The strategic minds behind it must have been Northern Catholic bishops (and especially Ever MacMahon, then bishop of Down and

Connor and later of Clogher, who was Eoghan Ruadh O'Neill's principal agent in Ireland). They naturally had special interests and particular ambitions. But if we want to find what was really in at the core, there is no substitute for the testimony of the professional poets. I would recommend the reader to consult Gofraidh Óg Mac an Bhaird, but unfortunately his work has not been published. *Do dhúisgeadh gaisgeadh Gaoidheal* ("The valour of the Gaels has been awakened") is a memorable example of the agitational poetry produced to incite and spread the rebellion in its early months. We can safely assume that in late 1641 and the early months of 1642 poems like this were produced over all of Ireland, although few of them have been preserved. There are surviving examples ranging from Donegal to Cork.

Éire arís d'fhilleadh orthaibh,
fine Gaoidheal gníomharthaigh

That Ireland shall revert to them,
the dynamic race of Gaels

– this is the aim of the rebellion (Gofraidh Óg). Or as elegantly expressed by Pádraigín Haicéad, *aithbheódhadh glóire Gaoidheal*, "revival of the glory of the Gaels". The appropriate English word would be restoration. On this the agitational poets leave no room for doubt. The rebellion was about regaining continuity with Ireland as it had been for centuries down to recent times. It was about reinstating Gaelic and 'Gaelicised' proprietors and expelling planters. Or to express things negatively, it was about destroying what was seen as the perverse and short-lived attempt to make Ireland British.

This is what gave the rebellion its energy. It is what motivated the majority of the rebels (who were 'Gaelic and Gaelicised') and sustained them afterwards in their long resistance. However, from the very beginning their rebellion was set in a context of great complexity. Catholicism, to start with, was part of what had to be restored:

Do chongmháil cáigh na gcreideamh,
d'ísliughadh uilc eithreigeadh

To maintain everyone in his faith,
to defeat the heretics' villainy

(Gofraidh Óg) – but the easy-going Gaelic Church was now led by men who had learned a much more ambitious religion in the Spanish territories. And one had to take account of the Papacy, whose ambitions were not bounded by the shores of Ireland. And even within Ireland the Catholic community included more than the Gaels. The Old English Catholics, the town Catholics – by and large they had not supported the great rebellion of forty years earlier, led by Hugh O'Neill. It would be well to plan this one carefully to try and draw them in! And that in turn raised the question of strategic support for the English king, who was then involved in a major conflict with his Parliament, and who had been plotting an Irish palace coup to replace the pro-Parliamentarian government in Dublin.

From the outset the strategic minds who guided the rebellion took account of these issues, which are reflected in some of the agitational poems. (Diarmaid Óg Ó Murchadha, addressing Donough MacCarthy of Muskerry in his ferocious "Burn Cork" poem, acknowledges Muskerry's desire to defeat the Puritans and indicates support for the English king.) Their strategic prudence bore fruit: astonishingly, an all-Ireland centre of Catholic political union was established. This Catholic Confederation had its base in Kilkenny, the heart of "Old English" Ireland. When in Kilkenny everyone talked proper, and "*in all of the documents connected with the proceedings at Kilkenny from 1642 to 1649 there is not a trace of the use of the native language among the Irish and Pale gentry who constituted the Confederation,*" according to Paul Walsh – this is true, I believe, yet it may be highly misleading.

But the complexities didn't end there. With the Thirty Years War continuing and another war just begun between Spain and Portugal, the fate of Ireland became a strategic concern for the European powers. There would soon be political influences from France, Spain and the Papacy (foreshadowed in Uilliam Óg Mac an Bhaird's poem, where he mentions that all of Europe knows about Ireland's martyrdom). Into this maze at its most involved came Conor O'Mahony with his drastic proposal of Irish independence. He intended to make an impact and he did, though not altogether the impact he had desired.

The introductory essay is meant to put O'Mahony's book in the context of Irish intellectual and political history. It was completed before I learned of the death of Breandán Ó Buachalla. I have criticised some of his opinions fairly robustly, so I should say that I think *Aisling Ghéar* is a book of considerable value. Ó Buachalla was determined to show that Irish Jacobite culture was part of the stuff of history. He would not let this body of thinking be ignored, dismissed or trivialised, and rightly so. But in an attempt to give deeper foundations to what was founded deeply enough, he misread the literature and politics of the first half of the 17th century, and that is what concerns me here.

I have drawn on Philip O'Sullivan Beare's *Catholic History*, John Callaghan's *Vindication of the Catholics of Ireland,* the *Rinuccinian Commentary* and various poems. These sources help to explain the writing of O'Mahony's *Argument* and the reaction which it received. Translations from languages other than Italian (for which I depend on Annie Hutton) and from books other than the Bible (where I use the Douai-Rheims version, for reasons explained in *Additional Details*) are mine unless otherwise stated.

Many people have helped me to produce this book. I was given very considerable help by James W. Castellan of the O'Mahony Society, to whom hearty thanks. Thanks also to Conor Lynch, Peter Brooke, Silvia Ruppeldtová, Angela Clifford, Brian Earls, Claudia Bubenik, Brendan Clifford, Jack Lane, Mary Doyle. Those mentioned bear no responsibility for anything I have written, and some of them may have strong disagreements. I am grateful to the staffs of the National Library, Dublin; Royal Irish Academy, Dublin; Österreichische Nationalbibliothek, Vienna.

***   ***   ***   ***

The book is dedicated to Denis Hurley,
with best wishes for a safe return to Carbery.

***   ***   ***   ***

CONOR O'MAHONY, THE 1641 REBELLION AND THE INDEPENDENCE OF IRELAND

Conor O'Mahony's *Argument Defending the Right of the Kingdom of Ireland, on behalf of the Irish Catholics against the English Heretics*, is one of the most controversial political works ever written by an Irishman. In the 1640s it became an international scandal. King John IV of Portugal issued orders that it be suppressed and removed entirely from his kingdom. King Charles I of England, acting through his ambassador, complained about the book to the Pope. The parallel Catholic government of Ireland, the Confederate Council based in Kilkenny, had it publicly burned by the hangman.

The *Argument* also became an issue in Irish politics. There was a developing conflict between those Catholics who supported the Marquis of Ormond (King Charles's Viceroy) and the anti-Ormondites, led by General Eoghan Ruadh O'Neill. Eoghan Ruadh was accused of plotting to become the ruler of all Ireland, and O'Mahony's book was said to be his political manifesto. A determined propaganda campaign was waged against it. Father Peter Walsh, the most eloquent writer and speaker on the pro-Ormond Catholic side, preached no less than nine sermons condemning it in Saint Canice's Cathedral, Kilkenny. Other zealous opponents included the mayor and burgesses of Galway. They announced that they too wanted to burn O'Mahony's work, but (as of September 1647) despite their best efforts they had failed to obtain a copy. As soon as they managed to acquire one they would put it in a bonfire – along with the author, if they could find him!

In turn, the book was used as a lever in the developing conflict between the pro-Ormond Catholic faction and Rinuccini, the Papal Nuncio. Rinuccini was accused of doing nothing to suppress the outrageous volume and being in agreement with its message. When the parish priest of Athlone was found in possession of a copy, the Nuncio allegedly protected him from punishment. Among Rinuccini's accusers was the English ambassador at Rome, who (partly on the grounds of his alleged sympathy with "this barbarous and bloodthirsty book") attempted to have him recalled from Ireland.

So what does this notorious volume say? It proposes Irish independence. O'Mahony urges the Catholic Irish to shake off the rule of the kings of England and elect a king of their own. Presenting the arguments in favour of English rule in Ireland, he refutes them systematically. He then demands that the logical conclusion should be drawn: that the Irish should resume their interrupted national monarchy. The candidates exist, he says; there are outstanding leaders of ancient royal blood, and it only remains to choose the right one.

At the outset O'Mahony claims that his book will be clear and scholastic, i.e. on a level with the best political writing in contemporary Spain and Portugal. Whatever else may be said, I think his clarity will be granted.

THE O'MAHONYS OF MUSKERRY

Conor O'Mahony was born in 1594 in Muskerry, Co. Cork. I have not found documentary evidence of his personal family connections. A contemporary of his, the poet Geoffrey O'Donoghue in not too far distant Glenflesk, was interested in the O'Mahonys, whom fate had linked in many ways with the O'Donoghues. There's an O'Mahony genealogy in Geoffrey's handwriting. He could have told us exactly who Conor was, but he does not mention him.

There were three O'Mahony septs which were settled in West Muskerry, a few miles south of Macroom, in present-day Kilmichael and adjacent parishes. In the opinion of Canon John O'Mahony, historian of the clan, the controversial author came from one or other of these three. The septs were called Clann Finghín (also known as *Uí Mhathghamhna Ruadh*, "O'Mahony the Red"), Clann Conchubhair and Uí Floinn Luadh.

However, the main body of the O'Mahonys lived elsewhere. They were settled in the area known as Kinelmeaky, around the present-day town of Bandon; we may call them the O'Mahonys of Bandon for convenience. Earlier they had been located further to the west, around Bantry, but the expanding MacCarthys pushed most of them northwards and eastwards. In times of upheaval the O'Mahonys tended to take the opposite side to those who had displaced them. "The enemy of my enemy is my friend": this meant that the enemies of the MacCarthys tended to be friends of the O'Mahonys. Particularly close political friends were the Norman FitzGeralds or Geraldines, who had been the bane of the MacCarthys' lives for the previous four centuries.

In the great political crisis of the 1580s it would have been prudent for the O'Mahonys to have varied this pattern. But they didn't. The

O'Mahonys of Bandon took the side of Gerald, Earl of Desmond, who fought the religious war which his cousin had foisted upon him to the point of complete ruin. The Munster Geraldines were destroyed and their enormous landholdings confiscated, forming the basis of the Munster Plantation. Since the O'Mahonys had been reckless enough to end up on the wrong side, when the rebellion was put down they too were dispossessed and their lands were given to Phane Beecher, the first of the West Cork planters.

The O'Mahonys refused to accept this result as final. They sustained a guerilla war, at one point burning Beecher's main castle at Bandon. Before long they managed to regain their lands, if only temporarily. In the spectacular Munster rebellion of the autumn of 1598 the Plantation was destroyed in a couple of weeks, with the planters being chased back to England or to the safe towns of Cork, Kinsale and Youghal. The Bandon O'Mahonys were prominent in the uprising and they were among Hugh O'Neill's staunchest allies when he made his tour of Munster in 1600, following up his success in the south (it had actually been his agents who sparked off the uprising). They also showed tenacity during the years immediately following, when the rebellion was savagely put down by Mountjoy. As late as 1603 they were still holding out.

Ultimately, however, the O'Mahonys once again lost most of what they had briefly recovered. They kept a foothold in the Bandon area, but the Plantation was restored and strengthened. Richard Boyle, the most active and resourceful property-grabber in the country, bought the town of Bandon in 1613; King James gave it a charter and Boyle induced some extremely hard-working English Puritan families to settle there.

The O'Mahonys of Muskerry, on the other hand, did not suffer confiscation before Cromwellian times. In 1598, when everyone else rose in rebellion, presumably they did also; afterwards, when the uprising had been put down, many of them turn up in the lists of those who received pardons – Mountjoy was handing those out in thousands in 1601-2. On these terms they held onto their lands for another half-century. But one assumes that young Conor O'Mahony grew up with a sense of danger. He must have been very well aware of the history and reality of plantation, the fate of his Bandon kinsmen, and the ominous future for his own community and family.

As regards his early schooling, I have no information. But it is likely that he was sent to one of the best schools available in rural Ireland

– that is to say, the schools maintained by the professional poets, the *filidh*. While this may be presumed on general grounds, there is something in his book which supports the presumption. Pointing out that examples of the deposition and killing of kings may be found in Irish history, he says: "*Let (the Irish) consult their own histories, which I do not have to hand right now.*" Since he does in fact have the Latin writings on Irish history at his disposal, he can only mean the annals and other historical sources in the Irish language. There is an implication that, though he does not now have access to these writings because he is abroad, he has read them at a previous time. But anyone who was not himself a qualified poet or historian would be likely to consult the Irish manuscript sources only in poetry school.

O'Mahony may have been taught by Fear Feasa Ón Cháinte, the outstanding poet of West Cork. Fear Feasa was close to the O'Mahonys, or physically close at any rate: he lived in a place called Curravurdy north of Bandon, in or around the O'Mahonys' territory. On the other hand, there were schools run by the O'Daly poets in Muskerry and Kerry. For example, there was one at Nohoval-Daly in Slieve Luachra; there was another at Kilsarkon, near Castleisland. Maybe Conor O'Mahony attended one of these.

In the poetry school he would have been trained in literary Irish; he would also have learned Latin, read Ovid and Virgil, and been introduced to the elements of Gaelic law. Scattered here and there through his book one finds snatches of poetry, more than would normally appear in a scholastic work of this kind (though even a top theologian such as Francisco Suarez might now and then quote a few lines from the classics). These verses are mostly from Ovid, modified or adapted on occasion.

O'Mahony was bright, he was presumably a younger son of a prominent family, and the question arose of his higher education. But if he were to be sent to Oxford or Cambridge (where a number of Gaels do turn up in the records of the 16th century) or to the newly-established Trinity College in Dublin, he would have had to accept King James as head of the Christian Church in Ireland. The alternative was Spain.

ON DEPOSING AND KILLING KINGS

In the late 16th century increasing numbers of young men from the lordly and poetic families began traveling to France and above all to Spain for higher education as priests. By about 1600 there were so many of them that within a few years a series of Irish colleges were set up in Spain, Portugal and the Spanish Netherlands. Conor O'Mahony entered one of these, the newly-founded college in Seville, about 1614.

An advantage of exile was that it gave freedom from conventional thinking, a longer and wider perspective. The Spanish offered new ideas, different from the kind of ideas one might find among poets at home. A poet such as Tadhg Dall Ó hUigín might urge, say, an O'Rourke to attack the Saxons, and quite ferociously too. But this was a position without a principle. When addressing a Burke the same Tadhg Dall could say, as in his notorious poem *Fearann cloidhimh críoch Banbha* ('Ireland is swordland!'): I challenge anyone to show that there is such a thing as inheritance of Ireland, other than taking it by main force; no one has lawful claim; the right of this territory is to be under whoever has might; fathers do not bequeath it to their sons; it cannot be gained at all unless gained by force; and the Burkes have the very same right as the sons of Milesius, the original Gaels, namely the right of conquest.

It was not that the Irish language didn't have words for the good or authentic ruler (*firfhlaith*) and the bad ruler or usurper (*anfhlaith*). But what was it that made a ruler one or the other? For example, the North and the South would never agree on which Brian Boru was; the O'Mahonys and the MacCarthys might have had different views on the Earls of Desmond. At the very least, Francisco Suarez made this question of rightful and unrightful kingship fresh and interesting. In 1613 he produced a book which is a major source for Conor O'Mahony and like O'Mahony's *Argument* had the distinction of being banned in two capitals (*Defence of the Catholic and Apostolic Faith, against the Errors of the Anglican Sect*: published, Coimbra 1613; burnt, London and Paris 1614). This was a reply to none other than King James I of England, who had published a book of his own addressed to the Catholic kings of Europe (*A Premonition to All Most Mighty Monarchs*), attacking the idea that the Pope had the right to punish kings and ultimately to depose them.

A king was a direct representative or "*vice-regent*" of God, according to King James. God, he says elsewhere, has made the king "*a little god on earth*". Suarez denies this outright in clear and uncompromising language. Kingship, he says, is not derived directly from God, it was given to the king by the people. And what the people gave they did not give absolutely or unconditionally. In extreme cases, when a tyrant king so fundamentally threatens their welfare that they are forced to defend themselves, they may take back what they have given. *"If the king turns his just power into tyranny, abusing it to the manifest ruin of the state, the people can use their natural power to defend themselves, which they have never surrendered."*

In his *Premonition* King James denounced this doctrine and called it a licence for sedition, because it implied that the people could refuse the king obedience whenever they liked. Not so, Suarez says. The people, having surrendered the right of ruling to the king, cannot take back this right except in extraordinary circumstances. But the ultimate right of self-defence, the right to prevent their own ruin, remains with the people always. And if the king threatens their ruin they may use it.

The Pope as well as the people has the right to depose kings in extreme cases. Suarez quotes a long list of historical examples where Popes deposed or excommunicated kings, including English kings. (He does not seem to include Henry VIII or Elizabeth – it was prudent to leave that much to the reader!) The Pope is God's shepherd: he is obliged to take care of the Christian flock, and like any other shepherd he cannot do this effectively unless he has powers of coercion. Above all, he needs to have the power to coerce kings. The king is a general example, and a heretical or perverse king puts his subjects in great danger; hence the Pope can deprive such a king of his kingdom, in order to save his subjects from peril.

This was far from being an issue of pure theory. King James's immediate predecessor, Queen Elizabeth, had been declared deposed by the Pope. So had King Henry VIII. Their subjects were proclaimed to be free from all duties towards them, and it was understood – and in the case of the FitzGeralds' rebellion, explicitly said – that Catholics resisting them or trying to overthrow them had the Pope's approval. (Those Papal Bulls are included here: Conor O'Mahony quotes them triumphantly word for word.)

The doctrine which had provoked King James's outrage most of all was that a tyrant king could legitimately be killed by his subjects. With a calm scholastic precision Suarez expounds the technicalities of how this may be done. Mere private authority is not sufficient, but only the authority of the *respublica*, i.e. commonwealth, and then only when it is necessary for the commonwealth's self-preservation. However, if the tyrant has no title to kingship, if he is a mere intruder, then anyone may consider himself licensed to carry out the commonwealth's will, as in the famous case of the killing of Julius Caesar. If the tyrant was a legitimate king originally, then he may only be killed by due process. (There is some irony in seeing Suarez spell this out for King James, considering what was to happen to James's son Charles.)

And where did this leave King James himself? Clare Carroll, one of the few who has noticed Suarez's influence on the Irish, says that *"Suarez specifically argues for the deposition of the King of England as a tyrant because he is the sort of tyrant 'who leads his subjects into heresy'"*. But Suarez does no such thing! To call for King James's deposition would go against the aim of the exercise. It would make the repeated personal appeals to the king pointless, and especially the crowning appeal at the end. There Suarez points out that Henry VIII was at first named defender of the faith and wrote excellent books against the heretics, but afterwards he left a deplorable example to England and the world. But James might yet turn out the precise opposite! *"Though in the beginning he was led astray by seducers and wrote against the Catholic Church, yet afterwards once having understood the truth, why should he not become the Church's keenest proponent and the restorer of good order in England?"*

The fact is that James was seen by the Papacy in a different light from Henry VIII or Elizabeth. During his period of rule as King of Scotland (1583-1603) he had not persecuted his Catholic subjects. When he became king of England in 1603 the Pope sent him a message of congratulations, expressing the hope that James would maintain his policy of mildness towards the Catholics. Hopes were raised still further by the fact that James's first major political initiative was to make peace with Catholic Spain.

However, James as king of England was in a different context. After Guy Fawkes's escapade (1605) he decided he had to make sure of his Catholic subjects' loyalty. In 1606 an Oath of Allegiance was published which they were required to take. The Oath denied that the Pope had any power to depose the King of England or promote rebellion against him, and it also included a fierce denunciation of the doctrine that princes excommunicated by the Pope could be deposed or killed by their subjects. It was this which eventually brought James into controversy with Cardinal Bellarmine, who condemned the Oath on behalf of Rome, and Suarez. But these polemics did not mean that the Church of Rome had given up hope of the Stuarts.

Suarez distinctly says that he counts James among the legitimate kings. Even a heretical king was legitimate until he was formally deposed. There is a procedure to be gone through, Suarez explains. The king will first be reproved, and if he responds to correction he will not be deposed at all. And even if a heretical king refuses to concede to pressure, the question is still wide open, because it will involve a strategic judgment of how that particular people's good can best be served. It is up to the Pope to decide not only when but whether.

The following is as far as Suarez goes in his king-baiting: *"King James, who denies the Pope's jurisdiction over the universal Church and especially over kings, shows too little concern for the power of direction. In fact he fears the Pope's coercive power, and most especially when it is taken as far as the deprivation of kingdoms, because while persisting in his error, he does not believe himself secure in his own kingship if his subjects believe that the Pope has such a power. Therefore, in order that he may freely persist in his blindness he wants to deprive the Church of Christ of all remedy against heretical princes."* The implied threat contained here does not mean that James's deposition is being called for currently. Quite the contrary!

Suarez took infinite pains to keep the king of England hanging on the hook which James was sooner or later supposed to get himself off. It was believed that Protestantism was nearing the stage of moral collapse and that under sustained pressure a Stuart king might one day decide, if only in his own political self-interest, to become a Catholic.

Others had done so before. A Protestant king of France, Henry IV, faced with a major Catholic rebellion and unable to take the city of Paris, had made a rational calculation that his best hope of ruling his kingdom securely was to change his religion. He summed this up in the famous words, *"Paris is worth a Mass"*. And however much trouble the Popes might afterwards have with Gallican Catholicism, this was a triumph for Roman policy. The grand ambition, however unreal it seems now, was to repeat that success in England. Suarez, Bellarmine, the Pope, all had their eyes on the same goal – that the Stuart king would be brought to the point of saying: London is worth a Mass!

Strong echoes of Suarez can be found in Irish-Iberian published writings of the next few years in Irish, Spanish and Latin. "*As deimhin gurab éxamhoil nemhionand an modh ar ar thionnsgnadar cumhochta spioradálta agus teamporáltha, ar an ádhbhar gurab iad an pobal tug do na ríoghuibh, nó dhá shinnsearuibh, a bhfuil do chumhachtoibh aca anois* (It is certain that the spiritual and temporal powers originated in ways that are distinct and different, because it was the people who gave to the kings, or to their ancestors, whatever powers they possess now)", said Flaithrí Ó Maolchonaire (*Desiderius*, Louvain 1616). King James had been led astray by bad teachers in his youth, Aodh Mac Aingil said, but he was not as bad as those heretics in the main tradition of Luther and Calvin; James had declared in his *Premonition* that he accepted the three Creeds and the first Four General Councils and the Church Fathers of the first five centuries, and now one must pray that he would be given the grace to accept all the remainder (*Scáthán Shacramuinte na haithridhe*, Louvain 1618).

The Spanish-language *Brief Relation of the Present Persecution in Ireland*, published in Seville in 1619, puts this persecution in a long historical perspective. Ireland has a glorious history that is independent of England altogether. Even in pagan times, the author says, Ireland was famed for learning, because it was the source of the culture of those Druids and Bards who are mentioned by Caesar etc. Later on, when the country became Christianised, Columbanus and other Irish saints made a deep impression on Europe. Ireland is still committed to the Catholic religion, and the English, who are trying to destroy that religion, are responsible for its miseries. It is true that the island was donated to the kings of England by Pope Adrian IV, who happened to be an Englishman himself; but it was expressly on the condition that the Catholic religion would be safeguarded and promoted. The recent kings of England have broken this condition by trying to do the exact opposite.

In Philip O'Sullivan Beare's *Compendium of the History of Catholic Ireland*, published in Lisbon in 1621, a further step is taken: legal thinking is used to attack the basis of English rule in Ireland. The English kings had violated the conditions on which Pope Adrian granted Ireland to King Henry II, therefore the grant itself was null and void. This idea is developed at length and the legitimacy of English rule in Ireland is rejected totally. Certain concepts of the law of nations and natural law are basic to O'Sullivan's work; evidently Spanish legal theory was one of the sources that fed his thinking, and Suarez's *On the Laws* (published 1612) was the most ambitious recent work. Clare Carroll has argued that O'Sullivan shows an alignment of views with Suarez and that *On the Laws* was a fundamental book for the historian of Catholic Ireland.

O'MAHONY IN SEVILLE

Life at the Irish-Iberian colleges was insecure at the best of times. And one might have to live through an outbreak of plague: the city of Seville had one in 1616. Students at the Irish College there, established in 1612, were living hand-to-mouth. The college's founder was forced to go begging door-to-door to get funds to support it. There was a problem of accommodation, and the administration was done by laymen who were later accused of stealing the little that was there. They were even said to have taken the donkey which was used to fetch water.

In 1619 the college, in a wretched state, was taken over by the Jesuits. The new principal took a robust approach to everything, student discipline included. The students were required to sign a document surrendering not just their personal property but even all their rights as students! Before long *"the sweet harmony of the house was disturbed"* by one Conor O'Mahony. He was at this stage already a priest; he had been ordained in 1619 before completing his studies, but for the moment he was staying on as a student at the college of Seville. However, during the following year *"Fr Conor Mahony, a priest of the college, gave serious grounds for expelling him from the college; but having repented and asked for mercy, he was allowed to stay on; because mercy is very much characteristic of the superiors of this house and the students have never found it lacking".*

There are no details of what O'Mahony had done. Later on he would be described as "*of choleric temperament*", i.e. he was impulsive and inflammable. Francis Finegan suggests two possibilities: firstly, he may have resented the Jesuit takeover and shown it. This might have been influenced by his association with Archbishop Flaithrí Ó Maolchonaire, which he mentions without giving details. For years Ó Maolchonaire had been involved in conflicts with the Jesuits who were administering some of the Irish colleges in Spain, particularly in Salamanca. He accused them of being pro-English, over-interested in money, biased in favour of merchants' sons and despising lads from the Gaelic families. It might be that this had something to do with O'Mahony's troubles.

Another possibility is that he may have been involved in faction-fighting with English students at the main Jesuit college in Seville. *"Such student trouble was endemic where Irish and English were educated in close proximity."* Anyhow, he was forgiven. And the

Prodigal Son, it seems, became a favourite, because after a further year he himself was received into the Jesuit Order in Lisbon!

Richard Conway, the Jesuit principal, also took an active approach to fund-raising. He targeted Irish soldiers and Irish merchants, aiming to get them to donate a part of their pay or profits. Conway also requested and received from the Pope permission for the fishermen of Seville to fish on six successive Sundays, with the proceeds from sale of the catch going to the Irish college.

Connected with this fund-raising campaign was the Spanish-language booklet already mentioned, *A Brief Relation of the Present Persecution in Ireland*, published in 1619. Here it is emphasised that the students were being trained to take their part in a life-or-death struggle of the Catholics of Ireland, who are equated with the native people of the country. Sketches are given of Irish history, the ancient as well as the recent. Ireland is said to have been in a happy state until the coming of the English. The English kings had received Ireland as a donation from Pope Adrian the Fourth, but on condition that the Catholic religion would be sustained and promoted; however, the recent monarchs of England had done precisely the opposite (a very important point in Philip O'Sullivan's book published two years later, and in Conor O'Mahony's book also).

The text is given of some recent proclamations by King James and his Irish Viceroy. The latest of these, dated October 1, 1618, commanded the Irish who were living on the planted lands in Ulster to remove themselves by the first of May following. The author of the *Brief Relation* (probably Conway) responds with what may be the clearest accusation in the literature of the time that the English were attempting to wipe out the Gaelic Irish. *"With this cruel edict the heretics have finally...removed the mask of pretence which they have worn until now in their proceedings in Ireland and elsewhere, proclaiming that they are not persecuting us on grounds of religion, they are not oppressing us, and they are merely trying to govern us as vassals in peace and justice according to the laws of the kingdom.... In their inhumanity and insolence these heretics were capable of going to this extreme, attempting something that has never been seen or heard among Christians, however hostile they may have been to one another...openly and tyrannically (the English) want to aggrandize themselves with as many lands and estates as they can, dispossessing the natives who have held them for three thousand years, and little by little they want to confiscate their lands throughout all of Ireland so as to expand their own sect and nation, introducing them in place of the Catholic nation and religion, which by this means they want to extinguish completely."*

Conor O'Mahony certainly read this *Brief Relation*, which he cites in his own book (where he refers to it as the *Relation of Ireland*). Quite possibly he helped distribute the booklet, which seems to have circulated widely. O'Mahony's college principal is also said to have written a history of Ireland which the Jesuit authorities refused to allow to be printed, in case it embittered Catholic relations with King James. In that respect Conway was rather an untypical Jesuit, but quite a typical Irish-Iberian.

There were many Irish-Iberian brains at work on the question of Ireland. Their masterwork is Philip O'Sullivan's large and uncompromising book, published two years later with a dedication to Philip IV. It is called *Compendium of the History of Catholic Ireland*, and I would say it is also a compendium of the historical thinking of the leading Irish-Iberian clerics: O'Sullivan Beare was a gifted writer, but his originality shouldn't be overrated.

The *Compendium* was soon circulating in Ireland. (Within six years of its publication in Lisbon Conall MacGeoghagan cites it in his English translation of the *Annals of Clonmacnoise*.) One assumes, however, that its greatest influence was abroad and especially in Irish-Iberia. Eoghan Ruadh O'Neill for one would have read this *History of Catholic Ireland*, and it must have shaped his ideas of the Irish past and present.

That it shaped the ideas of Conor O'Mahony is certain. He looked on this book as the bible of Irish history. His *Argument* takes the *Catholic History* as its foundation and draws upon it constantly. O'Mahony found it inspiring, quite as the author intended. O'Sullivan Beare was consciously aiming to inspire Irish officers, Irish clerics and Spanish allies for the new Irish war that sooner or later must come. He himself was a soldier in an interlude between wars, waiting for his own war and trying to prepare for it by his writing.

Astonishingly, most of the book has never been translated. (A century ago Matthew Byrne translated the Elizabethan sections.) Here I will draw mainly on the untranslated fourth and final volume, covering two-thirds of the reign of King James. I want to give some idea of how Conor O'Mahony, taking his overview from O'Sullivan, would have viewed this period. The *Catholic History* had a clear perspective even on recent events, enabling O'Mahony to make sense of his own experience.

Apart from that, O'Sullivan happens to be the author of the only broad survey of these events and times from an Irish Catholic standpoint. Would it be so surprising if here and there he had something of interest to say? (One of the official historians, Toby Barnard, entrusted with O'Sullivan Beare for the new *Dictionary of National Biography*, goes so far as to declare that the *Compendium* is *"a valuable corrective to the histories written by the victors"*. He forgot to put in one word: '*potentially*'! At least Barnard tries to rise above the level of journalistic propaganda, which is more than can be said for Hiram Morgan, author of a trivialising, sneering piece on O'Sullivan Beare for the Royal Irish Academy's disappointing new *Dictionary of Irish Biography*.)

PHILIP O'SULLIVAN BEARE ON THE PARLIAMENT OF 1613

> "In my three previous tomes I have explained how Ireland suffered calamities in war and peace under King Henry VIII and Queen Elizabeth. Now I must describe the exquisite contrivances and hellish inventions, unheard of in all the world, with which the English of the time of King James tried to destroy the Catholics of Ireland...
>
> The sum total of persecution consisted in implementation of a five-point policy. Firstly, to get rid of all Catholic Irishmen who were seen to excel in military skill and courage (whether they were old or new inhabitants, of the Irish or the English faction), executing them or throwing them in prison or driving them into exile. Secondly, to ban all the others from the exercise of arms and the discipline of education and (with their priests expelled) from the rites of the Catholic religion. Thirdly, to despoil them of their traditional rents and fortunes, reduce them to paupers, and make them resign public offices and administration, with English and Scots supplied to fill their places. Fourthly, to compel them to frequent the heretics' churches and acknowledge their ceremonies and swear that King James was the head and prince of the Church in his own kingdoms. Fifthly, to introduce the most savage possible laws against priests, and their harbourers and protectors, in the kingdom's assembly, known as parliament."

King James was a great disappointment to Catholics, because at the beginning of his reign he had raised their hopes. *"When originally James Stuart, King of Scotland, on his accession to the throne of England concluded a treaty with the King of Spain, it seemed to all Catholic princes that he was and would remain a Catholic himself. O'Neill and Rory O'Donnell and the other great Irish lords grasped the opportunity to adorn the churches, rebuild the monasteries and restore the worship of God to its pristine state... But James, having arranged the affairs of England and Scotland with the aim of not leaving a single vestige of religion in those lands, turned all his thoughts and his energies towards stamping out the Faith in Ireland and eradicating Ireland's Catholics."*

In July 1605 James declared publicly that he had no intention of allowing liberty of conscience to Catholics, and he commanded all Jesuits, priests etc. on pain of severe penalties to leave Ireland by the tenth of December following. O'Sullivan quotes this edict in full, in Latin translation. (He also cites official documents in connection with points 2, 3 and 4 of the five-point programme referred to above.)

Following the edict there were individual acts of terror against priests and their protectors, but these had little effect. The English knew that they had to remove the other side's champions, O'Neill and O'Donnell above all. They decided to involve the Ulster lords in a bogus conspiracy directed by one of their own agents. The Baron of Howth, Christopher Saint Lawrence, was ordered *"to invite those lords to rebellion and give information to themselves about the conspiracy. Christopher (according to report) cunningly tricked O'Donnell and Maguire from the Irish faction, and the Baron of Delvin from the English faction, into rashly expressing their inmost thoughts. (He did not dare to sound out the veteran O'Neill, a man of the highest prudence.) On learning of this the English resolved to seize O'Neill, O'Donnell and the others. O'Neill, warned by some English friends, with O'Donnell and Maguire then crossed over into France."*

By this escape, now known as the the Flight of the Earls, the English were cheated of their prey. Nonetheless they kept up the pressure, capturing Cormac O'Neill and O'Kane by treachery and despatching them to the Tower of London. Young Cahir O'Doherty, brave but reckless, was provoked into a rebellion which was bloodily suppressed. The way was then open for a general dispossession of the main Ulster lords and a plantation of Ulster, which O'Sullivan deals with under point 3 above.

Much work had already been done by 1613, but the Catholics of Ireland still stood firm. To cut the ground right from under their feet was the purpose of the Irish Parliament which was convoked in that year.

"Parliament – the word comes from French – if properly celebrated, I understand to be an assembly or convention of the high nobility and governors of a kingdom or dominion, who are enabled to take decisions concerning the state and introduce laws; or it is a senate convoked to decide on secular affairs. Since the whole people in a mass cannot easily be brought together for the tabling of laws, necessity obliges that there be a limited number of men, called parliamentarians or senators, who are authorised to pass or repeal laws and have the power of acting for the entire commonwealth. (Considering, however, that normally the majority of them are laymen, if they take it upon themselves to deliberate on spiritual affairs they can no longer rightly be called a convention or council, senate or parliament; they are rather a gathering of criminals.)

In Ireland parliament is celebrated with great solemnity and all orders in numerous attendance, either according to old tradition accepted by the leading men, or following the examples of foreign peoples. The power of casting parliamentary votes was afforded to those laymen who were of suitably illustrious rank: those who in modern Latin are called **dominationes**, in Spanish **señores**, in Italian **seignori**, examples of the kind being dukes, marquesses, counts, viscounts and barons. Above all, however, the most ancient of Ireland's high nobility, called **tighearnaí**, who were established through a long succession of time before the English conquest, made use of this right, though they have afterwards been repudiated because the English do not inaugurate them. For me this single fact is an argument of no light weight in favour of judging all the parliaments celebrated by English princes in Ireland as entirely invalid, since those who ought most of all to be parliamentary participants are excluded."

The English intention was to introduce anti-Catholic laws in Ireland, similar to those which were in force in England. But how could this be done unless the Parliament had a Protestant majority?

"The viceroy therefore ordered the local English Protestant prefects to have parliamentary deputies elected in towns and districts where English and Scots, or Protestants of English origin, lived and had civil rights. The prefects obeyed his commands, and if as many as one single Englishman or heretic enjoyed municipal rights in a town or district, they spared no effort to have that individual nominated as deputy. Electors were intimidated with threats and fines, or again they were gulled with deceitful promises; sometimes attempts were made to bribe them; and on occasion a Catholic's name was struck out from the roll of representatives and that of a heretic inserted."

Despite all this, the figures still didn't add up.

> "Whenever the viceroy, comparing the numbers of parliamentary Catholics and heretics, found that the former were in the majority, he would hold occult parliaments with his counsellors, where he would establish new heretical cities and administrative units by decree, to supplement the number of heretic parliamentarians. Since he needed towns and villages to which he might grant civic rights, he bestowed some on the fields and open plains, having had three or four huts erected. Wanting heretic citizens for these otherwise deserted towns, he made citizens for them out of English barbers, quacks, scriveners, solicitors, court janitors, and the like human scum, who had never set eyes on those places in their lives."

In the end the mathematics were right and the parliament could be held. As for the Catholic parliamentarians, though they expected the worst they had little idea of what was concretely planned. Eventually they acquired a written draft of the proposed new anti-Catholic law. This stated that all Catholic clergy had to be out of the kingdom within forty days, no others were ever to enter, and no person was to send his son to study abroad, or give any assistance whatever to anyone doing so. There were verbal reports, not confirmed in writing, of other anti-Catholic or anti-Irish measures to be tabled. *"Our parliamentarians decided they would resist staunchly, and if necessary be ready even to die."*

In May 1613 the Parliament opened. The assembly hall was in Dublin Castle, which was ringed by soldiers, creating an atmosphere of intimidation.

> "One of three royal judges launched into a speech of tedious length, praising an English knight called John Davies, a most obstinate heretic and bitter enemy of the Catholics and of all Ireland."

He finished by proposing Davies as Speaker of the Lower House, and uproar followed. Eventually *"a grave Irish knight"* rose to say that before any such election could take place the representatives of the false boroughs must be removed from parliament. The other side responded by calling on all supporters of John Davies to go next door for counting, and they left the room.

Finding themselves alone, the Catholics proceeded to elect Sir John Everard as Speaker, and he sat in the Speaker's chair. When the Protestants returned they demanded that he should surrender the chair to Davies. Everard replied that he had been elected Speaker by legitimate parliamentarians, whereas the Protestant candidate could not say the same.

> "Nevertheless, the heretics placed John Davies in his lap and on his knees, but our parliamentarians pulled him off. The Protestants were trying with might and main to dislodge Everard from the chair, while the Catholics tried to hold him there. With all the pulling and hauling Everard's robe was torn and he himself was flung to the ground. A few punches were landed on either side, allegedly. Things were close to the point where swords would have been drawn."

At that juncture the Catholics withdrew from parliament. Next day, when summoned to re-attend by the viceroy, they complained about the intimidating presence of soldiers and the violence to which Everard had been subjected by illegitimate intruders, who should not have been in parliament at all. They maintained their protest and refused to return.

The Catholic parliamentarians then presented a petition to the viceroy, which O'Sullivan gives in Latin translation. *"Neither by force nor persuasion can we ever be made to deviate a nail's-breadth from our religion."* Force, they pointed out, had been tried during the reigns of Henry VIII and Elizabeth, to no avail. The Catholics had hoped much from the clemency and humanity of King James, but instead they found that the king's ministers were reviving old statutes and other means of oppression. With heavy fines and impositions of various kinds they were being pauperised. Their sons were denied education abroad and they themselves were denied public offices – they could not so much as be justices of the peace! The prefectures of towns and cities were being taken from them and given to Protestants. Even Catholic tradesmen and craftsmen were suffering cruel exactions. But all of this would never deter them from their faith. And since Catholics were willing *"to give all due homage to James, our supreme king, without flattery, deceit or treachery, or conspiracy against his crown and sceptre"*, such oppression was absurd as well as futile.

> "Men of different ethnic groups have gathered in this parliament. Some of us are Irishmen alike by birthplace and ethnic stock; others by birthplace only, not by ethnic group; others again, conversely, by ethnic group, not by birthplace; and others finally neither by birthplace nor by ethnic origin, but by place of habitation. These differences of ethnic stock, birthplace, habitation, customs, mentality, are all dissolved and made one in this much at least, that they obey and submit to one supreme prince. And no one should doubt that authentic homage and

obedience can co-exist with diversity of religion, so far as our own ancient creed is concerned. In the same way as the natural body composed of many heterogeneous and dissimilar parts, flesh, bones, cartilage, muscles, nerves, is all together constructed, moved and governed, with the natural form, animated by the spirit, ruling over all its parts; so also the political body of the commonwealth, consisting of its various nations, which at this time differ in the idea and form of religion, may be ruled by one form of civil obedience, in no way feigned, under one sceptre of the King's crown, and in this way be adorned and increased."

This plea for a pluralist Ireland made no impression on Arthur Chichester, *"the most excellent viceroy"* to whom it was addressed. However, the parliament was stymied. It was not thought possible to proceed when such a large body of parliamentarians remained absent.

Did the King actually know what his Irish ministers were doing? Had he sanctioned their anti-Catholic policy? The Catholic parliamentarians believed that he hadn't, and they sent a delegation to London to present their complaints. King James at first received the delegates with apparent kindness, and four judges were appointed to go to Ireland and investigate the complaints. But in February 1614 James issued a warning to the complainants. They had presumed upon his mercy, he said, instead of receiving it in a spirit of gratitude; now they were pressing their complaints further and even attacking his viceroy. Let them know that the viceroy had his full support and confidence and was to be obeyed!

A dramatic confrontation followed between the king and the Irish Catholic barons. James attempted to crush them with a public rebuke at the English Parliament on April 21, 1614.

"You delegates from Ireland, I do not know how you have the audacity to appear in my presence, when you and yours are completely alienated in spirit from my religion and from me, and you are the most obstinate Papists... I will show that you are perfidious, false, and not true or integral subjects, but only half-subjects, or not even half. For while man consists of body and soul, you devote the entire soul, the nobler part, to the Pope, and to me you concede only the body, and not even that entirely; rather you divide it between me and the king of Spain, serving him with the body in arms, while leaving me the unarmed, naked, feeble, useless remainder."

This was too much for the baron of Delvin. Falling to his knees, he interrupted the king, saying that always he had been entirely faithful and ready to defend the realm, and he desired no more than the chance to be faithful to the king and at the same time faithful to God. James told him to be silent and continued his speech.

> "What reason can you devise, or why do you think that the government of souls was entrusted by God to the Pope? I declare before God, if by daily reading, frequent discussion, conversation with the most learned men and the most intense effort of thought, I became convinced that the Pope was Christ's Vicar on earth and that he and his predecessors rightfully claimed the authority which Christ delegated to Peter, then I would not only adopt his religion and follow its dogmas, but supposing I were the subject of a king who was hostile to the Papist religion, I would even kill my king if the Pope were so to command me. But far from it being the case that the Pope has the authority mandated to Peter or is entitled to govern or give precepts to kings, it is the height of stupidity and ignorance for you to believe this, gentlemen from Ireland!...
>
> In Rome you have Peter Lombard, whom you call bishop and doctor, and in Ireland you have the Jesuit Holywood, and they persuade you to send your sons to be educated in colleges overseas, so that afterwards they can return and set the whole kingdom in agitation, confirming you in your original obstinacy and calling you to conspiracies and rebellion, and confounding top and bottom by the Papal decrees that they carry round. I would have every right to punish this new and unheard-of crime, even with the avenging sword. But I have always condemned cruelty in other princes and I cannot approve it in myself. I do not thirst for my subjects' blood, I desire only their peace and prosperity. And so I have decided to reprimand you for your faults and your misdeeds, your own and those of the Irish generally, and to reveal to you my considered intention. I command that all Irishmen shall observe the and maintain the laws enacted in England in the second year of Queen Elizabeth's reign (1559) and whatever others are found to be necessary to eradicate the Papist religion, which until now you have stubbornly professed, perversely opposing my will. You are to receive these laws in the parliament where my good viceroy, who is here present and against whom you have falsely complained, along with others whom I shall designate, will preside."

With this King James concluded his performance, but an Irish baron was bold enough to deny him the last word. Christopher Nugent spoke up firmly, saying that laws such as these had never succeeded and never could succeed in Ireland. He begged the king to refrain: leave well enough alone and the whole kingdom would be tranquil and flourish.

Immediately senior members of the government and church of England were on their feet, demanding that Christopher be declared a traitor and sent to the Tower. Others spoke up for him, including Chichester the viceroy, who said he was a rash but loyal young man. The parliament was dismissed, and a few days later King James re-issued that recurring edict of his to the effect that Jesuits, etc. should be out of Ireland before the end of September.

The king apparently ruled that a few of the bogus parliamentarians had not been validly elected. But he now demanded that the Irish parliament should resume, with Sir John Davies as Speaker. The Catholic parliamentarians proposed a trade. They were ready to forgive the injuries they had suffered; they no longer wished to make complaints against the viceroy or other officials. But they could never agree to the proscription of Catholic priests. On the sole condition that parliament was not to deal with any religious issues, they were even prepared to accept Davies as Speaker and to tolerate the presence of the illegitimate parliamentarians in their midst.

> "Astonished by their response and even afraid that there would be a general Irish rebellion, the king dismissed our delegates with the order that they were to hold a parliament, where for the moment there would be no discussion of religion, but stabilising measures would be taken which pertained to the public benefit."

THE SPLIT IN THE IRISH CATHOLIC CHURCH

And now we come to the most revealing part of the story. I will give in full O'Sullivans's Chapter 8 of this section, and the gist of his Chapter 9. What they show is a political split of major importance in the Irish Catholic Church.

> *"What Was Done In The Irish Parliament*
>
> The delegates returned to Ireland with the viceroy and made haste to hold the parliament, as the king had commanded. In this assembly the Catholic senators accepted as colleagues not only those illegitimate senators whom the king had confirmed, but even those whom he had invalidated. They wished to be seen to obey the king's orders and to show that they were mindful of the privilege which the king had granted them, that the issue of religion would not be discussed. Firstly,

however, they made a public declaration that they were doing this without prejudice and on the proviso that the issue of religious controversy would not be raised. They were not saying that the illegitimate senators or Sir John Davies had been ascertained to be legitimate and were now judged or pronounced to be true senators. If the issue of religion were raised, they would denounce these senators as illegitimate and would not consent to their presence, nor would they accept their decrees as valid or hold a parliament along with them. And on this basis our deputies did indeed hold a parliament with those heretics; even if nothing plainly against the Faith was decided there, nothing pious or religious was done there either. The king who had suffered religion not to be dealt with in parliament was voted an enormous sum of money. The properties of O'Neill, O'Donnell and other Catholics were declared by the heretics to be forfeit to the treasury; the Catholic senators remained silent, confirming the proscription by their tacit assent.

But surely that proscription or confiscation should have been opposed by Catholic parliamentarians? The opinion of our clergy was divided on this matter. The worse part overcame the better, because the opinion which prevailed was that in the conditions of the time Catholic parliamentarians could not resist the proscription. Those lords had already been deprived of their holdings, which were occupied by the king, and nothing could obviate the proscription, nor could the proprietors be restored, since it was believed that this could not be done except by the king's favour or by force of arms; and therefore it was more prudent to cooperate with the king, so that he would be milder towards the Catholics. If they had not been persuaded by this faction of the clergy, the Catholic parliamentarians would have tried to obstruct the proscription, as the other faction of the clergy maintained they should.

The Archbishop of Tuam's Letter Against The Proscription

Flaithrí Ó Maolchonaire, an Irishman, Franciscan monk and Archbishop of Tuam, a highly learned man, wrote a letter from Spain to a friend in Ireland, where he shows by the most powerful arguments that this proscription or confiscation of the goods of Catholics was unjust and immoral. It was written under another name in Spanish, with authorities supplied from Sacred Scripture. We give here a Latin version, with no change made in the content.

"I have received the letter you sent me, dated December 24, where you inform me about what has been done so far in that anti-parliament of yours;

and I too praise to the heights the constancy of the Catholics, which you trust in so much, and if the whole world were to admire and extol it I would be immortally glad. There are few who have higher regard for those people than I do. But let me explain to you what I think about the matter: their constancy seems to me less glorious when I think that these same Irishmen (to the best of my knowledge) were the cause of the Christian religion in Ireland being brought to such dire straits. Not alone did they fail to give aid to the Catholic faith, which their brothers and countrymen had undertaken to defend against Queen Elizabeth, but they helped to break the strength of those who were determined to restore that religion to its pristine state and splendour. Their attempt could have been successful, were it not that certain Catholics (why I do not know) opposed them and gave most powerful support to the enemy, helping them to drive the defenders of the faith from their possessions and leave them in profound ruin....

Nevertheless,... I do not deny that they would have shown an example worthy of immortal praise if they had not wavered from that constancy which they had begun to show... But I am afraid they may prove more infirm and inconstant than that. You say in your letter that in place of a Catholic they have accepted a heretical magistrate who has done little good for the kingdom, and given consent to the new deputies illegally elected: that is no small degeneration from the original constancy of the Catholic spirit. With their connivance, those invalid and illegitimate deputies are seen to confirm by their authority and presence all the evil to which that assembly has given a firmer foundation.

My fears are increased considerably by what you have written about the confiscation. Not all of them, you say, were agreed about this, and you yourself appear to be in two minds, but seemingly you think it should not have been resisted, lest those who desired it might have been offended. Why? Will those people not also be offended and angry if the Catholics refuse to swear that the king is head of the Church? Tomorrow will they give consent to the proscription of their own goods? Surely you can see how weak and unworthy such thinking is for Catholics? How can we consider them good Catholics, if this is the counsel that they put into practice?...

It is known with certainty throughout the whole kingdom (or so I have been told) that those men whose possessions were forfeited to the treasury had been received with honour and accepted in friendship by the king, their possessions remaining with them by virtue of the new monarch's benevolence. And if afterwards they emigrated from the kingdom, wishing to vindicate themselves from the calumnies of envious men who strove to incite the king's anger against them, or attending to the salvation of their souls and wanting to lead free and Christian lives in other places, by doing so have they committed the crime of lése-majesté? On what other grounds have those Catholics come to the conclusion that these men, whom they saw to be reconciled to the king, afterwards fell into wrongdoing worthy of the punishment of proscription?

> Were they perhaps apprehended in the act of crime? Have they been formally and duly convicted with confessions in court and with clear and indubitable proofs? It stands to reason that this proscription is gravely wrong, especially when the law by which we are forbidden to take their goods from our neighbours is not merely a part of positive law, which the prince is therefore free later on to repeal or to observe less strictly and meticulously towards his subjects." "

*** ***

Ó Maolchonaire's letter, dated March 1, 1615, Valladollid, may be found translated in full in C. P. Meehan's *The Fate and Fortunes of Hugh O'Neill*. These extracts from O'Sullivan's *Catholic History* – as already noted, the only broad survey of these events from an Irish Catholic perspective – do not square with the picture of Irish attitudes that Breandán Ó Buachalla has painted. The Irish were not settling down under their legitimate Stuart king quite as snugly as he likes to claim. (Those who were most loyal to James had been loyal to Elizabeth too, as Ó Maolchonaire observes bitterly.)

In the Irish Catholic Church there were two factions, to use O'Sullivan's word, which competed with each other for influence and sustained their vigour down to the 1640s. In O'Sullivan's book we see them sharply and clearly defined. One of them was led by Peter Lombard, Archbishop of Armagh, based in Rome. For the medium term this faction seems to have aimed at a pluralist Ireland, as outlined in the Catholic parliamentary deputies' letter to Chichester, quoted above. O'Neill and O'Donnell were to be sacrificed for the greater good, and the Catholics of Ireland would go to all possible limits (short of abandoning Catholicism) to convince King James of their loyalty. This faction had its strongest influence among the clergy in France and in particular orders, most notably the Jesuits, and in Ireland mostly among Catholics of the towns, the Norman lordships, and the South.

The other faction was led by Flaithrí Ó Maolchonaire, Archbishop of Tuam, based in Spain. Ó Maolchonaire came from Roscommon, from a leading family of poet-chroniclers, and he himself was a recognised master-chronicler before he took to the religious life. He was over 30, and apparently posted to Spain on diplomatic business for the O'Donnells, when he entered a seminary in Salamanca. In 1598 he returned to Ireland, where he made an extraordinary impression during the second half of the Nine Years War. O'Neill and O'Donnell were eager that he should be made a bishop, and in 1609, through their influence, he became Archbishop of Tuam. For the twenty years that followed he was one of two great powers in the Irish Church, Peter Lombard being the other. Throughout that time he was consistently hostile to the policy of pragmatic accommodation with the Stuarts. This is brought out in an important new book by Benjamin Hazard, *Faith and Patronage: The Political Career of Flaithrí Ó Maolchonaire.*

Ó Maolchonaire aimed at the restoration of the exiled northern earls and their successors, by one means or another but most probably by armed force. Spanish aid would be crucial. The idea of strategically abandoning O'Neill and O'Donnell was seen as cowardly and contemptible. Ó Maolchonaire's faction had its greatest influence in the Spanish lands, also notably in the Franciscan Order, and in Ireland mostly in the North and among the Gaels.

The crucial word in these descriptions is 'mostly'. Conor O'Mahony was not a northerner, and he became a Jesuit, yet without doubt he belonged to the Ó Maolchonaire faction. He tells us only one thing about his period in Spain and that one thing is tantalising: *"Flaithrí Ó Maolchonaire, Archbishop of Tuam, a man of profound learning and piety, with whom I had friendly dealings once in Spain, died in exile..."* What were those friendly dealings? He gives no hint.

Ó Maolchonaire was well known to the English government, by reputation at least. *"Although he was a Franciscan monk and bound to that rule of life, he was known by the king's ministers and officials to be more interested in provoking war,"* Peter Lombard complained; he seemed to blame the Plantation of Ulster on the choice of archbishop for Tuam!

For decades afterwards Ó Maolchonaire was the O'Neills' chief diplomat at the Court of Madrid. He remained ever on the alert for conflict between England and Spain, because it might make possible another Spanish-backed invasion of Ireland. As late as 1627 he was presenting a plan to Philip IV for an invasion, to be led by the current O'Neill and the current O'Donnell.

Peter Lombard and his faction systematically opposed the appointment of men linked with O'Neill as bishops. They claimed that this was injurious to Irish Catholic interests, because it would upset the Stuarts and make them less disposed to be tolerant. But the other faction also had influence at Rome, and the Lombard faction's efforts were not successful. Rome understood that the Irish Church couldn't do without Gaelic-Iberian zeal if Catholic Ulster and Connacht were to be effectively led.

Ó Maolchonaire's faction had its intellectual powerhouse in the College of Louvain. (In the 1640s there were prominent clerics in the Northern Half who were marked by its influence.) Louvain was the most dynamic of the Irish colleges overseas, intimately linked with the Irish poetic families, a pioneer in the publication of Irish-language books and the collection of Irish history and antiquities. Flaithrí Ó Maolchonaire was its founder and guiding spirit.

He was closely connected with Philip O'Sullivan Beare, and he appears as a prime authority in the concluding pages of the *History of Catholic Ireland*. But I think he must also have had a wider influence on the book's content. Furthermore, without his influence the dedication to King Philip IV would probably have been impossible. In Spanish territory, which Lisbon was then, one did not presume to publish a *History of Catholic Country X*, including ferocious criticism of a major European power, with a dedication to the Most Catholic King, unless one had first ensured the Most Catholic King wouldn't mind. And who could make the request? Not just anyone! O'Sullivan must have had a powerful patron working in his favour at court, and Archbishop Ó Maolchonaire is the likeliest.

*** ***

With the account of King James's parliament O'Sullivan's history is effectively at an end. He brings the story up to December 1618, when he's finishing his writing, making it clear that he sees no essential change in English policy towards Ireland. The first chapter of his brief concluding section is entitled *The English Revert to the Original Persecution.*

However, the period 1615-1618 gets only perfunctory coverage. There is nothing in the book about a recent cultural conflict of great importance: *Iomarbhágh na bhFileadh*, the Contention of the Poets of North and South. This Contention, principally sustained by Tadhg Mac Dáire Mac Bruaideadha of Thomond, a poet whose literary skills O'Sullivan Beare admired, is to be taken very seriously. It is important not so much for what it explicitly says as for what it reveals. It is an ominous black cloud passing over Ireland, a cloud that will be seen again in the 1640s. (In parenthesis though, let us report an expert opinion, pronounced with an air of authority: *"Taken as a whole this elaborate debate on a non-issue is a reminder of the preference for solipsistic artifice that continued into the last decades of the Gaelic order."* (S. J. Connolly, *Contested Island: Ireland 1430-1630*). This is an appropriate opinion, and readers who want to be in the mainstream of Irish historical culture must be advised that they should hold it.)

O'Sullivan Beare does not mention this poetic conflict. But when he remarks that

> "the kings of England, having taken possession of the government of Ireland, should have composed and repressed the provincial dissensions and conflicts; on the contrary, they themselves, tainted with the filth of heresy, inflamed and increased them",

maybe he nonetheless has the Iomarbhágh in mind.

One more extract from O'Sullivan is worth giving here, on the subject of social change in King James's Ireland.

> "I will not list here the numbers of Connachtmen and Munstermen who were expelled from their holdings, while men of the baser sort, grown wealthy and landed, are now created barons and earls. I give one as an example of all: Richard Boyle, at a time I myself remember, about 24 years ago, was so poor that he couldn't even buy himself shoes. He was assistant to Nicholas Renning, who held a particular office where he was charged with investigating which titles had lapsed or devolved to the right of the Crown; officially he was called the Escheator. This Nicholas is still alive and has always been and still remains a man of slender fortune, because he did not know how to swindle others. Richard Boyle was in his service and became his scribe and notary. Having a clear perspective on the individual cases, he applied his arts to picking up anything he could here, there and everywhere, so that now he is the richest man in the kingdom (after Chichester, who was viceroy for 12 years), and recently (1616) he was raised with great pomp to the rank of Baron of Youghal. And thus Ireland's miseries out of misery make wealthy and honoured men. There would not be time enough to tell the stupendous frolics of fortune in Ireland, or the effects of tyranny rather; should anyone want to tell the story at length, there is material enough to go on to infinity."

O'MAHONY IN THE AZORES AND LISBON

In 1621 Conor O'Mahony was received into the Jesuit Order in Lisbon. He made his profession on St. Patrick's Day, taking the religious name of Cornelio de São Patricio. And it seems that he stayed in "Portuguese territory" ever afterwards.

Having taken his vows, he completed his studies at the Jesuit universities of Coimbra and Evora. By 1623 he was back in Lisbon as Prefect of Studies at the Irish College. Two years later the Jesuit superior in Ireland was writing to the Order's General, asking for Father Cornelius Mahony to be sent back to Ireland. The General expressed his agreement, but said it would be up to the Portuguese. In the event, O'Mahony was not sent to Ireland – probably, Francis Finegan says, because the Order in Portugal had spotted a man of talent and decided to keep him.

But no Jesuit could be perfectly sure of where he would be the following year. A Portuguese Jesuit could be sent to any part of the former Portuguese empire, and that was spread over three other continents. In a certain sense Portugal still had its empire, though not formally, since it no longer had its own monarchy. The Spanish kings were now kings of Portugal also. In 1580 Philip II of Spain had put together a sizeable army, apparently with the intention of sending it to Ireland to fight alongside the FitzGeralds in the Desmond Rebellion. But the Portuguese royal succession was in crisis, and Philip instead sent his army to occupy Portugal and solve the succession crisis in favour of himself.

Only one of the Portuguese pretenders was prepared to put up a fight, and his forces were defeated within Portugal in a matter of months. The rebels held out for a couple of years more in the Azores Islands in the mid-Atlantic. Otherwise the Portuguese parliament, nobility, church leaders and pretenders peaceably submitted to Philip and his successors. Portugal was given a good deal of autonomy and for some decades it was a trouble-free part of the Spanish kingdom.

It must surely have crossed O'Mahony's mind that he could be sent to Brazil, either to convert the native people to Christianity or to minister to the Irish (because some of the many Irish who were flocking into Portugal had gone on to Brazil as a land of promise). Africa and India were other possibilities. In the event he was merely sent a third of the way across the Atlantic, to the Azores. Less than two centuries previously these islands had been uninhabited, till the Portuguese began to settle them; now there were Jesuit training colleges in Angra on Terceira Island and Ponte Delgada on St. Michel. One might suppose that being sent to the Azores was some kind of punishment, but according to Finegan—

> "a professorship in the Azores was usually a junior appointment where a young man was tried out with the prospect of promotion to a chair of more importance in metropolitan Portugal, whether at Lisbon or Evora or Coimbra".

Anyhow, O'Mahony was sent there about 1626.

He taught Moral Theology at the island colleges. On September 2, 1630 he was at the college in Ponte Delgada when there was a powerful volcanic eruption. The earth opened and 90 unfortunate persons were burned alive. *"A river of burning sulphur mixed with gravel swept all before it to the sea, where pumice stone floated as light as cork on the surface. Thunders and flashes filled the air. Father Cornelius stood his ground at the college till morning, hearing the confessions of the terrified multitudes".* The Portuguese Jesuit chronicler says he was *"a great solace to all".*

Presumably it was in the Azores that he wrote a book on speculative and moral theology which apparently was never published but survives in manuscript, *Tractatus Theologici Speculativi et Moralis*, dated 1629. After six years he returned to Portugal, soon to become Professor of Moral Theology at the University of Evora. Three years later he was transferred to Lisbon, back to the Irish College, where he taught Scholastic Theology from 1636 to 1641. By this stage he was something of a leading light and occasionally he was asked to give formal opinions on questions involving moral law, or on whether a particular manuscript should be published as a book.

Though far from Ireland, he was not out of touch. There were channels by which a supply of Irish news reached Lisbon and O'Mahony would have had access to the best of them. What did he make of the condition of his native land in 1640?

By then the dynamic Earl of Strafford had left his mark on the government of Ireland. He had cut out a lot of the nonsense. Three or four years before his arrival, Richard Boyle (the spectacular upstart mentioned by O'Sullivan Beare, who had since progressed from Baron of Youghal to Earl of Cork), taking his turn at Lord Justice, had indulged himself by smashing up St. Patrick's Purgatory, and suchlike. But what political purpose was served by displays of bigotry? Strafford scorned to persecute people on purely religious grounds, since it was futile. However, this did not mean that the promotion of Protestantism had ceased, much less that the policy of 'civilising' Ireland had been abandoned.

"*The greatest seventeenth century exponent of 'civilisation' through conformity with the Church of England and, above all, plantation was Lord Deputy Thomas Wentworth, later Earl of Strafford*", we read in no less authoritative a source than the Oxford History of the British Empire. *"He believed that the settlement of English colonists remained the best means of* **'civilising... this people, or securing the kingdom under the dominion of your imperial crown.'** *He continued that* **'plantations must be the only means under God and your Majesty to reform this subject as well in religion as in manners.'** "

No doubt the unreformed majority were glad to be less harassed as Catholics. But they were not less harassed as Gaels. Strafford's many plantation projects threatened whatever they still possessed, and daily they were coerced to conform with an alien system and culture, daily undermining their own. The imposed new order was characterised, according to Flann Mac Craith, by

Síorchumdhach reacht gan riaghail,
nós nuaidhe gach aoinbhliadhain...

upholding law without principle,
new custom every year...

(The reader, if well adjusted to modern times, may wonder what is wrong with changing the social values yearly, but it must be emphasised that Mac Craith regarded this with horror.)

Gofraidh Óg Mac an Bhaird, who would be a notable voice of the rebellion, has poems also from the preceding peacetime. One of them shows him in search of a hero who could hold out against near-irresistible pressure. He believed, or hoped, he had found one in Maol Mhuire Mac Thoirdhealbhaigh Mac Suibhne (almost certainly one of the numerous MacSwiney rebels of 1641). The poet's image of his hero may be heightened, but his description of the general state of affairs reiterates what we find again and again in Irish-language testimony from the reigns of Kings James and Charles, so frequently that – whatever

Breandán Ó Buachalla may say – it overwhelms any contrary views. Gofraidh Óg presents the negative process at an advanced stage. English right, established by English might, prevailed in a horrible peace:

Atáid, gá truaighe pudhar,
lór gach lá dá laghdughadh,
dá gclódh i n-éigean 's a n-olc,
fá bhrón nach éidir d'fhurtacht.

Siothcháin cirt Gall 's a gcogaidh
ní h-ualach nach árdobair,
idir uaislibh Gaoidheal glan
guais-neimh d'aoinfhear a n-iomchar.

Every day – what more grievous loss? –
they are reduced considerably;
oppression, injustice grinds them down,
and their grief cannot be relieved.

The peace of English right and war –
that load is an enormous labour!
That right and might are a deadly burden
for any man of the noble Gaels!

PORTUGUESE INDEPENDENCE

In December 1640 there was a revolution in Portugal. A group of discontented nobles decided to repudiate the sovereignty of the kings of Spain and restore the old monarchy. After an uprising in Lisbon the most eligible pretender, the Duke of Braganza, was crowned as King John IV of Portugal.

The restored monarchy had much popular support, but the nobles were divided. It was only to be expected that Philip IV, "The Most Catholic King", would have his fanatical partisans, and especially among the clergy. A group of diehards, who included bishops, conspired to kill the just-crowned king and his closest supporters, but their plot was discovered. Since the affair was so serious, the new government ignored the usual procedure of letting clerical criminals have immunity from punishment by the state. The rogue bishops were arrested and tried and sentenced to life imprisonment.

This showed determination on the revolutionaries' part. They knew that Spain was determined to crush them; they would have to fight on all fronts, and the propaganda war would be crucial. If only a case could be made, there were excellent chances of recognition by Spain's enemies and rivals. France, England and Sweden were positively inclined because of strategic interest; recognition by the Pope would take longer, but that too could be worked on, and for the moment toleration would suffice. The Popes were realists and ultimately they would recognise any durable Catholic power.

The outstanding propagandist of the Portuguese restoration was Antonio de Sousa de Macedo. He was a civil lawyer, highly versed in theology, as a top civil lawyer had to be. His principal work of restorationist propaganda is cited several times by O'Mahony, who on one occasion gives him a warm word of praise. *"With his accustomed erudition"* – it's the kind of compliment scholar friends liked to pay one another. I think at the very least it is likely that these two were well acquainted.

De Sousa was secretary of the Portuguese legation which arrived in England in March 1641 (in spite of the Spanish who, knowing the significance of this, had sent seven frigates to intercept them.) The secretary's first task was to satisfy King Charles about Portugal's new king's legitimacy. Charles demanded a written justification and he was given a very polished statement in Latin. Among other things de Sousa assured him that the Portuguese did not want to disturb the existing peace between England and Spain. All they wanted from England was friendship; they did not need military aid or money.

From 1642 de Sousa himself was head of the London embassy. He became one of Charles's favourite ambassadors, doing whatever small services he could for the king in his struggle with the English parliament. He did have some sharp exchanges with the parliament, in particular because of his practice of allowing local Catholics to come to his house to hear Mass. But all parties were content to give him every facility for carrying on his anti-Spanish propaganda campaign, with the option of having his books conveniently printed in London. At least three of his works appeared with London imprints in the years 1642 to 1645, one of them an enormous tome of 800-odd pages. (For the sake of politeness though, he had his most scurrilous book published in Lisbon under a pseudonym.)

Juan Caramuel Lobkowitz (1642), written – in Spanish for added provocation – against a leading Spanish propagandist, presents the basic arguments which are repeated at greater length in *Lusitania Liberata*, and which we also find in O'Mahony's book in suitably adapted form. De Sousa's key claim is that King Philip II of Spain usurped the crown of Portugal by force. The right of succession belonged to Duchess Catarina de Braganza; she afterwards transmitted her right to her eldest son, who in turn passed it on to his own eldest son, the current King John IV. Granted, these princely persons had sworn oaths of loyalty to the kings of Spain, but this was of no importance because of the violence and duress which had been involved. The Portuguese royals protested that they had taken their oaths under duress, and by these protestations they preserved their right.

Furthermore, there could be no question of the Spanish having acquired prescriptive right through the length of their occupation. Firstly, prescription did not apply to kingdoms. Secondly, even if it did, at least a hundred years would be required for prescription to take effect, and the Spanish occupation of Portugal fell considerably short of that. Thirdly, even if time enough had elapsed, there could be no prescription because the original occupation was enacted in bad faith, when Philip II knowingly usurped the right of Catarina de Braganza. And bad faith annuls the right of possession forever.

But finally,

> "even if the king of Spain had possessed a right to the Portuguese succession, it is notorious that his ministers have sold justice, tyrannized over the people and reduced the administration to chaos, without his Majesty being able to remedy this, and by these means they have reduced this glorious kingdom to such a miserable state that his vassals, deserting the prince under whose power they were being ruined, may elect a new one who will rule them as God commands".

De Sousa covers the same ground exhaustively and exhaustingly in *Lusitania Liberata* (1645). Structurally it is similar in some ways to O'Mahony's book, though O'Mahony's is much smaller in scale. *Lusitania Liberata* begins with two preambles on the topography and history of Portugal. It comes rather as a shock to discover that the history of Portugal begins at an earlier time than Conor O'Mahony, or indeed Geoffrey Keating, claims for the history of Ireland – 143 years after the Great Flood, beating Ireland by a clear century and a half!

The Portuguese monarchy is said to be the oldest in existence. Anciently it had peaceful trading relations with Carthage, and some

Cathaginian merchants settled and formed coastal communities in Portugal. Unfortunately this brought in the Romans, who disrupted the monarchy's continuity; only in the 11th century was it properly resumed. The story is carried down to the last King Henry, whose death brought on the succession crisis which Philip II of Spain resolved with his invasion.

The titles of the three major sections, amounting to the great bulk of the book, will give an idea of the contents:

> Book I. *"Explains the disputed royal succession after the death of King Henry. Presents the claims of the parties aspiring to the succession. Concludes that the crown belonged to the Most Serene Catherine, Duchess of Braganza."*
>
> Book II. *"Shows that even if the kings of Castille had possessed the right to the crown of Portugal (as they unjustly pretend), they would have forfeited it through their unjust means of occupation, retention and rule. Proves that the Portuguese with full justice could exclude these royal persons, both from the causes already mentioned and also from natural defense and for the good of the Catholic religion."*
>
> *Book III. "Narrates the restitution of the crown to the legitimate king John IV. Shows that no prescription or oath is an impediment to this. Concludes that the liberty of the Portuguese has been rightfully acclaimed and stabilised by victories, to the applause of the whole world."* (An Appendix follows, giving some details of prophecies of the Portuguese restoration.)

Though de Sousa gave King Charles a copy of *Lusitania Liberata*, the book itself takes for granted a Catholic readership. On the second page, for example, it is casually remarked that the Spanish propagandists argue like heretics. No heretic, however, needed to fear that de Sousa would attack him: he had quite enough to do attacking Catholic Spain!

Interestingly, he devotes some pages to an English Catholic pamphleteer who had written in support of the Spanish claims. This 'mercenary' was identified only by the initials R.H.; failing to discover who he was, de Sousa concluded that he must be *Ridiculus Homunculus*. Unfortunately, R. H. was all too typical of the many English Catholics who had been deceived by hypocritical Spanish propagandists. These Englishmen swelled the pro-Spanish faction, in hopes that Spain would help them, but the record of Spain's kings should have led them to expect otherwise. For example, Philip II had helped Elizabeth, though a

Protestant, to gain the crown of England, because at all costs he wanted to exclude Mary Queen of Scots, whose election could have led to an English-French union of crowns. And the same Philip, having raised an army against Elizabeth on the Pope's authority, converted it into a force for oppressing Portugal! (This was the army which was supposed to go to Ireland to help the Geraldines.)

Flinging himself into this enormous work of polemical scholarship, de Sousa kept up his morale while doing his miserable duty. *"For five years I have not seen the sun as God made it; I have spent five winters in which the days are bright nights and five summers in which the days are dark; in the winters I was always trembling with cold and in the summers with pest; the men I meet are at least half drunk, and my only recreation has been the hope of getting back to Portugal"* (Letter, January 25, 1646). He also complained that *"the old English histories are very badly written and contain no details, and certain it is that this nation has no talent for writing on any subject."*

Another inspiration for Conor O'Mahony was the *Just Acclamation of His Most Serene Highness John IV of Portugal* by Francisco Velasco de Gouveia (Lisbon 1644). The first part of this book is devoted to proving: *"That the kingdom of Portugal has legitimate power to acclaim a king who has the legitimate right to be such; and to deprive of the kingship whoever does not have that right and has been intruded, without requiring the authority of the Pope or any person whatsoever."* Suarez is quoted repeatedly. Indeed one can say that his thinking on kingship, outlined earlier, forms the foundation of the whole book.

The five section-headings of the first part show how Suarez could be used in the cause of revolution:

> "1. *That the royal power of kings resides in the peoples and commonwealths, and is received from them immediately.*
>
> 2. *That after the peoples have transferred the power to the kings they still hold it habitually and can reassume their power whenever it may be necessary for their self preservation.*
>
> 3. *That the kingdoms and peoples can deprive intruder kings and tyrants, denying them obedience and submitting themselves to whoever has the legitimate power of reigning there.*
>
> 4. *That kingdoms, even those which are Catholic, are not normally but only in certain cases dependent on Papal sanction in order to deprive tyrannical and intruded kings and to acclaim those who are legitimate.*

5. That the kingdom of Portugal had legitimate power to deprive the Catholic King of Spain of possession of that kingdom and restore it to His Most Serene Highness King John IV."

The second part treats the legalities of succession in great detail. After 400 pages it is duly concluded that Philip II was a tyrant in Portugal due to defect of title. Then, almost as an afterthought, there are two brief sections devoted to the argument that Kings Philip II, III and IV ruled Portugal in a tyrannical manner, and on this heading also they could justly be deprived of possession.

The third part argues on similar lines to de Sousa that the Spanish have not acquired prescriptive rights in Portugal and that formal declarations of loyalty made to the Spanish kings by the Portuguese parliament or by anyone else can in no way impede the right to acclaim King John IV.

De Gouveia quotes mounds of scholastic literature in support of his statements. *Lusitania Liberata* takes this practice to an even further extreme. In fact, compared to his Portuguese trail-blazers Conor O'Mahony goes easy on the supporting authorities. But one had to pile them up now and then if one wanted to make an impression in scholastic culture. De Sousa scoffs at R.H., the English pamphleteer: *"You will hardly find him citing a text or a Doctor for any point of substance."*

As for the merits of these arguments: they must, of course, be taken in their context. If one were to take them out of context, one would have to say that the Portuguese arguments were mostly weaker than Conor O'Mahony's arguments for Ireland – or rather Philip O'Sullivan's arguments, which O'Mahony reformulated. (An exception is the issue of prescription. It was certainly easier to argue that Spanish power in Portugal had never had enough time to settle in.)

One recent writer suggests that a damaging attack could have been made on O'Mahony by pointing to the fact that the Irish lords accepted Henry VIII as their sovereign at the time of 'Surrender and Regrant'. As a matter of fact, I think O'Mahony simply forgot to include a mention of Surrender and Regrant in the hurry of compiling his book. Philip O'Sullivan mentions it, after all, and it isn't clear why O'Mahony should reject his mentor's lead on this one single issue of Anglo-Irish history. What O'Sullivan says is that Surrender and Regrant was a fraudulent exercise agreed to by the Irish lords under duress (i.e. threat from King Henry's army), therefore it had no validity. And this was the invariable Portuguese response to the limitless evidence of the peaceable collaboration of practically everyone in Portugal with the three Philips for the six decades after 1580 – violence had been threatened, implicitly if not explicitly, so no agreement was valid and everything was null and void. (Or, as de Sousa said in *Juan Caramuel Lobkowitz*, even if obligation arose as a consequence of such agreements one could get rid of it in Confession.)

On some points one might say that the Portuguese had a very weak case. However, they did have their "nine points of the law" – they actually had a king and were keeping him on his throne. They pressed their arguments, whether good or bad, vigorously and tenaciously. Their political effort was united and sustained; last but not least, they were successful in war, defeating the Spanish at the Battle of Montijo in 1644 (the "stabilising victory" referred to by de Sousa). All in all, it is not surprising that somebody should think of them as a model.

I should mention here that one of the rising stars in Portuguese politics after the restoration was Irish. He was known as Domingos do Rosário, but originally he was Daniel O'Daly, of the family of poets based in Kilsarkon, near Castleisland. His father had been the faithful secretary of Gerald, the last earl of Desmond. Daniel went abroad to study, became a Dominican monk, and in the 1630s showed his organising abilities by managing to found two Dominican houses in Lisbon, one of them for the Irish. This involved direct negotiation with King Philip IV of Spain, and for the second foundation he was required in return to go to Ireland to recruit soldiers for the Spanish service, which he did. When the restoration came in Portugal he changed his loyalties smoothly and began rising high. About 1644 he became the Queen's confessor. He was therefore already very influential by the time Conor O'Mahony began writing his book.

THE 1641 REBELLION

Less than a year after the Portuguese restoration, there was a rebellion in Ireland which not only spread throughout the country in a matter of a few months, but also drew into it the town Catholics and even most of the comfortable, the Anglicised and the scrupulously royalist among the body of Catholic lords. An all-Ireland leadership body was established, the Catholic Confederation based in Kilkenny, which effectively was an alternative parliament and government.

This course of events, in my opinion, should be thought of as breath-taking and astonishing. If ever there was something which didn't have to happen, which was the opposite of inevitable, then surely this was it! The town Catholics had kept a good distance from Hugh O'Neill, and they might have kept an even greater distance from Phelim of Dungannon, initially the foremost of the O'Neills, who spearheaded the uprising during its critical opening months. And so might a solvent, well-positioned and well-connected lord such as Donough MacCarthy, Viscount Muskerry. They were drawn into the rebellion. And somebody planned it so.

But who? Who were the planners, the strategists?

Of course, 1641 sustains any amount of conspiracy theory. There is evidence that King Charles himself had been conspiring to overthrow the existing Irish government. But he most certainly did not conspire at a generalised Gaelic rebellion. What the king wanted was a palace coup, to be organised by the Earls of Antrim and Ormond, which would remove the Irish Chief Justices, supporters of his rogue Parliament, and install a government loyal to himself. Phelim O'Neill, or anyone of his ilk, had not been invited to participate.

There were many allegations that O'Neill claimed he was acting on royal commission, but I am not sure whether they were founded on more than parliamentarian black propaganda. If O'Neill did make this claim, he was lying. He had no such commission, but the king's known intrigues would have made the assertion plausible. And this same assertion was allegedly repeated by others throughout the country as far as Kerry (where Pierce Ferriter, besieging Tralee Castle, reportedly said that he had the king's commission to do it). It does seem beyond doubt that the rebels affirmed their loyalty and goodwill to the king again and again, wherever English-speakers might hear them.

In fact, right from the outset the rebels tried as far as possible to conduct their rebellion so that other Catholics would know they were welcome to join them and would have acceptable political grounds for doing so. This is clear from the depositions made later by Protestant witnesses; and it is clearer still from the agitational poems produced early on in the rebellion.

One could view it differently. All of the credit for spreading the rebellion might be given to the bigoted Irish Chief Justices, Parsons and Borlase. John Callaghan makes this case with his typical clarity.

"In the year 1641 certain noblemen in Ulster, the northern province of Ireland, taking advantage of the growing disturbances in England, decided to throw off the heavy yoke under which this nation had groaned for a hundred years and more". Their ambitious attempt to seize Dublin Castle was betrayed and came to nothing, but they managed to create great disorder in Ulster. However, in Callaghan's opinion the 'Duumviri' (Chief Justices Parsons and Borlase) could easily have suppressed the Ulster rising. Instead they preferred to foment it, hoping that it would end in a general confiscation of the Catholic noblemen's lands.

Throughout the rest of the kingdom the Catholic nobles, living quietly in their homes, heard that the Ulstermen were in arms. All of these nobles were perturbed by the news, afraid that through the fault of some private individuals all of the Catholics would be treated with fiercer savagery than usual by the heretical ministers. Hoping to avert this disaster, many of the nobles and magnates hurried to Dublin and went to the Duumviri, calling for arms and asking that the suppression of the disturbances in the province of Ulster should be entrusted to themselves. But Parsons and Borlase spurned the help which these Catholics offered, making it plain that so far as they were concerned all men of the Catholic communion and all natives of Ireland were suspect, and they did not think it wise to give arms (without which the enemy might be provoked, but not effectively fought) to those who were requesting them. It was not only the nobles, but all Catholics throughout the kingdom of whatever condition, who took note of the heretical magistrates' treachery and found it frightening. They understood that they would end up in a bad state unless they took measures in good time. Puritan policy was more and more tending towards the suppression of royal authority and the introduction of another form of regime; so that this could be done the more easily, the Catholics (since they had the name of being more faithful to their majestic religion than any others) would be uprooted and driven out of the three kingdoms.

Their fear was intensified by the chance capture of letters from Puritan magnates, where it was indicated that as soon as possible Papists would be compelled to renounce their faith or else be transported to New England, thereby making space for many new colonists from England to be transferred to neighbouring Ireland.

These and innumerable other complaints which they had suffered for a long time already, being oppressed due to hatred of their nation as well as of their religion, eventually weighed so much with the Catholics that many of them, even before consulting together or forming coalitions, decided that the issue must be settled by war."

And from this grew the Confederation of Kilkenny.

Unquestionably the Chief Justices helped to concentrate Catholic minds. But in Callaghan's account there is something missing: the element of active agency. The rebellion was consciously spread and actively propagated throughout Ireland. It was argued for and explained, it was justified on grounds of principle, it was defended on grounds of policy. There is intelligence in this rebellion, and note that it is intelligence based in Gaelic Ireland. Peter Walsh, one of the few Catholics who could never accept the rebellion's legitimacy, saw it essentially as a Gaelic movement and a Gaelic political achievement. The Gaelic rebels, he said (his exact words are quoted later on in this book), persuaded the rest to join in, rather against their will.

One doesn't get much of a sense of this from Breandán Ó Buachalla. In *Aisling Ghéar* he presents his own special variant of the "new British history", which treats Ireland as a subordinate element in the overall Three Kingdoms politics. The 1641 rebellion, he tells us, was one element in the intricate military strife of the three kingdoms. He is therefore not very anxious to spotlight historical sources in the rebels' language. Unlike other historians he does quote something from two of them (by Haicéad and Uilliam Óg Mac an Bhaird), but only as much as may confirm his presuppositions.

But for someone who feels the need to know, those agitational poems which were written late in 1641 and early in 1642, inciting the Gaelic nobility to rebellion, are priceless evidence. I know of six or seven of them, though probably other examples survive. Two of these poems were printed in my edition of Geoffrey O'Donoghue; another is in Pádraigín Haicéad's collected poems; one other was published in *Ériú* in 2002. The remaining two or three have not been published until now, as far as I know.

I hope to write more about 1641 elsewhere. For now I will simply give a few verses from one of the agitational poems written in 1641-2, by Gofraidh Óg Mac an Bhaird. Better than any State Paper that is likely to be found, it illuminates the rebellion. It reveals what the rebels most want, what fuels their movement, what they think others will be ready to fight for. To restore honour to the nobility; to protect Ireland against distress; to maintain all in their faith; to put an end to the heretics' evildoing; to put everyone in his ancestral place:

Do dhuisgeadh gaisgeadh Gaoidheal
fada anonn bhus neartmhaoidheamh,
an bhuaidh rolonn rug an ceart,
tug a h-onóir san uaisleacht.

Do tógbhadh meanma mac rígh,
do reacadh tlás ar thréinbhrígh,
ciodh acht guaisbhearta gníomh dte,
díon na h-uaisleachta an eirghe.

Do coindleadh coindle an fheadhma,
tanaig claochlodh cinneamhna,
ar neart láimhe gibe bheas,
as sé bhus sáimhe suaimhneas.

Ar feadh Éirinn theas is thuaidh
tré ar adhain innte d'anbhuain,
beag tarbha acht armghníomh re h-eadh
ag daighdhíon Banbha ar buaidhreadh.

Do chongmháil cháigh na gcreideamh,
d'ísliughadh uilc d'eithrigeadh,
gá dtamaid dá d'treidhibh gill
tarnaicc ar eirigh d'Éirinn.

Eireochaidh dháibh na dheadhaidh
uaisle innse Mhuireadhaigh,
go dtí i ndiaidh a dtuile treas
biaidh gach duine na dhileas.

The heroism of the Gaels has awakened
– long will it be celebrated!
Right has made its own of martial virtue
and given back honour to the nobility.

Kings' sons spirits have been lifted,
weakness has been changed for strength and vigour;
what now but the perilous resort to battle?
Nobility's safety is the uprising!

The spark of power has been kindled
and fate has been transformed:
whoever now depends on the strength of his arm,
he will have the soundest security!

Throughout Ireland north and south
(with the fire that has been kindled from her torment),
there's little profit now but in deeds of arms
to defend Banbha soundly from distress.

To maintain everyone in his faith,
to defeat the heretics' villainy:
– what more need I say of Ireland's noble lords? –
that is what those who rose resolved upon.

And the noblemen all over Muireadhach's island
will rise in rebellion after them,
till following the deluge of their battles
everybody will be in his own.

In a word: restoration. The Gaelic civilisation restored and an end made to the project of making Ireland British. That is what 1641 was about.

Ó Buachalla says that at first there was a defensive and preventive uprising, paradoxical as that might sound. But as it spread it slipped out of the leaders' control and became vengeful, bloody and sectarian. The rabble (*daoscar*) came into their own, with unbridled millennial aims (*aidhmeanna ainsrianta miléanacha*): to drive out the English, to drive out the Scots, to drive out all of the Protestants, to recover the ancestral lands, and to take revenge for the dishonour and oppression of the Gaels.

In fact, while revenge is not highlighted in the agitational poems and while there is more mention of restoring Catholicism than of extinguishing Protestantism, otherwise the above would not be a bad description of their message. The poets who wrote them, highly trained and cultivated masters of language, would have been surprised and not well pleased to find themselves described as spokesmen of the rabble. (As a matter of fact, Ó Buachalla's rabble has names like Maguire, McDermott, Nugent and MacMahon in the Protestant depositions which he cites as evidence.)

But if the poets are to be seen as rabble-rousers and Maguire, MacMahon etc. as rabble, it isn't clear why the Catholic hierarchy also shouldn't be labelled as rabble representatives. Because in March 1642 they declared that the uprising was justified, and that Catholics must assist it on pain of excommunication. And it surely had become a riot of the rabble by then, if it ever did.

At the point when the hierarchy intervened, the defensive war on behalf of the king was being turned into a religious war, Ó Buachalla says. But this was precisely the point at which Donough MacCarthy, Viscount Muskerry, joined the movement. And MacCarthy himself explained that he joined it on the understanding that it was a defensive war which had support of the king as one of its main objectives. And afterwards defense of the king's rights was included as one of the three pledges of the Confederate Oath, second only to the liberty of the Catholic Church and preceding the rights (or "immunities") of the Irish nation.

Although the leaders were firmly in support of King Charles, some of the rabble expressed the wish to have their own king of Ireland, Ó Buachalla tells us. According to the depositions, this king might be variously O'Neill (Phelim or Eoghan Ruadh) or Maguire. From the agitational poems I am in a position to increase this list of names to at least six. The king of Ireland might also be O'Donnell (Seán Mac Aodha or an Calbhach Rua), or MacCarthy.

Ó Buachalla finally becomes uneasy about his contrast of leaders and rabble and himself volunteers the statement that it is over-simplified. But nonetheless he insists that the distinction is valid to this extent: it identifies two large groups that had different aims and strategies within the common ideological framework of religion and royalty. He then blithely continues with his contrast of leaders and rabble as if his concession were irrelevant. According as the war continued uncertainly and haphazardly and the Kilkenny Council became ever slower and more inefficient, the leaders – under pressure, we are led to understand, from the rabble – were laying down ever more extreme conditions. And with that Ó Buachalla makes the giant leap from 1642 to 1649 and frees himself from his difficulties by bringing in Cromwell, the great simplifier.

This contrast of leaders and rabble is baseless. I suppose it would be going a bit far to say that there was no such thing as rabble in the rebellion, there was only royalty. But it would be nearer the mark.

In three of the agitational poems (and the six I have mentioned can only be a small fraction of the poetry which was then produced) three different lords, two from Tirconnell and one from Muskerry, are encouraged to hope that they might be kings of Ireland. Academic experts will tell us that these things were impossible and were known to be so, and could not have been taken seriously by those involved. They are missing the point. In Gaelic Ireland, which did not take its kings in a line of primogeniture, it could not be so clearly preordained that this or that lord would be king and this or that other would not. The example of Brian Boru was known to all. What was most important was that each considerable lord should be given a sense of his potential and reminded that he was royalty.

The depositions which Ó Buachalla cites suggest that there were other poems made also to Phelim O'Neill, to the Lord Maguire and probably many more besides, declaring that they would be king of Ireland, and that this was repeated among their followers. And this in fact fuelled the rebellion and inspired people to fight. But what ultimately mattered was not that all of these people should be kings of Ireland, but that they should be effective kings of Tyrone, Tirconnell, Fermanagh, Muskerry, Carbery and so on, as their ancestors had been. Such kingship could be compatible with having the English king as overking (two somewhat ambiguous lines near the end of Diarmaid Óg's poem can certainly be taken to mean allegiance to King Charles and support for him against the Puritans). If Charles Stuart was prepared to repeal Poynings's Law and the measures against Irish Catholics and generally to leave Ireland alone, why shouldn't he be accepted as a High King?

Some may say that the Gaels had no right to expect that they could live as they once had lived, or revive the old glories. *Aithbheodhadh glóire Gaoidheal*, "the revival of Gaelic glory", which Pádraigín Haicéad held out as a prospect, was impossible. Times had moved on, change was inevitable, and all that. But it should be acknowledged that even if this was true objectively, subjective awareness lagged behind. The Gaels of the 1640s were not as wise as their critics are now. They didn't know they were history's castaways. It never occurred to them that the new implanted culture of constant acquisition and improvement was a model for Ireland and indeed for the whole world. From their point of view it was only a perverse interlude. (That is explained very clearly in Gofraidh Óg's other poem *Deireadh flaithis ag féin Gall* ("The rule of the English bandits is at an end").

The strategists of rebellion knew they were launching their great venture in a complex context. Presumably they had all read the *Catholic History*. They knew what O'Sullivan Beare is at pains to emphasise, that the last great rebellion, that of Hugh O'Neill, had been fatally undermined by a lack of support from part of the Catholic population. The town Catholics, the less Gaelicised of the Old English, even the more Anglicised and comfortable Gaelic lords – what could be done to secure their support this time?

Appealing purely and simply to their Catholic loyalties might not suffice. But just at this moment, by great good fortune, the king of England was in fierce confict with his Puritan parliament. To launch the rebellion in public support of the king and sustain this position afterwards was a strategic masterstroke. Without that it would never have been possible to forge an all-Ireland rebel confederation encompassing all of Catholic Ireland, apart from a few hyper-scrupulous lords and clerics such as the Earl of Clanricarde and Peter Walsh.

In May 1642 the Irish Confederation was formed in Kilkenny as an oath-bound league of Irish Catholics. Each member pledged himself by oath to defend three things even at the sacrifice of his fortune and his life: the liberty of the Roman Catholic Church; the person, inheritances and rights of Charles our king; and the legitimate immunities and liberties of the Irish nation. Breandán Ó Buachalla, when describing the Oath, leaves out this bit about the immunities of the nation, in case it should seem to detract from the Confederates' royalism. But we mustn't ignore that important third principle. It is actually *aithbheodhadh glóire Gaoidheal* in Kilkenny-speak, in formal dress, presenting itself in proper and decent English.

One must say that it isn't a piece of empty rhetoric. It was interpreted to mean the repeal of Poynings's Law (which subordinated the Irish Parliament to the English Parliament), Irish government offices to be held only by Irishmen (who after the repeal of the anti-Catholic laws would generally be Catholics), an end to Strafford's plantation projects and no others to be undertaken, and so on. All of these things were demanded in February 1644 by the Irish Catholic delegation, led by Donough MacCarthy, who met the king at Oxford. What was envisaged was in effect a dual monarchy, something like the Austro-Hungarian Ausgleich of 1867, with the difference that the Irish only aspired to govern Ireland.

The formation of the Kilkenny Confederation is something astonishing, scarcely credible. It is too good to be true, as indeed the sequel showed.

The question to be considered here is how Conor O'Mahony would have viewed that sequel, i.e. the course of events in the rebellion up to 1645, when he was writing. It is easy to guess but difficult to prove. O'Mahony presents the issues with drastic simplicity. He sticks to the main point: Irish Catholics are "waging a sustained war against the English heretics" (Sec. 44); "(fighting) a just war for the Catholic faith, for your beloved country, for your lives and fortunes" (*Call Action*, sec. 12). On the other hand, he says right at the introduction that certain Catholics, *"to preserve their fragile temporal comfort",* do not defend their country as they should. It is all kept at a very general level.

However, it becomes clear in passing that he actually had a good deal of detailed information about the course of events in Ireland. His information extends as far as September of the year in which he is writing, 1645, when Malachy Queally, Archbishop of Tuam, was killed by the Parliamentarians (mentioned in *Call to Action*, sec. 11). One can assume that there was a substantial supply of Irish news reaching Lisbon and that O'Mahony had access to the best sources

I think he would have agreed with many of the views expressed by the Papal Nuncio Rinuccini in his Report to Rome in March 1646. Rinuccini drew a very clear picture which is worth looking at closely. But first of all, if only for the sake of contrast, let us peruse his official Papal instructions (probably drafted by Luke Wadding, a Waterford Franciscan who was highly placed in Rome), where the tone is much more south-east-of-Ireland and town-Catholic. Which is not to say that grand visions are lacking.

PROBLEMS OF INVADING BRITAIN

Rinuccini's instructor begins with a sketch of Irish history from the time of Saint Patrick. All that interests me here is the time of the Stuarts and after. There was a period of intensive persecution of Catholics during the reign of King James, but it did not last very long. Anxious to find a Catholic princess as a marriage partner for his son, James thought it better to slacken his anti-Catholic measures, *"and on the marriage of the Prince to Henrietta Maria of Bourbon, sister to Louis XIII of France, he granted to all the Catholics in his dominions the free and unconditional exercise of their religion. Affairs were in this state when Charles I succeeded to the throne and with it to the hatred which James, his father, had borne to that sect of the heretics who, following the pure doctrines of Calvin, under the name of Puritans, separated themselves from other Protestants."*

An account is given of Charles's conflicts with English Puritans and Scots Presbyterians, an unbroken chronicle of follies and misfortunes. The crowning disaster was the execution of the *"wise and far-seeing"* Earl of Strafford, *"the most faithful and the ablest minister of the King"*, whom Charles was obliged to sacrifice. Puffed up with success, the Parliament drastically reduced the King's powers and confiscated his revenues, and they committed themselves to wiping out the Catholic religion completely in England and in Ireland also.

This made the Irish Catholics think about rebellion, even if many of the leading nobles lacked courage. *"A few bold spirits"* forced the issue. Though they failed to take Dublin Castle, their rebellion was forceful enough to spark off a rising of the Catholics in general.

> "The rising, at first doubtful and tumultuous, was gradually organised into a well-arranged movement by the prelates and other clergy, who willingly gave both advice and assistance. But seeing that the army was led without military skill, its movements guided without knowledge of civil or political government, the bishops convened a council in the city of Kilkenny in April 1642. At this national synod they declared, first, that the rising was justified, and that its sole object was the preservation of the Catholic religion, by ensuring the public and unrestrained performance of its rites throughout the island; secondly, in order to unite all the disaffected into a strong religious confederacy, they introduced a form of oath which, administered in the first instance to the members of the assembly, was afterwards to be taken by all who desired to join the party before any active measure should be taken; and thirdly, a proclamation was issued for the general assembly to meet at Kilkenny in the following May, to decide on the form of government they should adopt."

All the noblemen of Catholic Ireland came to this assembly and elected a Supreme Council, which took over the powers previously held by the King's Irish Viceroy. The armed forces were organised as four provincial armies, each commanded by its own General. The Supreme Council, which included both noblemen and bishops, dealt with all civil business; ecclesiastical business was given over to the bishops exclusively. Many churches and cathedrals had been repossessed and hopefully more would soon follow, and in Catholic-held territory the Church was completely free. Monks went around in their habits, public religious processions were held, etc.

> "I must observe that the first and greatest object of your Excellency must be to establish in Ireland an unalterable right to the public exercise of the Catholic religion. To this object all your skill and energy must be assiduously devoted."

The writer takes it for granted that establishing the free public exercise of the Catholic religion in Ireland implies that there should be a Catholic Viceroy. Currently there was a Protestant Viceroy, the Marquis of Ormond. If he were to turn Catholic that would be very advantageous: Rinuccini is encouraged to explore possible means towards his conversion, and mention is made of relatives and others whose influence might be employed. But Ormond as he is now will not do. This is soon spelt out: *"You will endeavour to unite the clergy among themselves... Although the greater number are warmly interested in the enterprise, timid men are not wanting, nor even some who, preferring a private and undisturbed life to the public weal, are unhappily indifferent on the subject, nor think it of importance that a Government under a Catholic head be established in the island, provided the private celebration of Mass be not forbidden by the heretical Viceroy."*

Rinuccini's first duty, then, concerns Ireland. But in a separate memorandum it is made clear that Ireland is only one square on the chessboard, and the adjoining square is actually more important. So the big question is raised: how can the strength of the Catholics of Ireland be used for the benefit of the Catholics of England?

> "This may be done in two ways: first, that the Irish should include in the articles of accommodation with the King some conditions in favour of the English Catholics."

But this might be counterproductive, making the Irish Catholics look like political gamblers who do not care about the King, and the end result might be to strengthen those who oppose peace with the Irish in any form.

> "A second way would be to insist on terms which would secure the Irish in their property, and enable them to send a considerable army into England to the assistance of His Majesty; with this army the

English Catholics would unite, and thus form together a Catholic *army of the two nations, by means of which they might do some signal service, and thus find favour with the King, despite the malice of all their enemies."*

But how was this Irish Catholic invasion force, united with English Catholic auxiliaries, to be effective? The writer lists seven conditions. Firstly, *"that the Irish army shall never agree to land in England with less than ten or twelve thousand effective men, that they may be able to defend themselves without danger of being cut to pieces by the English, who serve the King."* (One's first thought is that this could be a translator's error, but the Italian original says the same and if anything more emphatically. The sixth condition, below, confirms the point. To all appearances, Rinuccini's instructor is saying and means to say: the first danger the King's Irish auxiliaries will face is of being massacred, or betrayed and led into massacre, by their English Protestant royalist allies.)

Secondly, the Irish would need control of two well-fortified seaports, with Irish-appointed governors, for disembarkation. Thirdly, the army's generals and all subordinate officers would be Irish-appointed. Fourthly, the Irish generals would obey no orders except those which came direct from the King. Fifthly, the Irish army would keep together always in one body. Sixthly,

> "that permission and authority from the King be accorded to the English Catholics to form themselves into a body of cavalry proportionate in strength to the Irish infantry. This condition is so essential to the Irish Catholics that the King cannot refuse it, as they are so hated by the English Protestants that they would be in constant danger of treachery if moving with cavalry commanded by Protestant officers."

And seventhly, since the Irish general would need to be able to trust this English Catholic cavalry general, he would have a veto on his nomination.

Reading these elaborate preconditions, did Rinuccini wonder how firmly his instructor had a grip on reality? Did he reflect that it might be no easier for King Charles to give over two of his western ports, supposing he still had two to give, to the Irish, than to include some universal Catholic relief measures in an Irish treaty? Yet there were important issues here. The King was indeed hoping for military assistance from Ireland in conjunction with an Irish peace. But how could Irish Catholic troops be landed safely in England, and once landed how could they do the King good service? (The precedents were discouraging. A few years previously contingents of Irish Protestant troops had been sent to help the King; they had deserted in large numbers to the Parliamentarian side; those who did not desert had made no great showing in battle, and the English Parliamentarians who fought them did not accept that the laws of war applied to anyone from Ireland.)

Of course, none of this could be attempted unless there was agreement between the Irish and the King. And here we find that the writer sniffs Conor O'Mahony's idea somewhere in the breeze, and he wants Rinuccini to oppose it.

It would be unwise, he says, to try to change something or other in the form of the Irish government, because this might force the King to give up on the Irish Catholics and make peace with his Parliament. The Irish, who till then had fought a just war purely for the sake of religion, could fairly be represented as rebels if they demanded more. There is also the danger of embarrassing the Pope:

> "His Holiness, sending at this juncture a Nuncio of eminence with money and other supplies to the Irish... (might seem as if) not content with the establishment of religion, (he) sought to incite the King's subjects to open rebellion against the temporal crown, and to divert them from their legitimate subjection to His Majesty... Your Excellency can do nothing more effectual to help them in this work, or more worthy of apostolic zeal, than to seek to hold them firm in loyalty and temporal obedience to their King, and consequently, to cut short any new or political propositions, which might create a shadow of suspicion to the contrary."

Perhaps there are no such ideas in the air just now, the writer says, but this may change.

> "It may be that at present the Confederate Catholics of Ireland have no other thought than for their religion; still, when united into one powerful body, and accustomed to govern themselves, they may readily, and with some prospect of success, become ambitious to throw off the Royal yoke; therefore they will need to be restrained..."

In the Secret Instructions this warning is repeated forcefully.

> "Let him promote the interests of the Catholic religion in such a way as to show he considers it one with the English Crown, and hold firmly to the principle that at no time could he wish its yoke to be thrown off, nor ever hearken to propositions which tend to the contrary."

But it wsn't going to be easy to reach agreement with the King if the precondition was Catholic emancipation. And even if Rinuccini were to prove a skilled negotiator, initially at least his appointment was bound to make things more difficult.

In the Spring of 1645 there were stories going around London – or at any rate they were told to Antonio de Sousa – that the Pope was on the point of donating Ireland to King Philip of Spain. Since every Spanish success was a loss for Portugal, it was in the Portuguese interest to help prevent this. De Sousa reported to Lisbon that neither Charles nor his Parliament was likely to be able to resist the Spanish, and the best way to pre-empt a re-donation by the Papacy was for King Charles to reach agreement with the Irish Catholics. Charles indeed had plans, but to do anything about anything he desperately needed money!... There was interest in Portugal's Infanta as a marriage partner for Charles junior if her dowry was generous enough...

The sensational tales in London must have been connected with Rinuccini's appointment. He was named Papal Nuncio to Ireland in March 1645, though for various reasons he only arrived in the following October. This was a very striking papal intervention in English/Irish affairs, and many were unsure how to read it. And the question is: when Conor O'Mahony, fired by enthusiasm and urged by friends, as he tells us, began writing his *Argument* in the year 1645, did he know that the Pope had appointed an Italian Archbishop to go to Ireland with substantial aid in money and arms for the Catholic forces and orders to give them strategic political direction? He must certainly have known by the time he finished. But although he records the other Papal interventions in Ireland, down to the blessing of Eoghan Ruadh O'Neill in 1642, this one is studiously avoided.

Though not all of the Catholic lords and prelates of Ireland wanted an energetic Nuncio, none of them tried to obstruct him openly. He was warmly welcomed on arrival. Even John Callaghan, his fiercest Catholic critic, admits that much. However, there can be no doubt that the people who wanted him most were northern. The importation of an activist Papal Nuncio was the last spectacular move of the northern strategists, their attempt to regenerate the rebellion and restore its momentum. Of course, this was possible only because the Pope considered it good for global Catholic and papal interests. But it is certain that Rinuccini didn't come to Ireland without being asked for.

But how would he see his duty? To what ends would he try to guide the Catholic movement? Would he choose to treat it as an instrument in the Church's larger strategy for the recapture of Britain, as advised by his instructor?

The northern strategists were confident that in all the circumstances this Italian Archbishop could come nearest to leading Ireland as they believed Ireland should be led. For their part, they were prepared to offer him background knowledge, explanation, perspective and counsel. He knew, of course, that he was supposed to keep an independent point of view, but wasn't it natural to listen? A newly-arrived Italian who was supposed to lead Ireland needed all the help he could get!

Four months after his arrival in Ireland (March 1, 1646) he sent a report on the state of the country to his cardinal-supervisor in Rome. The document shows him deeply frustrated with the state of Irish Catholic politics, and in the intensity of frustration he was thinking dangerous thoughts.

Rinuccini began by complaining that the Supreme Council had grown too big, and this had produced three major evils. The most obvious was the gross waste of time and inefficiency. But the other two were by far the most serious: firstly, Ormond's supporters were packing the Council; secondly, and related to this, a dangerous split in Irish Catholic politics was deepening.

> "But the two less apparent evils became beyond comparison the most grave. The first, that the Commissioners having to treat for the peace of Dublin and of England with the Marquis of Ormonde, it was so managed, under the pretext of sending deputies who were agreeable to him, that members were always chosen who were well affected to his party, and the consequence was to fill the Irish Council with the favourites of that faction, the prime cause now, and perhaps for the future, of all the turbulence and misery of this kingdom. The second was having increased the division between the old and the new Irish, which will always be the greatest obstacle to the progress of religion; the old, perceiving that the Council, to please Ormonde, was by degrees becoming entirely composed of their adversaries, are alienated in heart, and wish for disturbances in the hope of recovering some of their power. This wide division has been the origin of the great diversity of opinion which prevails on the island.
>
> Now the old nobility, to increase their power, have contrived to draw to their side the clergy, and with these have declared that if they

cannot obtain a glorious peace, they would much rather go to war. Their opponents on the contrary are suspicious of the clergy and wish for peace on any terms, not being ashamed to declare that if they obtain the free exercise of the Catholic rites at home, they would consider it superfluous and unjust to ask for more. The old Irish awaited with the utmost impatience the arrival of a Nuncio, supposing that he would have orders to exclude all thought of peace and think solely of war. I have had no little trouble in persuading them to the contrary, and ridding myself of the importunities of those who persist in believing that I brought money to raise a Pontifical army, not so much to fight against the Puritans, as to put an end at once to any treaty or agreement with the King. The opposite party by no means welcomed my arrival, as they knew I should not be disposed to purchase a peace such as they desired, and would accept none unless favourable to religion; hence in order to diminish the credit of my authority, they have actually spread a report that I am come to take temporal possession of Ireland for His Holiness, and that Father Scarampi had been sent on before to see if such an attempt would be practicable. Finally, the principal desire of the old Irish is for the splendour of religion and the equality of the nobles, while for the others, the satisfaction and advancement of Ormonde constitute their great aim."

When Rinuccini refers to the old Irish, he means the Ulster Irish plus like-minded people in the South (O'Sullivan Mór, O'Sullivan Beare, the O'Donoghues of Kerry, dissident MacCarthys, the O'Moores and O'Byrnes of the Midlands/South Leinster etc.). One can justly complain that the term 'old Irish' oversimplifies things when used to describe one of the two great Catholic political factions. Donough MacCarthy, the most powerful old-Irish lord in South Munster, was actually the leader of the opposite party, the pro-Ormond faction; and as for North Munster, its most powerful old-Irish lord was outside of Catholic politics entirely: Murchadh Ó Briain, Lord Inchiquin, was the military leader of the Munster Protestants and at that time an ally of the Parliament.

Thirty years previously Tadhg Mac Dáire Mac Bruaideadha, leader of the southern side in the North-South Contention of the Poets, in his victory poem claimed to have upheld the honour of the entire Southern Half of Ireland (Leath Mogha) against the Northern Half (Leath Chuinn). He named one by one the specific clans whom he thought were indebted to him. Taking south Munster, there were the MacCarthys in their various branches in Magonihy (Kerry), Carbery and Muskerry; the

McDonaghs, O'Keeffes and Callaghans; the O'Mahonys, McKennas, O'Sullivans, MacGillacuddys, McAuliffes, O'Donoghues, Mac Fineens. Moving on to Thomond, he naturally claimed that the O'Briens above all were his debtors; also mentioned were the O'Kennedys, McGraths, O'Mearas, O'Herlihys, Hogans, O'Cassins, MacNamaras, O'Clancys, O'Heas, MacCoughlans, O'Deas, O'Carrolls and O'Haras. Additionally Tadhg declared that some of the Old English lords had become assimilated to Leath Mogha through their female ancestors: two important examples were the Butlers, Earls of Ormond, and the Burkes, Earls of Clanricarde. Making all due allowances for dissidence, it is certain that many of the old-Irish clans mentioned above supported Donough MacCarthy throughout the 1640s, and some of those in Thomond would have supported Inchiquin.

However, Rinuccini can be forgiven for the way he uses 'old Irish', because the Ulstermen were using the equivalent term *Sean-Éireannach* in the same way (as evidenced, for example, by Ó Mealláin's Diary). What is interesting is that he sees the Ulstermen as having won the support of the clergy – by which we should understand "the best of the clergy". He is somewhat uneasy about this politicised clergy and the desperate state of mind of the Ulstermen, but mainly he likes them and they like him too. And dialogue is occurring. He mentions the energetic ex-Louvain man, Ever MacMahon, Bishop of Clogher, as one of those who have properly high ambitions for the state of religion, but says he is dominated by political concerns. Yet who else is likely to have impressed on Rinuccini this particular sharply-drawn outline of Irish Catholic politics?

As for the other faction, they weigh upon his mind, they haunt and obsess him, and will throughout all his time in Ireland. Have they not allowed the Marquis of Ormond to waste irreplaceable time and precious Catholic resources?

> "It is evident that if at the beginning of the war the Irish had steadily continued to take possession of all the fortresses of the kingdom, and especially of Dublin, they would now be masters of the whole country and by professing in virtue of their oath to hold all for the King, in effect excluding the Puritans, from whom no concessions could be hoped for religion, they would have served their cause better than by truces and treaties which have not even saved them from being called rebels by His Majesty and all England.
>
> It was the Ormond faction who, partly under the pretence of neutrality

and partly to please the Marquis, introduced by little and little the cessations with the Protestants, much to the injury of the common cause, as they have interrupted the course of victory, checked the first ardour of the people, and wasted the means which might have been employed against the Puritans; since during the three years of truce it has been calculated that a large part of the revenue has found its way into the hands of the Marquis, which would otherwise have passed into the hands of the Irish, and might have absolutely terminated the war.

The military negotiation, then, tends chiefly to the conclusion of the long-desired Ormonde peace, to be followed by the appointment of the Marquis as general of the whole army, and thus give him all the glory and all the fruits of the whole enterprise."

The Confederation's army, or armies rather, are all a mess. The Generals are a law unto themselves, but to make matters worse they have rivals (as in the case of Eoghan Ruadh and Phelim O'Neill, whose rivalry cripples the campaign in Ulster), or they obstruct one another for political reasons (as in the case of Preston and the extreme Ormondite Castlehaven at the siege of Youghal). As for religion, most of the bishops, and still more so the monks, show a lukewarm spirit. They think it is fine to have Mass said in private houses, and the 'lower orders' feel the same way. Rinuccini feels that the Irish in general are strangely inert and unindustrious, satisfied always with the barest minimum – apart from climate and coldness of the blood, he thinks it may be a result of the centuries of English oppression. Under firm direction he believes they are capable of better. In fact, all of the most serious problems could be solved if just one single obstacle was removed.

"As all the disturbances take their origin from one source only, that is the faction of the Marquis of Ormond, it is manifest that this once remedied whatever disorders there are in the three estates might be repaired at one moment, because if the Supreme Council had wished or would wish to secure Dublin, and have the Marquis as their colleague but not as their superior, one could have formed at once, and could even now form, a union between them and the nobility of the kingdom from which the political government would acquire sufficient strength, and resolutions would be promulgated with common consent and approval."

The war against the Parliamentarians would then be pursued strenuously, without caring about what the Marquis thought. And the currently timorous clergy,

> "freed from the thought of having to consult with the Viceroy day by day on the condition of religion, would defend it everywhere and strengthen themselves so that they should never lose ground, assured that when the King was in a state to make concessions, he would do so with the good faith due to an armed people resolved to obtain them by every means in their power."

But ultimately all of this may be purely theoretical. So impressed is Rinuccini by the strength of the Ormondites that he feels they could well be politically invincible. But if the King's position in England collapses, surely they too will topple. His frustration is such that he cannot refrain from putting this thought into words.

> "As there is no human force that can either destroy or weaken this Ormond League, it has often occurred to me to question whether it would be better for this country that the King of England should regain his power, or that the Parliament by his ruin should become masters of Ireland. On the one hand I think with respect to the Faith, it would be more secure to treat with a Prince not unwilling perhaps in this matter to yield all in his power convinced of the fidelity of the Irish; with a Catholic wife, and on a friendly footing with all Catholic princes. But on the other hand, I am alarmed by the general opinion of His Majesty's inconstancy and bad faith, which creates a doubt that whatever concessions he may make, he will never ratify them unless it pleases him, or not having appointed a Catholic Viceroy, whether he might not be induced by his Protestant ministers to avenge himself on the noblest heads in Ireland, and renew more fearfully than ever the terrors of heresy.
>
> Therefore I am disposed to believe that in considering the subject of religion, which grows and is purified by opposition, the destruction of the King would be more useful to the Irish. In this case a union of the whole people to resist the forces of Parliament would immediately follow, and by choosing a Catholic chief or Viceroy from among themselves, they would establish according to their own views all ecclesiastical affairs, without danger of being molested in the execution of their designs by the Protestants or their adherents. Nor am I daunted by the apprehension generally entertained of a sanguinary war waged against Ireland by the King and Parliament united, inasmuch as if money be supplied from abroad, the kingdom is not so destitute of men but that it could defend itself against very large armies. In this case also it would so move the compassion of His Holiness and other princes, that as Christianity could not have an enterprise more important

or meritorious than this, so the people would live in the assured belief that they would never be abandoned by the goodness of the Holy See and the piety of Christians."

From this position Conor O'Mahony should be visible on the horizon! A Nuncio who thought like this would not be well-equipped to *"promote the interests of the Catholic religion in such a way as to show he considers it one with the English Crown"*, as stipulated by his instructions. Rinuccini was suspect on this point from the beginning, and suspect he remained. But how realistic were those instructions of his: on the one hand he must be emphatically royalist, on the other hand he must prevent any peace except on terms which the King (conferring with Donough MacCarthy in Oxford) had rejected as politically impossible even in the Spring of 1644, and which had not become more politically possible in the two years since: the complete emancipation of Catholicism in Ireland, with all that this implied? As John Callaghan demanded: if you couldn't or wouldn't make any realistic peace with the King, didn't that suggest you were thinking of a separate Irish monarchy, or of Ireland being transferred to some other monarch's domain?

And what was so frightful about submitting to Ormond? his adherents asked. The man had merits that could be listed at length.

> "Besides his illustrious family and ample fortune, (he shows) supreme fidelity to his legitimate prince, supreme humanity towards all upright Catholics, incredible graciousness, unshakeable firmness of word and promise, prudence without vulgarity, far-sightedness in adversity, modesty in prosperity, remembrance of things done by followers in their duty, forgetfulness of injuries, elegance and brilliance of speech, eminent distinction of mouth and entire body: apart from religion, everything that is worthy of a leading man",

in Callaghan's words. And furthermore: Ormond had never expelled Irish Catholics from their lands and replaced them with English Protestants, though he might have done so profitably; his entire county now was no less inhabited by Catholics than in his father's time; he had always admitted Catholics and Protestants into his family and never asked anyone to change religion; he had even continued paying the pensions to Catholic clergy, including the Archbishop of Cashel and the Bishop of Waterford, which his Catholic father used to pay!

Rinuccini tried to see his opponent clearly. He noted that Ormond had political ability and considerable personal charm; probably he also had considerable personal ambition.

> "After deliberating on the course he is likely to pursue in case the King be entirely ruined, I have taken care to show to all who are likely *to report my words to him, how much more useful and glorious it would be for him to declare himself a Catholic, rather than pass over to the Puritans as it is reported he is about to do."* If Ormond became a Catholic he was sure it would only be a "Paris is worth a Mass" type of conversion, purely opportunistic. Ormond by all accounts was a convinced Protestant and his Catholic relatives and associates were not capable of unsettling his convictions.

The Marquis, it was thought, hoped to use the peace for political advantage.

> "He has therefore heaped promise on promise to his adherents; and as he knows the tenacity with which the Irish hold to their religion, it is said that he has granted every facility to its exercise, not only by words and declarations of tolerance, but by a general clause introduced into the articles of the peace, which declares that with respect to the Catholic religion he consents to all the conditions which may be approved by the King in favour of everyone. His faction, deluded by such promises and deceived by his manner, protest that no event could be more favourable to religion than a union with the Marquis, and that it would be better to rely on him even in ecclesiastical matters, rather than stipulate for them one by one, and that in short the kingdom could not be in a more secure or more enviable position than under his care and providence, and in trusting to the magnanimity of the Marquis."

The magnanimity of the Marquis! There it was in a nutshell: the attachment of most of the Catholic Supreme Council to this Lutheran was so **positive**! Here was something more than the weakness of spirit and timidity that Rinuccini had been warned to expect. Why did they so want to submit to this heretic, what was the compulsion they felt to please him? That this Protestant lord should count for more with the Catholic government of Ireland than he himself did – he, the Papal Nuncio! The tone of his words quoted above is rather pessimistic, but Rinuccini, given half a chance, was determined to fight.

REVIEW OF THE ARGUMENT

It is time for a brief review of the book which Conor O'Mahony, writing at furious haste, had by then concluded and may already have handed over to a printer. The author was in good health, a contemporary Jesuit source tells us; on the evidence of his book he was also in high spirits. By then he was no longer teaching. In 1641 he had ceased to lecture at the Irish College, in circumstances which are not known. *"We know simply that he was transferred to the Professed House in Lisbon and henceforth laboured as an* ***operarius*** *with the duty of administering the sacraments and preaching"*, Finegan says. This may explain the implied complaint in his foreword that he doesn't have enough leisure for compiling his book: he wishes he could spend as long in the libraries as some other learned doctors.

Following his opening address to the Catholic Irish and his foreword to the Catholic reader, he gives a summary account of pre-Norman Irish history, which is declared to be uncontroversial. With minor qualifications this is true, or it was true then. His source here is the Norman writer Gerald of Wales, whose account is used also by the other writers whom O'Mahony quotes in support.

Interestingly, O'Mahony gives most space to the pre-Milesian period. O'Sullivan Beare ignores this period entirely – logically enough, because what did the Parthalonians or the Nemedians have to do with the history of Catholic Ireland? In the course of time the Milesians, and they alone, had converted to the Catholic faith, and O'Sullivan Beare was writing for their descendants. He therefore remarks that Gerald has a brief account of pre-Milesian history, which is also contained in very old manuscripts, but for most of his own readers this would be a waste of time (*otium*). But O'Mahony had before him the just-published polemical masterwork of independent Portugal, *Lusitania Liberata,* which began by tracing the history of Portugal from the year 143 after the Flood. And he must have said to himself: Ireland has an antiquity almost equaling Portugal's!!! – now there's something to be proud of, that much needs to be said!

O'Mahony changes only one thing in Gerald's account, and it corresponds to one of Geoffrey Keating's two main criticisms of Gerald's pre-Milesian history. According to Keating, the story of Cessair's occupation of Ireland prior to the Flood should not have been presented as though Irish historians believed it, since it was only a literary fiction. O'Mahony obviously thought the same and he omits this story. Apart from that he follows Gerald faithfully, including in his treatment of the Tuatha Dé Danaan, who are almost entirely ignored. This was the second target of Keating's criticism. The man who gave Gerald his information must have been blind or stupid, he said, to omit such an important invasion! I think it is more likely that Gerald's informant was prudent: he knew that the Tuatha Dé Danaan were a group of the old gods and he mightn't have wanted Gerald to become too interested.

When we turn to O'Mahony's First, Second and Third Sections, where he sets out his opponents' four arguments for the validity of English rule in Ireland and responds to the first two, the importance of O'Sullivan Beare's *History of Catholic Ireland* becomes clear. I leave it to others to do the detailed matching, but anyone who compares O'Mahony's Sections 17 (Henry II's war was unjust), 18 (Pope Adrian's Bull was obtained falsely) and 31 (the Bull's conditions were broken) with the *Catholic History*, tom.2, bk.1, ch.7 will see that he is paraphrasing O'Sullivan when not quoting him word for word. The argument in the Third Section is taken further by producing a series of later Papal Bulls, some of which declare that the subjects of King Henry VIII and Queen Elizabeth are freed from their allegiance (so implicitly the Irish are freed from English rule!), while others give encouragement and blessing to Irish rebels.

In the Fourth Section, arguing that English rule was not validated by Irish acceptance, he quotes O'Sullivan Beare's statement that Henry was accepted by the Irish lords not as king of Ireland but as papal prefect and collector of Peter's Pence. Again, in the Fifth Section, where it is argued that the English have no prescriptive rights, one of the strongest points is O'Sullivan Beare's: English rule in Ireland was never tranquil or settled, because at all times it was interrupted by Irishmen waging just war. Throughout the book two other Irish writers, Richard Stanihurst and Peter Lombard, are cited as supporting authorities. Their role is purely to back up O'Sullivan Beare; they contribute very little independently, and that little (e.g. the story of King Murchadh, Argument 95) could just as well be left out.

The Fourth and Fifth Sections are legalistic, and here we see the influence of O'Mahony's Portuguese models. Great numbers of authorities are cited, but it is fair to say that the most important of them all is Suarez.

In the Sixth Section O'Mahony tells his opponents that even if all their objections were valid, even if the English kings had legitimately held Ireland, they could still be expelled on the grounds that they had become heretics and tyrants. Drawing heavily on Suarez, he argues firstly that kingship is a human institution, conferred by the people. However, if the king threatens the people with ruin, they may take back what they have given. And if this is legitimate even when the people are faced with material ruin, how much more so when the ruin threatened is spiritual! Heresy is tyranny, so the heretic king may be treated in the same way as the ordinary tyrant.

He then presents an enormous catalogue of kings who had been deposed by their peoples and/or killed. No doubt he was worried that many of the Irish Catholics thought of the English king as something approaching "a little god on earth", in the words of King James. O'Mahony wanted to bring him down from that pedestal. There were readers whose instinctive reaction might have been that deposing the king was 'unheard-of', but with his numerous examples he hoped to convince them that the opposite was the case. (The grim catalogue is varied with a narrative of the misdeeds of a king who wasn't deposed, though the author says he should have been: King Henry VIII, whose scurrilous biography is transcribed from the English Catholic writer Nicholas Sanders.)

There are many more examples he could give, but for brevity's sake he is leaving the Greeks and Assyrians out of account. In Lisbon's libraries there are chronicles of all the world, unfortunately with one important exception: Ireland. He cannot avail of the Irish histories at present. Consult them for yourselves, he tells his readers at home; they are by no means lacking in stories of kings losing their kingdoms. (And certainly this is so, even if Geoffrey Keating's exuberant claim is not to be taken too literally: defending Brian Boru against charges of being an usurper, he says that there wasn't one in seven of the Milesian kings who hadn't killed the king before him!)

O'Mahony's Call to Action follows. Here he takes the step which Philip O'Sullivan Beare had not taken: he calls on the Irish to elect a king of their own. Irishmen, do as the Israelites did in the days of Samuel!

He is most ingenious in finding Biblical examples to develop the Ireland-Israel comparison, which was well-known already in Irish-language writings. One example is from the *First Book of Kings*, where the men of Jabes come to the heathen King Naas and say to him: Make a treaty with us and we will serve you. And he replies: I will make a treaty with you to pluck the right eye out of every one of you and leave Israel a disgrace before the world! – This part at least Rinuccini must have read with relish.

O'Mahony makes it very clear that he does not favour treaties with the heretics. This brings us to the most notorious part of the book, where he quotes the Irish Lord Justices' fantastically inflated figure of 150,000 Protestants killed in the rebellion. He claims that the Catholic side had not disputed this figure. So far as I know this is true, though certainly there were doubts. Even those who were ill-disposed towards the Catholics of Ulster, where most of the killing was said to have occurred, suspected some exaggeration. John Callaghan, writing in 1650, says that Phelim O'Neill with his raw troops *"had done many things against the English and Scots of Ulster... which (if the stories reported are true) a Catholic man should by no means be responsible for"*.

The Earl of Castlehaven, who was still more anti-northern, said later on in his memoirs: "*It is very certain that there have been great cruelties committed upon the English, though I believe, not the twentieth part of what is generally reported.*" Castlehaven's assertion holds up well in the light of estimates made by cooler heads from the 18th century on, which suggest that the figure of those killed was about 4,000, with about another 8,000 dying of rebellion-related causes such as exposure. To this it should be added that while the rebels from the beginning tried to rob the colonists of everything that they had, including their financial documents and their clothes, they did not normally try to kill them. The distinction which Domhnall Mac an Ghalloglaigh makes in relation to Leitrim – *"it is clear from the depositions that the Leitrim rebels were more intent on expelling the Protestants and seizing their property than on taking their lives"* – can be generalised. It was when the colonists themselves responded with local massacres that the rebels carried out the counter-massacres which then became notorious.

But O'Mahony takes the figure of 150,000 in earnest. Their side has admitted this, he says, and you (the Catholics) have not denied it. So then, continue the work well begun! Kill or expel the rest of the heretics also! Canon John O'Mahony comments:

> "This passage has been unfairly represented as an incitement to an indiscriminate massacre or assassination. But in the context – in the paragraph (19) preceding that passage and in the sentence following it – he is expressly speaking *of ordinary warfare."*

He is indeed speaking of warfare, but with the best will in the world I don't think one can call it 'ordinary'. The fact is that the man took his Bible a bit too literally. Like many others on both sides of the Catholic-Protestant divide, he thought that the biblical massacres were admirable and well worthy of emulation in suitable contexts.

For whatever reason, he seems fascinated with the arithmetic of the large-scale killing of idolators, heathens and heretics. He gives about five examples with figures from 23,000 to 100,000, ranging from Biblical events to the 13th century Albigensian Crusade. It may be that he always keeps in mind the proviso, "spare the civilians!", but he has omitted to say so. (True, he condemns the "detestable" words of the emperor Vitellius, *"The enemy dead are stinking nicely, the Romans will stink even better!"* However, this comment is taken verbatim from Suetonius.)

Canon O'Mahony is on firmer ground when he says that all this must be seen in the context of the example given by the English in practice and theory: murderous actions on the one hand, including the use of famine as a weapon of war, and murderous writings on the other. Edmund Spenser does not say "Kill them all!", but he says that it's OK to create a famine and starve everybody wherever anyone is still resisting. Stomachs that are strong enough for *A View of the Present State of Ireland*, which is reprinted time and again, will hardly be too upset by anything O'Mahony says.

Anyhow, with this leap into the jaws of Puritan propaganda O'Mahony made it easy for his enemies to represent him as "barbarous and bloody". In other respects the *Argument*'s author is anxious to secure himself against possible misinterpretation. He insists that he has nothing against Englishmen who are Catholics, much less against Irish Catholics of English extraction. While prescription does not apply to English royal rule, it does apply to the property of Catholics who arrived in Ireland as colonists or planters. Twenty years or ten is enough to confirm them in prescriptive right, O'Mahony says. Approvingly he quotes a statement by the Confederate Supreme Council forbidding any distinction to be made between Catholic Irishmen.

On the other hand, his concluding declaration that he has no animus against King Charles is not to be taken seriously. This is a purely technical disclaimer, as well as a provocation. At the beginning of *Lusitania Liberata* de Sousa likewise disclaims any malice against the Most Catholic King of Spain, and we know just how sincerely that was intended.

*** ***

"Who financed the production of the Disputatio?" Finegan wondered. *"Conor had no resources of his own. Was it maybe some of the merchant princes of the Irish seaports who traded at Lisbon? To such questions no ready answers are forthcoming."*

O'Mahony must have known from the beginning that his book could never appear under his own name, nor could Lisbon be given as the place of publication. But this problem was not a new one. For at least a generation Irish Catholic writers had been getting controversial books printed in Catholic territories where the authorities were content to know nothing, but did not want these books to disturb relations with England or provoke bothersome protests. What one needed to do was to think of a pseudonym, a fictitious printer and a German city. Favourites were Frankfurt and Cologne.

It is possible that our author was inspired by the example of a namesake, a Cork Franciscan called Francis O'Mahony, who may or may not have been a near or distant cousin. In 1631 Francis O'Mahony had produced a book called *Examen Juridicum*, a contribution to a controversy involving Catholic clergy in Ireland and Paris. The *Examen* appeared very quickly in reply to a document published in Paris in the same year, so presumably it was printed in Paris also. But the place of publication given is Frankfurt.

The *Argument Defending the Right of the Kingdom of Ireland*, according to its title-page, was printed by permission of superiors by Bernardus Govranus in Frankfurt in 1645. Contradicting this, the statement by the Portuguese king on December 5, 1647, that the book had been printed in Portugal, could be taken as decisive. However, for the sake of completeness I have checked the evidence at the German end, where the most extensive sources of information have no mention of a printer called Bernardus Govranus or anything similar.

R. A. Madden, who had some knowledge of Portuguese books of the period, says: "*From the typography, the binding and the quality of the paper I judge that the book was not printed in Frankfurt, but in Lisbon*". For good measure J. P. Conlon says that the watermark on the *Argument*'s paper is of a type well-known in contemporary printed books in Spain and Portugal, but no examples of this type are known from Germany. From all of this it seems reasonable to conclude that 'Frankfurt' is a fiction and the true place of publication was Lisbon.

Whoever he was, 'Bernard Gowran' was not much of an ornament to his profession. O'Mahony didn't have the option of correcting a set of proofs before printing, but he was able to check the printed pages before binding, and what he saw appalled him. Hastily he compiled an errata page, listing "the more important errors" and leaving the reader in no doubt of his feelings about the printer.

> "The pages of this book, though few in number, contain not a few errors which crept in because the author was not present and the printer was not diligent. The Catholic reader in the course of reading can fill in corrections for those which we note here and any others which he may find."

There are signs of last-minute insights and frantic last-second amendments. The original title read *An Argument Defending the Right of the Kingdom of Ireland, in Support of the Irish Catholics Against the English Heretics*, *written by C. M., an Irishman, Master of Arts and Theology*. But another title was produced which reads, *An Argument Defending and Demonstrating the Right of the Kingdom of Ireland, in Support of the Irish Catholics Against the Heretics*, *written by Constantinus Marullus, an Irishman*. The most important change here is the substitution of "English heretics" simply by "heretics". It suggests that O'Mahony was now worried he might be accused (as indeed he would be) of promoting ethnic hatred and inciting attacks on English-born or English-descended Catholics living in Ireland.

"*In some copies there is a second title, extending the initials C. M. into Constantinus Marullus*", Charles McNeill says. This implies that there are other copies which have only the first title. But in each of the two copies of the 1645 edition which I have seen both title-pages are included! This can hardly have been intended, so presumably it is one more mark of the printer's incompetence.

Very interesting is the expansion of "C. M." to "Constantinus Marullus", suggesting that O'Mahony wanted to leave a clue to his name (even though now, pressed for space, he had to omit his academic distinctions). On this the family historian remarks:

> "Certainly he selected a pseudonym not calculated to secure perfect concealment, as 'Constantinus' was one of the two Latinized forms employed for Conchubhar, a Christian name that had become almost peculiar to those who bore his surname at that period".

And 'Marullus'? What does that signify? It's a normal Latin surname, beginning of course with 'Ma...' But then why not 'Marius' or 'Marcius'? Or 'Marcellus'? Why '**Maru**llus' particularly?

One would expect the surname to have a special significance, to contain some identifying riddle. In Francis O'Mahony's *Examen Juridicum* the author calls himself **Ursulanus**. The name comes from *ursa*, Latin for 'bear', playing on *Ó Mathghamhna/Mathghamhain,* 'bear' in Irish. A year later his principal adversary in Dublin published *Arktomastix* – Greek for 'bear-whip'.

The reader may be able to come up with a better theory than mine. I can only suggest that our author would have been known in Muskerry as Ó **Ma**thghamhna **Ru**adh if he belonged to Clann Finghín, one of the three O'Mahony septs in Muskerry mentioned earlier. (Pushing this speculation still further, one might guess that he was a younger brother of Dermot O'Mahony, recorded as owner of the lands of Farnanes in the parish of Moviddy, who was leader of Clan Fineen from 1617 to 1663 and is known to have taken part in the 1641 rebellion. But I cannot show proof of this, and it remains true that the most we can safely say about Conor O'Mahony is that he was a Muskerryman.)

With his 'Frankfurt'-published book in his hands, O'Mahony went around Lisbon showing it to all and sundry. An English priest who saw it went to the English ambassador who denounced it to the authorities, and on April 6, 1647 it was officially condemned. By then O'Mahony had probably had it packed in barrels and shipped to its destination. In the autumn of that year we find that the *Argument* is circulating in Ireland. It is making some of the Irish authorities excited, and selected quotations giving the most outrageous bits are going the rounds (one of these lists of quotations is preserved in Clarendon's papers).

The *Argument* made its appearance in a fiercely divided Catholic Ireland. All the explicit evidence suggests that it mainly inspired a ferocious pro-Ormond counterattack. However, according to Peter Walsh there were "many copies in the Nuncio's time privately dispersed up and down among trusty men in Ireland, but not discovered or known by the contrary side until about the year 1647." Some of those trusty men may have found inspiration in the book for their political actions. It is possible that one of them was the poet Pádraigín Haicéad, whose adventures we will come to shortly.

FOR AND AGAINST THE 1646 PEACE

In the autumn of 1645 the siege of Chester was near the critical point. John Callaghan thought that this was a critical moment for Ireland also.

> "Chester, a maritime town in England, held by a Royal garrison and besieged by Parliamentary forces, was being pressed hard. Unless relief was sent it would soon be surrendered, causing irreparable damage to the King's party. The royal forces were diminishing daily, the enemy was every day growing: if the King succumbed, then the mighty English nation – populous, rich, warlike, with horses, arms, ships, all the necessities of war and especially money, which is war's sinew – would pour not one but many armies, if need be, into Ireland, and would wear down all that remained of the nation in a matter of a few months, and all the more easily since it lay wide open. There were some zealous people who seemed to want prospects for the militant Church, that it would be preserved and increase; but the Church is a society of mortal men, not of immortal spirits, and consequently if these men were exterminated by the violence of ferocious enemies, the Church too necessarily would collapse. Without doubt the Catholics of Ireland would be extinguished to the last one, or through fragile human nature, fear of punishment or bitterness they would abjure their faith, if the King in England were to perish or became debilitated. The security of the whole nation, along with religion, was at stake along with the prosperity of the King's Majesty. The King could not maintain himself unless he received reliable aid from Ireland, which would save him from his downfall, while at the same time the enemy, taken up with its domestic conflicts, would be averted from Ireland."

Chester fell in January 1646, but the Confederate Supreme Council was still determined to make an accommodating peace with the King. In a difficult position Rinuccini played for time, and time worked in his favour. During the few months that he gained all three of the functioning Confederate armies won important military victories. The greatest was Eoghan Ruadh O'Neill's victory over the Ulster-Scots at Benburb. And then the Supreme Council published its peace, according to which the Catholic religion for the moment would be tolerated and the Catholics for the moment could keep the churches they possessed; the King, when eventually he was free, would decide the outstanding issues, and maybe he would decide in the Catholics' favour. And his Viceroy, the Marquis of Ormond, guaranteed he would not obstruct any possible future concessions to the Catholics, if the King in the future were to make some.

Who was for the peace?

> "The most eminent and prudent men were well aware from their study of the situation that nothing could be more desirable than to enter into peace with the King's party, so that by jointly repelling the Parliamentarians, who were such bitter enemies of King, kingdom and religion alike, provision would be made for the security of the nation and religion, and opprtune aid would be given to the struggling King." (Callaghan)

And what about those who were not so eminent or prudent?

> "Any kind of war was more acceptable to the clergy than that peace, where no provision was made for retaining or recovering their ecclesiastical properties; there were needy men who were tied by debts to others, and even many nobles whose faith and fortune had suffered in the period of civil quiet, and under the cloak of religion these took the clergy's side. Besides, there was the populace, more religious than it was provident or prudent..."

Rinuccini, writing a report on the peace for Rome, says essentially the same thing, though in positive language. *"The most zealous towns"* have combined with the clergy against the peace. Also, *"the whole province of Ulster, and many of the barons of Munster, consider themselves especially aggrieved, because although by the terms of the peace the adherents of the Marquis are all to be restored in their possessions, no mention whatever is made of them."* Ormond, it was feared, would use the immense power which he gained under the terms of the peace to discriminate against or punish all who did not belong to his faction; *"the most ancient nobles"* were of this opinion, *"and if they had a leader they would without doubt combine to kindle a civil war."*

So then, the old nobility **did not** have a leader! They **did not** have someone who was capable of leading armed opposition to the peace. That was Rinuccini's opinion, and it's worth noting. I should say here that along with the 'old nobility' there were plenty of the 'new nobility', i.e. nobles of Norman families, who were of like mind. A memorable expression of the thought "If this is the peace, what did we have a war for?" may be found in Pierce Ferriter's elegy for Maurice FitzGerald:

M'úidh leat is mo shúil go mór riot,
san cinneamhain do chirrbhadh na cómhairle,
mar do rug an cnoc luch mar thóircheas,
is é seacht mbliadhna i ndiachair tórmaigh.

I looked for you and longed for you greatly
in the fate that overcame the Council,
as when the mountain bore a mouse
after seven years of labour pain.

Rinuccini himself came forward as the champion of all opposition. By a resolute assault he laid the Ormond faction prostrate. The Supreme Council was imprisoned, a new one was installed composed of his own men, and he became dictator of Catholic Ireland. At long last the Confederate armies could resume their suspended work! The time-wasting truces with Ormond would now cease, the Catholics would recapture the military initiative, Dublin would be taken, Ormond would be got rid of, a Catholic viceroy would be appointed, and finally with the entire island in their hands the Catholic forces would be ready to face whoever emerged victorious in England, whether King or Parliament, in peace or war as the case might be.

That was theory. In fairness, Rinuccini did his best to put it into practice. But as a result of his actions patterns began to emerge which he had not foreseen and which had unexpected consequences.

"Bádar Comhairle Cilli Cainnigh ag dénamh síthe la hIarla Urmhumhan, gan chead na Sean-Éirionnach, agus dá radha ris teacht chugtha. Do gheall dóibh go dtiocfadh. Do desuigheadh an Chúirt agus an Caislán 'sdo cuireadh geabhta núa súas arna nighe as ór fó chomhair an Iarla. Tainic an Iarla, 15 trupa agus dá mhíle coisigh. D'umhlaigh Comhairle Cilli Cainnigh, Tighearna Mhóta Goiréad, Donncha MaCártha, agus an tír uile dhó; agus ar mbeith réidh leis an tír do chuaidh go Caisioll Mumhan. Gabhsat Muimhnigh leis go luathgháireach.

Tarla mon am sin Caibidil ag a' Nunnsius i bPort Láirge. Do clos aca Iarla Urmhumhan a bheith san tír. Do chuir a' Nunntius fios ar chúig céad saighdiúir, agus do chuir litreacha go Gen Uladh a rádha ris teacht gona shlóightibh as in mBreifni...

Dála Iarla Urmhumhan ó do chuala Gen. Uladh thecht don tír agus eision i gCaisiol do ghlacadar teitheadh chugtha, cúig trupa déag agus dá mhíle coisigh. Níor ghabh dá bhaile féin go Cill Cainnigh ach go

Gabhrán...Leis sin do theithseat go Lelinn...go Ceatharlach...As sin doibh go hÁth Cliath....

Dála Gen. Uladh ar dtecht don tír...arna chlos don (Nunnsius)...(tánic) a Cill Cainnigh I gcoinne a' Ghen.

Tánic a Gen. Agus Sior Feidhlim agus na h-uaisle i láthair na ndaoine naomhtha 'sdo ghlacadar a mbeannacht. Do iarr a' Gen. caislen agus daighne na cathrach do thabhairt dó féin: "agus tugtar braighde na tire agus an bhaile so dam i. Donnchadh MaCártha, Tighearna Musgraidhe, Eamonn Buitléar i. Mac Tighearna Móta Goiréad, Sectarii na Comhairle i. Beliin, Sior Seon Beigneir agus ceither fir eile do mhathaibh na Comhairle agus na tire." Do chuir glés ar na braighdibh agus ar an mbaile ó sin amach.

(Diary of Toirdhealbhach Ó Mealláin)

("The Council of Kilkenny was making peace with the Earl of Ormond, without the permission of the Old Irish, and inviting him to come to them. He promised them that he would. The Court and Castle were decorated and a new gate with wrought gold was put up for the Earl to pass through. The Earl came with 15 troop of horse and 2,000 foot. The Council of Kilkenny, Lord Mountgarret, Donough MacCarthy, and the whole region submitted to him; and when he was finished with that region he went to Cashel. The Munstermen received him in high spirits.

It happened that the Nuncio was then at a Synod in Waterford. They heard that the Earl of Ormond was in the region. The Nuncio sent for five hundred soldiers, and he sent letters to the General of Ulster telling him to come with his forces from Breifni.....

When the Earl of Ormond heard that the General of Ulster was coming to the region and he himself was in Cashel, he fled with his fifteen troops of horse and two thousand foot. He did not go to his own town, Kilkenny, but rather to Gowran...Thence they fled to Leighlin...to Carlow...From there they went to Dublin.

When the General of Ulster came to the region...and (the Nuncio) heard of it...(he came) to Kilkenny to meet the General.

The General and Sir Phelim and the noblemen came before those holy men and received their blessing. The General demanded that the castle and strong points of the town be delivered to him: "and let the hostages of the region and this town be given to me i.e. Donough MacCarthy, Lord Muskerry, Eamonn Buitléar i.e. Lord Mountgarret's son, the Secretaries of the Council i.e. Belings, Sir Seon Beigneir and four other leaders of the Council and the region." He kept the hostages and the town in order from that time forward.")

Language befitting an O'Neill High King! One understands that troops must be properly spoken to, and in all probability this language was used by Eoghan Ruadh to explain things to his Ulstermen rather than directly in dealings with "the region and the town". Maybe one shouldn't take a speech to the troops too literally.

Yet the fact remains that from this time forward O'Neill appeared to convince everyone that he considered himself in a different category from the other generals, something over and above what they were; he had big ideas, uncomfortably big... How big? What ideas? The question was answered variously. But suspicion of O'Neill now became the most powerful weapon of the defeated Ormond faction, and they used it ruthlessly.

As a result, whatever chance there was of taking Dublin by a quick determined assault dissolved in the mists. The task was given to two armies combined: Thomas Preston's Leinster army and Eoghan Ruadh's. Preston and his men had lined up on Rinuccini's side – due, Callaghan says, to a mixture of spiritual terror and Spanish gold. But Preston's heart, or something more than half of it, was with the Ormond faction, and his ear was open to their warnings. They told him *"that O'Neill's march into Leinster with so powerful an army proved that the pretext of religion given by him and others was utterly futile; that the clergy were in fact bent upon making him master of that province for other purposes"*, Rinuccini wrote later. He believed that Preston had privately committed himself not to take Dublin. And the Leinster General's behaviour on approaching the city, when he neglected or else hindered the proper preparations, gives that suspicion credence. That he involved himself in a lively intrigue with Ormond is clear from Ormond's own correspondence, and Clanricarde's. (The Viceroy had a chance to change the political shape of Ireland, but he didn't take it.)

Fleetingly, Rinuccini himself became resentful of Eoghan Ruadh and his army. The Ulster General was highly insubordinate, acknowledged no superior and had the gall to let his troops refer to themselves as the Pope's Army. On one occasion when the Pope's Army had behaved particularly badly, a member of the Ormond faction led a group of women to the Nuncio's house and they demonstrated noisily outside his window. *"Hatred of these Ulster troops is the cause of all the dissensions"*, he concluded, adding prophetically, *"all future events will be influenced by it"*.

Preston, he thought, would not have been so open to intrigue with

Ormond were it not that *"O'Neill had given proof of his high pretensions and determination to restore the old Irish faction"*. High pretensions...? Now what did he have in mind by that?

Nor should one forget the little tournament of quatrains that took place in Kerry at some time during the 1640s, when the issue was who should control part or all of "the hand" of Ireland. It was then that Pierce Ferriter controversially declared:

> *Más é an leoghan cróga Gaedheal i gceart*
> *do bhéarfas fód glan Fódla fé n-a smacht,*
> *a bhfaice-se, a stóchaigh chróin noch téid tar lear,*
> *beir chum Eoghan Mór Uí Néill an ghlac.*
>
> If he's indeed the brave lion of the Gaels
> who'll bring the land of Ireland under his power,
> you ugly (English) masts going over the sea,
> give up the hand to the great Eoghan O'Neill!

To give "the hand" to Eoghan Ruadh – in context what did it mean?

ACCUSATIONS AGAINST EOGHAN RUADH

While the Dublin situation was in stalemate, Rinuccini tried to make political gains in Munster. He was able to have Muskerry deposed as General of the Munster army, with the Earl of Glanmorgan replacing him. (Frustrated by Ormond's time-wasting pedantry, Charles had sent Glamorgan as his own special envoy to the Irish Catholics in 1645. When the Irish Parliamentarians discovered compromising documents, the Earl was disowned by King Charles and left high and dry in Ireland. Soon he aligned himself with Rinuccini and became one of the Nuncio's most faithful agents. Rinuccini was planning to make him the first Catholic Viceroy. True, he was an Englishman, but Irish divisions were so bitter that no native Irishman could be credible in the role.)

But though Muskerry was deposed, his men remained in key positions, including that of Lieutenant-General. The Munster Army was riven by plots and counter-plots. Passive resistance was widespread. *"Only meagre forces assembled in that province"*, John Callaghan says.

There was a military genius on the other side who sensed his opponents' weakness: Murchadh Ó Briain, Lord Inchiquin. He immediately took the offensive, picking off a series of important towns without any reply from the Confederates. The Muskerry faction was then accused of sabotaging the war effort and effectively helping Inchiquin, so as to discredit Glanmorgan. A lively agitation got underway in the Munster army. It was led by one of the most fascinating poets of the period, Pádraigín Haicéad, who had already produced *Músgail do mhisneach, a Bhanbha* ("Rouse up your courage, Ireland!"), the outstanding literary blast against the 1646 peace.

Haicéad was one of three Dominican chaplains who were spearheading agitation against officers loyal to Muskerry. The first mention of this seems to be on May 24, 1647, when a letter from Clonmel Confederate Council to Rinuccini accused the three friars of *"seeking to render the King's authority which is entrusted to us odious to the people"*, causing jealousies in the army, and *"by their disorderly and irreligious way of life"* giving general bad example. Muskerry heads the list of signatories.

A few days later the Council sent another complaint to Rinuccini, this time concerning an agitation carried on within the Munster army by Colonel Richard Butler, who was trying to supplant Muskerry's man as Lieutenant-General. The three friars are said to be among the most active pro-Butler agitators.

Then suddenly Muskerry counter-attacked. On a day in early June he literally went to the army, spoke to the officers and convinced them. *"Within the space of an hour he secured the army for himself, and Glanmorgan was driven away."* Not a drop of blood was spilt. *"That most mild man and great lover of his country's tranquillity composed the sedition. He might then have destroyed his personal enemies with ease, but in his charity he preferred to forgive them."* However, a less forgiving spirit is revealed in the extraordinary letter to Rinuccini quoted in full below. It is dated June 17 (and incidentally it suggests that at that point there were in effect two Munster Confederate armies).

> "The forces which support Viscount Muskerry, and many people of great note in the province of Munster, state the following concerning the intention of General Eoghan O'Neill to invade their liberties and fortunes.
>
> 1. General Eoghan O'Neill is thinking in terms of being absolute ruler and sovereign of Ireland.

2. To this purpose he is recruiting an immense army, beyond the kingdom's capacity, for his own ambition and will, ignoring the decrees of the General Committees in this regard.

3. He has his supporters in all provinces and sustains those who are active on his behalf.

4. He does not obey the orders of the General Committees or Council unless they correspond with his inclination.

5. He writes fine words to the Council, but does as he pleases.

6. His forces are like enemy soldiers in the harm they cause (except that they do not kill), plundering everything and leaving nothing behind except desolation and hunger, taking away ploughhorses etc.

7. Many hundreds of families in the other three provinces have been ruined by their cruelty and depredations.

8. They utter strong words to the effect that they will extirpate the Anglo-Irish, and the same declarations can be heard from many of their clergy. O'Neill's disobedience at the time of the siege of Athlone has caused many people to fear that he is directing his activities towards domination and rule over all; no one can give credence, without fear of mistrust, to the letters or words of those who refuse submission to orders in the accepted manner of the kingdom.

9. On the pretext of O'Neill's authority, Terence O'Brien is now mustering forces against the Council's manifest prescriptions, and it is feared that others will do the same.

10. The parties which now follow Muskerry assert that, arising from the fact that a mutiny had been raised near Clonmel, on one or more occasions messengers were sent by those inciting the sedition to Eoghan O'Neill, calling him (as is thought) to come to their assistance.

11. His military forces despise the authority and commands of the Council, as may be seen in the Tirconnell regiment and Alexander MacDonnell's regiment, who have moved from this province against the express command of the Council and the will of the governors.

12. Under his orders, though prohibited by the Council, his army has intruded into various counties to the ruin of the provinces: in County Kilkenny, for example, last Easter, within the space of twelve days their pillaging caused losses of twelve thousand pounds.

Demands attached:

1. The parties supporting Muskerry, led by the reasons aforesaid – since they would face dangers and sinister plots in a great army whose officers, to the oppression of subjects and the ruin of the province, arrogantly invite General Eoghan O'Neill to support them – will have

good fighting morale only if the Council manages to stabilise the situation and make it safe, which will not be done by bare orders to that General, but only by placing the province in a state of defense against him, since they do not trust his words, his army or his good faith, nor do they believe their liberties, possessions and fortunes to be secure.

2. They desire that anyone from the army of General O'Neill who comes into this province without the consent of the Council shall be declared a criminal outlaw.

3. That all officers of the Munster army shall swear that they will prevent and prohibit any plan of the aforementioned Arch-strategist or his army which tends towards reducing the immunities of the province.

4. They are prepared to swear on the Holy Sacrament that in separating themselves from the remainder of the forces they have never had it in mind to coalesce with Ormond or Inchiquin, or to renew the old peace which was previously rejected, or any other form of peace contrary to religion, or to approve any other peace unless with the authority of the kingdom in the General Committees, but nonetheless they are resolved before God that they would sooner coalesce with Ormond, Inchiquin or the Turks than commit themselves to Prefect General Eoghan and his army to be destroyed and reduced to slavery.

5. They humbly represent that they do not enjoy so much favour and estimation with the Illustrious Lord Nuncio as others do who are less suited to serve Ireland than they are, being at the beck and call of General Eoghan O'Neill.

6. There are certain monks who maliciously instil in the Illustrious Nuncio's ears suspicions, fears and unfounded mistrust of their integrity as regards religion and country, asserting that all they do is attempt to form a union with Ormond or Inchiquin, or to introduce the old peace or a new one similarly noxious, and other rotten concoctions of the kind. Despite their vows and Holy Orders, no province in the state, whether military or civil, should be entrusted to these monks, but only whatever is to be done according to Eoghan's pleasure.

7. Three monastic priests, Fr Patrick Hackett, Fr Philip O'Dwyer and Fr David Roche, behaved as active incendiaries in raising the recent sedition at Clonmel, where they interfered in the taking of the Confederate Oath and asserted that some of the Confederates, and those men of no contemptible fortune, such as Dr Gerard Fennell and others, could legitimately be plundered. Even now they are daily spreading division and discord and attaching infamy to good men's actions and intentions, in this manner preparing the way for Eoghan

O'Neill and his partisans, so that they may be dominant in this kingdom. A complaint has been made to the Illustrious Nuncio about these monks, but hitherto no penalties have been imposed upon them as a warning to others, no mark of ignominy has been inflicted on their unbridled licence. It is a hard thing that a few monks, and irregular ones at that, should set the army alight and fix disgrace and opprobrium upon many faithful people in the province; and it is difficult to think of a way of subjecting them to the laws. To lay violent hands on them is not permitted, and to take legal proceedings to demand that just penalties be imposed on them by their superiors' tribunals would be a long-drawn-out form of redress, and great evils would grow in the meantime for the Irish people and the state.

8. Finally, those in the army who now follow Viscount Muskerry, and many men of integrity and opulence in the province of Munster, in all humility and for charity's sake ask the Illustrious Lord Nuncio that he may be pleased to form a benign opinion of their intentions and consider them to be acting as obedient sons of the Church of God and sworn confederates of the Catholic cause, and that the Illustrious Nuncio should closely examine both them and those others who talk so much of religion, and according to the end purpose of what is done should judge which of us are led more by pious intentions and less by personal advantage."

This astonishing letter contained a tacit proposal to Rinuccini. He was being invited to change halves: detach himself from Leath Chuinn and come over to Leath Mogha. (It seems he did not consider doing so.)

But also, of course, Rinuccini was meant to understand that his attempt to bury Muskerry's influence had failed, and he should now try to limit the damage. The point was driven home in a further complaint three weeks later, this time from the Council of Kilkenny. Haicéad, O'Dwyer and Roche were said to be raising sedition again and putting Munster in great danger, and the Nuncio was asked to remove them from the province altogether and have them sent to a monastery in Ulster or Connaught. *"The Nuncio acceded to (the Council's) wishes",* we are told. I take this to mean that Haicéad and the two others were removed from Clonmel and sent to another province.

Writing to his cardinal-supervisor six weeks later, Rinuccini obviously felt that his agitators had gone too far, and perhaps he was afraid that reports of their doings would reach Rome. In the Munster army, he said, *"suspicions and quarrels were increasing without limit, and things went so far that three Dominican friars, army chaplains, began putting it in many people's heads that it was legitimate to kill their officers and Muskerry himself, and not to obey the Supreme Council, which was seen as favouring these people. They defended these propositions with theological reasonings and propunded them audaciously, and anyone can well imagine the state of mind they induced in illiterates."*

Now given that Muskerry's letter accuses Eoghan Ruadh of seeking the kingship of Ireland, and given that the three Dominican friars are identified as his agents, the question arises whether they could have come under the influence of Conor O'Mahony's *Argument*, which must already have been in Ireland at that time. Because it is obvious who O'Mahony himself thinks should be king, though he never explicitly says so: that *strenuissimus et nobilissimus dux*, the renowned Catholic warrior who set off for Ireland with Papal blessing, Eoghan Ruadh O'Neill! And apart from the question of kingship, if anyone wanted theological reasons for refusing obedience to deviant Catholics or even expelling or killing them, he could find it in O'Mahony's book (for example, at the end of Section Three).

The connection has been assumed by Thomas O'Connor, who believes that the three Dominican agitators were fired by "enthusiasm for O'Mahony". But the question is not so simple. Did the Dominicans need lessons in political intolerance from a Jesuit? Surely their own order had literature written in this spirit, though I am not aware of any specifically dealing with Ireland. And surely Haicéad was close enough to this position in *Músgail do mhisneach, a Bhanbha*, written eight or nine months before. His prescription for relations with "*an Faction*"? *Obthar libh go bruinne an brátha*, "shun them forever and ever!".

Aside from that, I cannot find anywhere in Haicéad's poems or in his few extant letters an indication that he had a particular personal attachment to Eoghan Ruadh. Nor is there anything that seems to imply support for a separate Irish monarchy. He appears to hold firmly to the war aim as defined in Rinuccini's instructions. Those who made peace with Ormond in 1646 are condemned for breaking their oath *um cogadh do dhéanamh go cosnamh an chreidimh fhírinnigh in Éirinn*, "to make war till the true faith in Ireland is secured". On his death in 1649 Colonel Richard Butler (or Lieutenant-General, as Haicéad calls him) is praised because he kept his oath

> *gan chosg don chogadh go cosnamh a gcána*
> *'s a gcreideamh go réidh don chléir chráibhthigh.*

> not to cease from war till the pious clergy
> had their lands secure and their religion free.

So I think that the question whether Haicéad and his friends were inspired by O'Mahony's book must remain open.

HANDING OVER DUBLIN

Given time by the punctilious Ormond, Rinuccini was able to bring Preston back in line. With some effort Ormond might have budged him again. But the Marquis preferred to take his other option. It now transpired that those frightful Parliamentarians who were crucifying the King, whom it was so essential to combine against, who should have been stopped at all costs from taking Chester... were actually suitable people to receive the city of Dublin, lest it should go to the Catholics!

On March 6, 1647 Rinuccini noted that *"the Ormond faction (are) more than ever bent on depressing the clergy, Owen O'Neill and his army, and aggrandising the Marquis"*. But then came the news that the Marquis had given up hope of aggrandisement and chosen emigration: he had committed himself to give Dublin to the Parliament. Without hesitation his faction absolved him from all blame: *"The clergy, by rejecting the peace, have forced him to this step, and the Catholic religion will never flourish as it might have done under his administration."* To the impressionable Rinuccini at this juncture, *"it seems as if hope had utterly abandoned us"*.

Without any question, Ormond's handover of Dublin to the Parliamentarian forces in June 1647 was a disaster for both king and Catholics. The only question is who to blame for it: whether Ormond himself, or the Catholic Confederates under the command of Rinuccini?

John Callaghan, writing three years later, gives what is surely the best argument anyone can give for Ormond. It is only fair to quote it at some length.

> "The Viceroy, informed about all that was going on, received orders from the King that he should hand over Dublin and the other towns which he held to the Parliamentarians, if he was unable to hold them any longer. This message was painful to him, as indeed was the dire situation of the king. Charles, though he was the best of kings (if one excepts religion), was also the most unfortunate, deserted by his

subjects on all sides. In countless ways he was the sport of fortune, till eventually the Scots, whose good faith he had trusted in, treacherously gave him up to the Parliamentarians. After that he was held at Hulme, where he conceived some hopes of recovering his liberty, firstly through the people of London and soon afterwards through Fairfax himself, the commander of the Parliamentary Army.

Through Sir George Hamilton, the king was informed by Ormond of the state of affairs, the straits to which the Viceroy found himself reduced: since all that he had was being spent to pay his soldiers, he no longer had anything left to maintain himself and he could see no other way towards reconciliation with the Catholics, dominated as they were by the party of the Nuncio, to whom all thought of peace was utterly alien. He would therefore necessarily have to give up the towns, since he could not defend them without soldiers and he could not maintain soldiers without money to pay them, which he did not have. Let his Majesty therefore decide to which party he should give Dublin, the capital of the kingdom, and the other towns committed to him, which he was unable to hold any longer.

The king – whether it was that he suspected the loyalty of the Catholics, who were under the dictation of a foreign Nuncio, or that he did not dare do otherwise, lest he be treated more severely by the Parliamentarians – ordered him to make whatever agreement he could with the Parliamentarians and hand over to them the towns which he could no longer retain.

Knowing very well the Parliamentarians' treachery, the Marquis received this order with dismay. But what was he to do in this quandary? – persuaded as he was (whether rightly or wrongly, let others decide) that the Nuncio was resolved and eager to transfer the kingdom to some foreign sovereign.

He was motivated also by the king's authority: to disobey it would not only be reprehensible but also highly dangerous, because the Parliamentarians might treat the king as the guilty party, if his viceroy surrendered the towns not to them but to the Catholics, and punish him cruelly. He therefore approached the Parliamentarians and negotiated with them for the surrender of Dublin and those other towns which hitherto he had faithfully and laboriously preserved for king and (if the Irish would only appreciate it enough) for the nation."

Quite possibly Ormond believed that Rinuccini had designs of detaching Ireland from England. He had certainly said so. When he made his first contacts with the Parliament in the autumn of 1646, he and his Council of State informed the king *"that the Irish having perfidiously violated the Peace, had begun a new War, to wrest the Kingdom from his Majesty, and transfer it to the King of Spain or the Pope; to avoid which, they were forced to apply themselves to the Parliament"* (Richard Cox). Be that as it may, Ormond knew very well that there was a large body of Catholic Irishmen who were anxious not to be party to anything of that kind, General Preston being currently their key representative. But in dealing with Preston, and indeed with "the Irish" generally, he was either a narrow-focused Irish Protestant or a pedantic Englishman. He was not capable of shaping something larger.

(The Spanish Pope, as a matter of fact, had been checking out options. Noting the collapse of King Charles's position and the seemingly amenable spirit of Irish Catholics, and possibly influenced by the rumours getting back to him of what he was supposedly doing, he felt tempted. He thought about doing for his own country what Adrian IV had done for England.

According to Karin Schüller, in April 1647—

> "*the Conde de Oñate reported (to Madrid) on the possibility that the Pope would either donate Ireland to Philip IV or proclaim his illegitimate son Don Juan José of Austria King of Ireland. Luke Wadding, who was representing the Confederation of Kilkenny in Rome, was not made privy to these plans, which were initially to be kept in strict secrecy. However, the Spanish Council of State rejected such plans unanimously. Spain had too much on its hands just then to be able to conquer Ireland. It would involve a great war of conquest with an uncertain outcome, since the united English-Scottish forces were extremely strong. Apart from that, it would mean a breach of the peace with England. In Philip II's time Spain had intervened militarily in Ireland and the only result had been "that a great deal of money was spent without anything being gained". King Philip IV took the same view as his Council of State."*)

THE CAMPAIGN AGAINST O'MAHONY'S ARGUMENT

1647 was a ruinous year for the Confederates. *"In the space of four months the Catholics lost two entire armies"*: the Leinster Army in July, destroyed by the Parliamentarians under Col. Michael Jones; the Munster Army in November, routed by Inchiquin at Knockanoss, near Mallow. The only one left intact was the army of Eoghan Ruadh, who according to Callaghan *"had been summoned to be told by the Most Reverend*

Nuncio and the Bishop of Clogher that committing himself to battle with the enemy was most strictly forbidden: as a result Jones devastated wide regions of Leinster with impunity".

Eoghan Ruadh certainly played the role of Fabius. There were possible battles with Jones that he avoided: for this he was mocked by the Parliamentary pamphleteers, and he even infuriated people in his own army. Their feelings are memorably expressed in *A óga do ghlac na h-airm* by Toirdhealbhach Ó Conchubhair, who says that although he is just a private soldier, given a chance he could do what these Spanish-trained officers do:

Gidh nár dheachas riamh tar tuinn
d'fhoghlaim catha nó chomhluinn,
mar chách féin do-ním fo seach
an retréat scaoilteach scannrach.

Do fhedfainn gidh lór d'allás,
dá dtugthaoi dhamh úghdardhás,
go dteichfinn d'aon-Ghall tar lear
le seisir gníomh-ghann Gaoidheal.

Although I have never gone overseas
to learn warfare or combat,
like everyone else I make in turn
the scattery, panicky retreat.

I'd guarantee (though it's much to boast!),
if I were given authority,
to flee overseas from a single Gall
with a half-dozen action-grudging Gaels.

O'Neill played safe. He did not try to conjure new Benburbs out of nothing. But surely he needed glorious victories if he was to achieve what his enemies said he sought, the kingship of all Ireland?

His alleged royal manifesto, O'Mahony's *Argument*, was being furiously attacked in the autumn of 1647. *"The ill-willed and the Ormond faction make use of it to serve their own purposes"*, Rinuccini said, *"to increase the general hatred against the ecclesiastics and the people of Ulster."* The book was said to be an Ulster-clerical production, designed *"in order to bring round men's minds to make a king of O'Neill, in whom the two conditions, to be a native of the country and of ancient blood, are combined."* Rinuccini, however, declared that O'Neill had never had such ambitions, so far as he knew.

In a furious protest to the Pope the English ambassador in Rome said that this *"barbarous and bloodthirsty book"* had confirmed a suspicion already current: that Rinuccini had a secret mandate to change the government of Ireland and separate the island from the English Crown! This was first of all suggested by his treatment of Ormond, whom he had forced against his will and inclination to give Dublin to the Parliament, to the King's enormous detriment. And now O'Mahony's book had been disseminated throughout all Ireland, and it was tolerated by the Holy See! Rinuccini was accused of doing nothing to suppress the book and refusing to let the secular authorities punish John Bane, parish priest of Athlone, who was found in possession of a copy.

From his precise description it is clear that the Nuncio had acquired a copy himself. His comments are lively and thought-provoking, but ultimately neutral. Maybe his heart was with O'Mahony, while his head told him this could not be.

On September 11 *"the mayor, sheriffs, burgesses and commonalty of the town of Galway"* took the opportunity to affirm their loyalty to King Charles and to say *"that we do utterly detest and abjure the said damnable and seditious book, and the doctrine therein contained"* and would burn both book and author *"if we light on them"*. The book received much attention in Kilkenny also. It was publicly burned by the hangman, by order of the Supreme Council, and the Franciscan Peter Walsh attacked it in a series of sermons preached on nine consecutive Sundays and holy days in St Canice's Cathedral.

Walsh was a very able polemicist and his account of what he said in those sermons, contained in *The History of the Loyal Remonstrance*, constitutes the most forceful reply to O'Mahony's book on record.

> "He hath by manifold arguments... sowed the seeds of a civil, cruel and perpetual war among the Roman-Catholic Irish nation in general... Hath not he evinced clearly, if we believe himself, that the Kings of England have been all along these 500 years meer Usurpers of Ireland? And consequently that all, at least those of either Old or New English, or other Foreign Extraction, living in Ireland, and deriving originally and only their titles or rights from those Kings to the lands possessed by them in that country, must be likewise unjust possessors? And

therefore also, that the more ancient natives of Ireland, otherwise called the old and meer Irish, retain still fully all the ancient right which their predecessors enjoyed before the conquest of Henry II in the year 1167, or thereabouts?... Now who is ignorant that the far greater part of the Roman-Catholick Nobility, Gentry, and other proprietors inhabiting and possessing quietly great estates when the war begun in 1641, and before even time out of mind, and most of them for hundreds of years, derive their extraction from those old English, or other foreign Conquerors under Henry II, and his successors, in the Conquest of Ireland? And we have already seen, that an honest author C.M. hath warranted his kindred of the more ancient and meer Irish (as they are commonly called) of the lawfulness and justice, and equity also of their forcing out of all possession those unjust inheritors, and putting them all to the sword, if they did resist."

One might say that this is unjust, because O'Mahony firmly denies that his arguments have these implications. He distinguishes between the prescriptive rights of the English kings to the kingdom, which he rejects, and the prescriptive rights of Catholics of English origin to their properties, which he accepts. Ten or twenty years are enough to validate those rights, he says, and these possessors must not be disturbed. He even quotes with approval statements by the Confederate Council to the effect that no distinctions shall be made between Catholic Irishmen.

However, Walsh claimed that this was inconsistent with the main message of the *Argument.* He was speaking to people's fears, and he would have been heard and heeded by the more Anglicised of the Old English Catholics above all. As Carte put it, the *Argument*—

"made the confederates of English descent, whose extirpation was thus openly advised and encouraged, more desirous than ever of a peace, which was never more necessary for the king's affairs, than it was now become so for their own preservation."

(Rinuccini believed that the real cause of the outcry over the book was property. Many wealthy Catholics had picked up some of the confiscated church properties, and they felt threatened. *"(If) the heretical King is not a legitimate sovereign... this would bring overwhelming ruin on all who hold ecclesiastical property from him, as they infer that their titles also would be illegitimate, and that they would be forced to make restitution."* Rinuccini didn't actually want to seize their ill-gotten gains: he had power to give dispensations and very much wanted to do so. But *"not one of them believes me!"* – the possessors of church properties did not want them confirmed by dispensation, because they saw dispensation as a trap. *"This, the real and perilous stumbling-block in this country, will at all times give rise to suspicion and dissension"*, he prophesied in his characteristic way.)

In his sermons Walsh responded to the criticisms O'Mahony had made of conquest, popular acceptance and prescription as justifications for English rule in Ireland. Being implacably opposed to Papal interference in Irish or English politics, he scorned to use any argument based on the Papal Bull *Laudabiliter*. But the other three arguments he considered valid.

> "After I had shewn the insignificancy of the solutions given in that book to the three main arguments, proving the lawful right and just title of the Crown of England to the kingdom of Ireland, viz. Conquest, Submission and Prescription (for that of Pope Adrian's Donation I valued not) and consequently had confirmed those arguments, I enlarged my self further on another, even a fourth, late, and indeed insoluble argument, proving against this vain babbler, and wicked scribbler, that in case all his solutions were admitted, yet he had nothing to say, nor could find any possible way to evade the perfect, full and free both acknowledgement and obligation of the late Oath of Association, made and taken, yea, so often renewed by the Roman-Catholic Confederates of Ireland, by their Archbishops, Bishops, Earls, Viscounts, Barons, Knights, Gentry, Commonalty and Burgesses, even by all their Three Estates Spiritual and Temporal in their National Assemblies, nay, even principally and in the first place by all the chief men of the meer, or most ancient Irish (those very and only authors indeed of the Insurrection in October 1641 and consequently of all the Civil Wars that followed) being they were the men that drew (if not in a great measure forced) the Descendants of the old English Conquerors to rebel, or join with them in that unhappy war, and to that end, of themselves freely and voluntarily first in the said year 1641 framed that Oath of Association to persuade not only those other natives, but all the world, they notwithstanding their taking arms against oppression, did religiously acknowledge Charles I of England to be their lawful king, and holily swear true allegiance to him, and his lawful heirs and successors the kings of England, as the undoubted, just and lawful kings of Ireland too, however otherwise known Protestants. This was the argument that in the last place I insisted on as absolutely unanswerable, though we did (which yet we could not) freely grant, that all other were avoidable."

This was a strong argument, though Walsh was mistaken in thinking O'Mahony could have found nothing to say in reply. What O'Mahony would certainly have said is that all oaths of allegiance given by the Irish to the kings of England had been given under duress and were therefore null and void. This was true of the Confederate Oath also. Even in the circumstances of rebellion, before the Catholic Irish were aware of their own strength or before they fully understood their rights, the reality of duress was still there. At any time they had the right to abjure their unfreely-given oaths and reclaim their rightful independence, following the example of the Portuguese. Most certainly the Portuguese had sworn many oaths of loyalty to the three Philips, but now they scorned these supposedly binding commitments as made under duress and were maintaining an independent kingdom.

Nevertheless, taking Ireland as it actually was, I think Walsh's argument was strong. It was true that Eoghan Ruadh owed nothing at all to the King of England, but like everyone else he had taken the Confederate Oath:

> "I, N.N., swear before Almighty God and his angels and saints that I will defend the liberty of the Catholic, Apostolic and Roman Church, the person, inheritances, and laws of our Most Serene King Charles, and the legitimate immunities and liberties of this nation, against any and all usurpers and invaders, at the risk of all my possessions and even of life itself".

In correspondence he had insisted that he really and truly meant it.

Replying to critics like Walsh and Callaghan, one might say that King Charles was in second place. But if one had sworn to defend his inheritances, how could one honourably try to depose him from one of his kingdoms? Besides the argument based upon duress, there was another obvious reply. One could say that loyalty to King Charles was based on the assumption that he would know how to keep his major kingdom in order, that he wouldn't lose sovereign power in England to a gang of fanatics. If he lost effective support and became a mere captive in England, then the Irish must be permitted to shift for themselves. I presume that Eoghan Ruadh and his agents argued on these lines in 1648-9 when they were negotiating with the Cromwellians, but somehow Irish lords didn't find the argument convincing. In fact, Ormond's agents were able to exploit old jealousies of the O'Donnells and other Ulster lords and win them to their own alliance.

Eoghan Ruadh would have known what had happened to the mighty Wallenstein, less than twenty years before. After Wallenstein was seen to break with the Emperor Ferdinand II, and when he was believed to be preparing a separate kingdom of Bohemia in alliance with the Emperor's enemies, parts of his army began to melt away (as much of Eoghan Ruadh's melted away in late 1648 and early 1649, when he was severely isolated from the Royalist mainstream), his most trusted commanders began playing a double game, and men were found who had the will and opportunity to murder him – including his long-serving Irish mercenary Walter Butler.

However, there was another reason why Eoghan Ruadh could not have launched a campaign for kingship in late 1647, when Conor O'Mahony's book came into currency. It had to do with the character and make-up of Ireland.

There's a moment in O'Sullivan Beare's *History of Catholic Ireland* when he mentions something that **isn't** in the Papal Bull *Laudabiliter*, though he obviously thinks that it might occur to the reader (because Nicholas Sanders had asserted it in print): *"Did the Pope make an Englishman lord of Ireland so as to put an end to the conflicts of the Irish nobles? No – there is no mention of any such thing in the letter."* And again near the end of his book he says, *"The kings of England, having taken possession of the government of Ireland, should have composed and repressed the provincial dissensions and conflicts; on the contrary, they themselves, tainted with the filth of heresy, inflamed and increased them"* for their purposes of divide-and-rule.

Now it is obvious that in late 1647, even with a deadly enemy seizing important positions in Ireland, these old dissensions were aflame – and a claim to the kingship of Ireland would inflame them further, and not to O'Neill's advantage. Eoghan Ruadh in one aspect might have been proud and arrogant, but mainly he was a cautious realist. He presented no such claim (an attempt was made to entrap him, the Rinuccinian commentary tells us, but evidently it failed) nor to the best of my knowledge did any of his supporters. Conor O'Mahony's thoughts, for the moment, had fallen on barren ground.

'DUBLIN IS WORTH A MASS!'

The remaining four years of the Confederate War are not really within the scope of this book, so I will limit myself to a few brief notes.

When the armies of Leinster and Munster were destroyed in quick succession *"that did not trouble the Most Reverend Nuncio and his partisans, it was said, because their judgement was that everything would crumble to the advantage of Eoghan, who alone had his forces intact"*. But although this was said, it had no basis in fact. Rinuccini wanted and needed Catholic victories, not Catholic defeats. Though he kept on trying, by the end of 1647 his strategy was in ruins.

Of all the things he set out to do, he succeeded only in one: getting rid of Ormond. Once Ormond was removed from the position of Viceroy, he assumed that the Ormond faction must collapse. Not so! With Ormond exiled in France his Catholic supporters were regaining political strength, even as the military position weakened.

In the following year, 1648, there was an amazing political turnaround, and it centred on Murchadh Ó Briain, Lord Inchiquin. From the very first months of the rebellion this man had led the Munster Protestant resistance. For the previous four years he had backed the Parliamentarians, attracted by their vigour, and he had made himself the terror of the town Catholics. But now...

> *A Mhurchadh Uí Bhriain tá fiadhach ar Ghaedhalaibh*
> *le h-ocht mbliadhain i ndiaidh a chéile,*
> *is mithid duit stad is teacht chun réighteach,*
> *is léigheamh id chairt do cheart ar Éireann.*
>
> Murchadh Ó Briain, who's been hunting the Gaels
> for eight years continuously,
> it's time for you to stop and reach an agreement
> and read in your charter your right to Ireland!

Inchiquin was aware of being a chartered man, that is to say, he held his lands and titles and arguably even his age-old right to Ireland as an O'Brien (in the contemporary context that might mean being appointed Viceroy) under the kings of England. But what if his allies now were intent on destroying the monarchy altogether? People connected with Muskerry, that most resourceful politician, were pressuring him by all possible means to change sides:

Ná bí meallta, hám ná tréig-si,
ná creid feasta do mhalairt an tsaoghail,
idir dhá stól do thóin má léigir,
d'éis do leagtha budh deacair duit éirghe.

Ní beag súd sa ndubhairt riot d'fheachuinn,
amharc id thiomchuill, moill ná déan-sa;
an aghaidh do ríogh má bhír i gcéidiol,
***all your deeds believe are treason**.*

Don't be tricked, don't give up your judgment,
don't trust any longer to the change of fortune;
if you lay your backside between two stools,
after you're flattened you'll find it hard to rise.

There are many who have told you to watch out,
look around you, and do not delay;
if you stand against your king in an armed conflict,
all your deeds believe are treason.

The verses above are from a poem by Seán Ó Críagáin, where he tells Inchiquin that his support for the Parliament has caused general disaster; that his subordinate officers (*"Broghill of Cork"*) are undermining him in London and soon neither he nor King Charles will have any political power at all; that the English will cast him aside once he has served his purpose; that even if he should remain on top he will be hated so bitterly that he'll never be able to lay his head to rest...

Féach id dheoidh is romhat a n-éinfheacht
is déan an chomhairle is cóir do dhéanamh;
lean do ríogh i ngach áit da ngéabhann,
is tréigh an aicme nách tabhair dó géilleadh.

Look at the same time behind and before you
and make the decision it is right to make:
follow your King wherever he may go,
and abandon the group that would not submit to him.

If anyone needs proof that the spirit of Richard Cox remains strong among present-day Irish historians, I reply: this poem, which I published ten years ago in my *Contention of the Poets*, remains unknown.

Inchiquin took the plunge, renounced the Parliamentarians, made a ceasefire with the Confederates, and committed himself to enter a new royalist alliance – to be led by a returned Ormond! And Clanrickarde also committed himself. For years he had held apart from the Confederates, keeping more or less neutral, but now he assumed command of the Confederate army in Connaught.

At this stage – quite as Tadhg Mac Bruaideadha might have prescribed it! – the major powers of Leath Mogha were ranged together. But Inchiquin brought his extreme prejudice against Leath Chuinn into the alliance, where there was quite enough of that prejudice already. The dynamic *Murchadh na dtoiteán*, "Murrough of the burnings", might have done good service by keeping Munster securely in Royalist hands. In fact, he confirmed his old cronies as governors of the southern towns – for years they had been Parliamentarians with him and now they pretended to be Royalists with him, but only until the critical moment came when they could opportunely change sides yet again. Brian Boru's descendant was not worrying about things like that: he was impatient to lead his army up north to start harassing Eoghan Ruadh. He did more in that line than he ever managed to do against the Parliamentarians.

Eoghan Ruadh, still loyal to Rinuccini who had condemned the agreement with Inchiquin, became very isolated. Bits of his army began peeling away and joining the Ormondite alliance. Even the O'Donnells were going missing!

(The catastrophes of 1647 made the individual lordships feel the need to take care of themselves. They began doing so in the South after the battle of Knockanoss (November 1647). Following up his crushing victory, Inchiquin made settlements one by one with the South Munster septs on quite stiff terms. O'Sullivan Mór alone held out until he got the terms he thought himself entitled to.

Similarly, when Ormond built his new royalist alliance his agents won support in Ulster piecemeal. They guaranteed that whoever defected from Eoghan Ruadh would be confirmed in possession of his lands, etc. All of the O'Donnells, it would appear, made this bargain in the course of 1648 and early 1649. A bitter poem from this time declares that Eoghan Ruadh is the only true son of Ireland left and all the rest are bastards:

> *Do shénsat Pádraig ar mhír*
>
> They have rejected Patrick for a morsel!

Quite possibly Gofraidh Óg Mac an Bhaird's poem *Treoin an cheannais Clann Dálaigh*, "Clann Dálaigh (the O'Donnells) are the mighty leaders", was composed at this crucial juncture. The recipient is An Calbhach Ruadh Ó Domhnaill, to whom Gofraidh Óg had addressed another poem right at the start of the rebellion, urging him to get involved. An Calbhach's character hasn't changed: he is lazy and easy-going by nature, and once again it has to be spelled out for him that real achievement requires hard effort and if finally he is to have security and ease, then he must accept some temporary suffering and hardship. By now he does appear to have military experience:

Dearna corcra ó chaitheamh sleagh,
bráighe dhonn ó dhath mháilleadh

Hand purple from throwing spears,
neck coloured brown from the helmet!

but the lack of detail suggests he may not have done all that much.

Anyhow, Gofraidh Óg is insistent that he should not make peace with *sluagh longlíonmhar Lonndan*, "London's army with its many ships", rather he should hold out for their complete expulsion from Ireland. And it just so happens that the illustrative story chosen is the conflict between Conn of the Hundred Battles and Eoghan Mór, who was also known as Mogh Nuadat, as told in *Cath Maighe Léna*: how Conn originally drove Eoghan from Ireland; how Eoghan spent nine years in exile in Spain, while Conn was consolidating his power at home; how Eoghan then returned with *buidhean adhbhal ón Easpáin*, "a frightful band from Spain"; how Conn *d'eagla easaonta*, "for fear of disunion", gave half of Ireland to Eoghan, and this division into halves, Leath Chuinn and Leath Mogha, was maintained for fifteen years; how eventually, as Conn had hoped, Eoghan's Spaniards became sick of peace and wanted to leave Ireland; how Eoghan on a visit to Dublin saw that Conn had many more ships in the harbour than he had, and demanded half of Dublin Harbour or it would be war; and how Conn now opted for war and defeated Eoghan and killed him at the Battle of Magh Léna.

Ionann breathnughadh dá mbrath,
Conn Céadcathach 's an Calbhach,

roinn 'r a cheartfhonnaibh ní chuir,
ná Goill eachtrannaigh Eoghain.

Their attitudes, one feels, will be alike,
Conn Céadcathach and An Calbhach:
he too does not divide his rightful lands,
nor do Eoghan's foreign strangers!

One could argue forever about what is being said here, how much is being implied, and whether Eoghan – who at all times is mentioned respectfully, as the hero of *Cath Maighe Léna* should be – is thought of as having a present-day reincarnation. But what one can certainly say is that the focus on Tír Chonaill has become exclusive. Counter-Reformationist thoughts and larger ideas about the condition of Ireland, which were earlier blended into the basic thinking on Tír Chonaill, are dispensed with now. This is even more emphatically true of Somhairle Mac an Bhaird's magnificent elegy for Aodh Buidhe Ó Domhnaill (Hugh Boy), colonel of the Tirconaill infantry regiment, who was killed somewhere in Wexford in the late months of 1649 – not during Cromwell's storming of Wexford Town, as I suggested in *The Poems of Geoffrey O'Donoghue*, but in the weeks that followed, because Ormond's correspondence makes it clear that Aodh Buidhe's regiment was assigned to defend New Ross. Aodh Buidhe is said to have fought throughout all the four provinces of Ireland, and he had, as a matter of fact, visited all of them during his time in Eoghan Ruadh's army. But the poet by triple repetition gets the message across that this fighting in Munster, Leinster, Connacht and Ulster was all in done in the interests of defending Tír Chonaill.)

"During 1648-9 Eoghan Ruadh was in constant negotiation with Cromwellian leaders such as Monk, Jones and Coote, from whom he occasionally received supplies of arms; through his envoy in London, Abbot Crilly, he sought to make a permanent peace with the Parliament and offered to join the Parliamentary side on certain conditions, pointing out that he had experience of different forms of government on the Continent; the Vicar General of his Ulster Army, Edward O'Reilly, later Archbishop of Armagh, was accused then and later of Cromwellian sympathies." (Ó Fiaich).

For this the Kilkenny Council (September 30, 1648) duly declared him a traitor and rebel against the King.

The Parliamentarians operating in Ireland were already showing a taste for massacre – which Eoghan Ruadh's army never did, one should note. (Ó Mealláin, writing in 1647-8, denounces Parliamentarian massacres both of civilians and captured soldiers, and challenges anyone to come up with an instance where the Irish side broke the military code. No such instance is given in a recent detailed study of the conduct of the war.) With hindsight, the idea of a general settlement between these two sides seems far-fetched. But Eoghan Ruadh surmised that the Parliamentarians might be inclined to make peace as political realists. Weighing their reasons of state, they might decide that Ireland was more trouble than it was worth and that pacts could be made even with an O'Neill!

King Charles was then nearing the end. From February 1644, if not earlier still, he had been hinting that he wanted Ormond to settle on his behalf with the Catholics, promising them something like emancipation – a deal on which he fully intended to cheat. By 1648 he was desperate enough to spell this out for Ormond literally. The Viceroy could go as far as he liked, without worrying that his commitments would ever be honoured! There was no point, however, in saying such things to Ormond, since he wasn't the kind of loyalist who will play these dangerous games.

But in the late months of 1649, having thrown away his own army at the disastrous siege of Dublin and with Cromwell descending on the land, even the pedantic Viceroy finally understood that to isolate Eoghan Ruadh was suicidal. So he made an offer that an heir of the great O'Neills could accept. Eoghan Ruadh, who was then near death, responded by sending substantial forces south for Ormond's disposal. Those troops were outstanding in the anti-Cromwellian resistance. No other commander came near to matching the achievements of Hugh Duff O'Neill at the sieges of Clonmel and Limerick.

Ireland had incredible fighting stamina and reserves, but a leader was needed who could keep O'Neills and O'Donnells together and above all who could pull Leath Chuinn and Leath Mogha away from their fatal enmity and focus all their energies against the invader. A king of Ireland? Yes, indeed, in principle, certainly! Without forgetting the large dissident presence in the Southern Half, one could say that Ormond was Leath Mogha's candidate for a kind of kingship of Ireland – it was thought he could become a more Irish type of viceroy, a more authentic leader of all Ireland under the English overking.

But Ormond did not grow naturally into the role that the tireless Muskerry fashioned for him, because psychologically he was too English. He was Strafford's protegé and essentially he too, like his mentor, thought that the Irish needed planting, Protestantising and civilising. MacGeoghagan calls him "*a more zealous Protestant than an able minister*", which hits the mark. As overall leader he was hardly inspiring, since he failed wretchedly to take back the city of Dublin from the Parliamentarians to whom he had given it. Having led the defence against Cromwell without distinction, he returned to France in September 1650, accompanied by Inchiquin. But those who admired him and loved him, who were certain that he and he alone was the destined man of Ireland, were nothing if not persistent. In May 1651, after Muskerry had scored some military successes in Munster, there were moves to bring Ormond back yet one more time. But given that Protestant royalist support had by now melted away, this time he was asked **to come over as a Catholic**!

His agent in Ireland wrote to assure him that if he arrived as a Catholic and remained Catholic **even for the space of one year**, the Ormond faction would now sweep all before them! The person who forwarded this letter (Ro. Allen) enclosed a note of his own: *"Your excellency's speedy arrival here is wished beyond all measure by all your friends."* Hopefully their expressed wishes *"will not only call you home with expedition, but also remove all obstacles, working in you that honourable resolution of Henry the Bourbon in choosing to hear one Mass rather than to hazard his kingdom".*

Dublin is worth a Mass! – These letters were intercepted, but even if they had reached him it is hard to imagine Ormond responding. He would scarcely have considered taking the advice. Besides, even though I think the idea was a good one, it was one of those good ideas that come too late. Now if Ormond, immediately after Rinuccini's departure from Ireland in February 1649, had made a political change of religion and come forward as the leader of Catholic Ireland – that would have been interesting!

DANIEL O'DALY

The book that Conor O'Mahony had written was briefly very embarrassing to the state of Portugal. Nevertheless, it may have occurred to the reader that if an Irishman was king of Ireland, then the King of Spain couldn't be. So the question arises whether some of those friends who, O'Mahony tells us, urged him to write his book, had larger political designs. So far as that goes, I have not found evidence and I would not expect to discover any.

In January 1650 Daniel O'Daly (Domingos do Rosário) was preparing to go to Ireland to recruit men for deployment in the continuing war against Spain. Existence had become harsh or even impossible for large numbers of soldiers as the war in Ireland dragged on. Various continental Catholic powers were interested in these men's services, and Portugal was one. However, O'Daly warned King John IV that it was difficult to win the Irish to the Portuguese service because of their existing pro-Spanish inclination. They would need to be shown that the Spanish were hypocrites and had never given effective aid against the heretics, and some well-trained Irish priests should be sent from Portugal to assist in this task.

At this time O'Daly was also in contact with Charles II, the exiled King of England, and while he was in Ireland he intended to see if anything could be done on Charles's behalf. It seems, however, that after elaborate preparations O'Daly didn't have time to go to Ireland. About August 1650 he wrote a letter to Ormond apologizing for not being able to meet him, and explaining that in his opinion Ireland ought to be an autonomous kingdom. Charles Stuart should be its king, but the English ought to have nothing to do with its government.

Previously he had said to Charles that—

> *"the government and settlement of that kingdom consisted principally in the fruition of the privileges of a free kingdom, as Ireland is deserving it better than any of H.M.'s dominions for to show themselves more loyal in their later revolutions for which they should not be of worse conditions, rather larger privileges for the future example and consequence. I added how it would be against natural law that a kingdom should be under another but only dependent from their king immediately, according to the conditions of all nations. Whereunto I found His Majesty well-disposed, but his council most averse, whom I cannot blame herein for not concurring to deprive themselves of the government and disposition of that kingdom."*

Ormond, he thought, could make all the difference, and O'Daly appealed to him to think of his country's rights and dignity. But Ormond had no ear for anything like that. He was far from thinking that Ireland didn't need English tutelage, and apparently he was indignant that Charles Stuart had given this presumptuous friar a hearing.

After a few rounds of naval conflict with Cromwellian England, the Portuguese signed a peace treaty in 1654, and afterwards (to the horror of the Pope) they were trying to construct a quadruple alliance of England, France, Portugal and Sweden. At this stage Daniel O'Daly was the central figure in Portuguese diplomacy. Though extremely busy, he still found time to write his fascinating *History of the Geraldines*, published in Lisbon in 1655.

The question of English right comes up very soon in his introduction. Rhetorically he claims that he doesn't intend to discuss this, and first of all he will not express an opinion about whether that English pope was biased.

> "Far be it from me to examine whether flesh and blood prompted the Vicar of Christ to bestow on a king of his own nation the island of Erin, on some vain and unfounded representations. Historians of great weight have asserted it. I enter not into the controversy, neither do I intend to assert that the head of the Church was deluded by the false statements of Henry, nor to argue with the Church concerning the justice of the case…."

Nevertheless, in due course he concludes that *"it is manifest that the first and second pretexts on which the grant made to King Henry was founded – namely, to enlarge the territories of the Church, and to announce to a rude and ignorant people the Christian faith – must have been false and delusive."* The further pretexts of rooting out vice and subjecting the people to law were equally fictitious. He tells the story of how Archbishop Lawrence O'Toole attempted to mediate between King Henry and the Irish High King Roderick, and comments: *"After the English had been 11 years in Ireland, neither people nor clergy acknowledged them as masters or conquerors."*

In general,

> "I have not the heart to question the right of English domination over the Irish people, for, cursed as it has been, a possession of over five hundred years has confirmed it. But there is one subject which I will not hastily dismiss, to wit, the utter recklessness of honour and principle on the part of our tyrants, and the fortitude and constancy with which the Irish have sustained "the burden of Babylon". "

Following the history of the Geraldines, O'Daly gives a summary account of Catholic Ireland down to Cromwellian times. For the earlier period he depends a good deal on Philip O'Sullivan, whose history he recommends warmly. When dealing with the 1640s he is exceptionally careful not to get involved in the political controversies among Catholics, beyond saying that such divisions are very destructive. One need hardly say that the *Argument Defending the Right of the Kingdom of Ireland* is never mentioned.

The Portuguese maintained good relations with the Stuarts despite their diplomatic dealings with the Cromwellians, and there was a happy ending with the marriage of Catarina de Braganza to Charles II in 1662. Antonio de Sousa considered this to be O'Daly's greatest diplomatic achievement for Portugal. But at heart, de Sousa thought, Frey Domingos would have preferred to do something for Ireland: he was a patriotic Irishman who wanted nothing more than to serve his own country.

O'MAHONY'S LAST YEARS

Conor O'Mahony seems to have lived untroubled in Lisbon until his death in 1656. King John IV had wanted him chastised, since his publication had caused the Portuguese state "*greater care than is expected*". The king turned in exasperation to the head of the Portuguese Jesuits, demanding that something should be done with the author, given that he was a Jesuit and therefore the state couldn't touch him. But it seems that O'Mahony was protected by his superiors and was not punished.

Two years after his book had been condemned in Portugal, a Jesuit catalogue gave the following character sketch: "*Excellent intelligence; good judgement and prudence; sufficient experience; excellent proficiency in scholarship; choleric temperament; excellent talent for writing.*" During the 1650s he was still being asked to give formal expert opinions on whether learned works of theology were fit for publication.

Though his book was banned in the kingdom, he retained copies and was happy to show them and to claim his authorship. He presented a copy to the Bishop of Ardagh, who had come to Lisbon in exile from the Cromwellians.

According to M. Gonçalves da Costa, in King John's letter of September 29, 1648 to the Portuguese Jesuit Provincial it is said that

O'Mahony had published a second tractate on the same subject. Unfortunately, da Costa does not give the king's exact words and I have not been able to check the documents cited. But I think this may be a misunderstanding based on the *Argument*'s two different title-pages. At any rate, if a sequel was published I have found no reference to it anywhere else. The statement by both Prestage and da Costa that a Portuguese translation of the *Argument* was published is certainly due to confusion: they did not realize that Marullus/Marlow/Mahony and Cornelius de são Patricio, mentioned in two different decrees by the Portuguese king, were one and the same person.

O'Mahony died unexpectedly at São Roque in Lisbon on February 28, 1656.

His book still came up in controversy for some time afterwards. In the fierce political disputes among Irish Catholics abroad, which began in Paris and Brussels in 1649/1650 while the Cromwellian War was still in progress, the *Argument Defending the Right of the Kingdom of Ireland* was referred to as a kind of landmark. People accused their opponents of holding this author's scandalous opinions, or worried that they themselves might be thought to be in his camp because of certain other views that they held.

Clarendon, writing about 1660, claimed that "*this book, so barbarous and bloody, is as yet credited by the Catholics and Apostolics (in Ireland)*", though I don't know what basis he had for saying so. But certainly it surfaced again as a political issue. There was a fresh proposal to burn the offending text in 1666, when a national convention of the Irish Catholic clergy met for the purpose of formulating a declaration of loyalty to King Charles II. The tireless Peter Walsh – as a friend and follower of the Viceroy, the Duke of Ormond, he had an important part in making the convention possible – called for a number of things to be done, including that this particular book should be burned and anyone possessing any copies should be ordered to put them in the fire. Of Walsh's various proposals, this was the only one on which he received complete satisfaction.

In 1827 there was a comical epilogue, when 100 copies of the *Argument* were reprinted in Dublin by a man called George Mullen. His purpose was apparently to show what ghastly creatures the Irish Papists were when given sufficient freedom. Hopefully, influential people who read this book might think again before allowing Catholic Emancipation!

In 1845 R. A. Madden, who was in Lisbon researching something about Portuguese Restoration politics, stumbled on King John IV's order banning the *Argument*. He searched in all the bookshops of Lisbon but couldn't find a copy. Eventually he found one in the National Library of Portugal and was kindly permitted to take it away to his lodgings for ten days – "*a fitting example for public libraries*," he says! (It appears that Madden brought the book back, or anyhow this obliging National Library still possesses its copy – two copies in fact, catalogued under *Hiberno, C. M.)* Madden couldn't deny that the *Argument* was powerfully written. But, himself living in the atmosphere of Young Ireland, he found the sentiments reprehensible – of use, he thought, only to anti-Catholic bigots.

And Madden's response, I think, was typical. The later independence movement found no inspiration in this book and it was not reprinted. The reason is obvious: between Eoghan Ruadh O'Neill and Pearse/Connolly there had been Tone, Davis and Mitchel. An exclusively Catholic state was not desired and a book which linked such a state with the cause of independence could not be welcomed. (Suarez was quoted quite a lot around 1921, as anyone may see by consulting *Studies*, but not Conor O'Mahony!) In recent times only his fellow-Jesuit Francis Finegan had the boldness of mind to look at the book in context and try to make a reasonable judgment.

Nonetheless, as Finegan has already pointed out, there was a core in O'Mahony's work that would stand the test of time: the idea of Irish independence. Whatever else they did, the events of the 1640s dug deeper the gulf between England and the majority population in Ireland. No form of English politics would prove able to bridge this gulf. Conor O'Mahony's pioneering proposal is fascinating, and he would be the first of many who asked (with 'republic', if need be, in the place of 'king'):

> *"Why should Ireland (which had 190 kings before the coming of the English, and besides is a much more distinguished kingdom, and in temperateness of climate, fertility of the soil, fruitfulness and abundance leaves England and Scotland far behind) – why should Ireland be without a king of its own?"*

DISPVTATIO APOLOGETICA, DE IVRE REGNI Hiberniæ pro Catholicis Hibernis aduersus hæreticos Anglos.

AVTHORE C. M. HIBERNO

Artium, & Sacræ Theologiæ Magistro.

Accessit eiusdem authoris ad eosdem Catholicos exhortatio.

FRANCOFVRTI Superiorum permissu typis BERNARDI GOVRANI.

Anno Domini 1645.

Original Title Page

CATHOLICIS HIBERNIS vtriusque ordinis Ecclesiastici, & secularis C. M. temporalem, & æternam felicitatem optat, & precatur.

PATRIÆ adiuuandæ zelo, & amicorum precibus commotus hanc de Iure Regni uostri Apologiam, & Exhortationem scripsi, & vobis omnibus (qui in virtute Dei custodimini per Fidem in salutem paratam reuelari in tempore nouissimo) *dedicare volui, vt virtute, & fortitudine, qua Regnum nostrum hæreticis, magna ex parte, eripuistis, & in Chatholicam libertatẽ asseruistis, eàdem ius á me illius in hoc opusculo explicatum contra eosdem hæreticos, eorumque fautores defendatis, & doctrinam Exhortationis executioni mandetis. Omnes enim tenemur iure diuino, humano, & naturali Religionem Catholicam, & patriam dilectam defendere, pro qualitate, & possibilitate vnius cuiusque; alij enim armis, alij literis, alij pecunijs, personis, & comeatibus auxilium conferre debent, vt præclarissimum opus libertatis nostræ inceptum ad optatum finem perducatur; ad quod perficiendum non parum iuuare poterit scientia iu-*

stitiæ

A page of text from the original edition

An Argument Defending The Right Of The Kingdom Of Ireland, In Support Of The Irish Catholics Against The English Heretics

by C.M., of Ireland,
Master of Arts and Sacred Theology

followed by the same author's

Call to Action, Addressed to the Irish Catholics

In Frankfurt, by permission of superiors,
printed by Bernard Govran
1645

TO THE IRISH CATHOLICS

of both orders, clerical and lay, C.M. wishes and prays that you may have temporal and eternal happiness.

Enthusiastically wishing to help my country and responding to appeals by friends, I have written this vindication of the right of our kingdom, followed by a call to action. I wish to dedicate it to all of you who have been sustained by the power of God through faith in the salvation which will be revealed at the end of time. I hope that by the bravery and fortitude which you have shown in seizing our kingdom, or the greater part of it, from the heretics and establishing Catholic liberty there, you may defend that same right, which I explain elsewhere in this booklet, from the heretics and their supporters, and put the doctrine of my call to action into practical effect. All of us are obliged by divine, human and natural law to defend the Catholic religion and our beloved country, according to the rank and resources of each particular individual.

Some should help with arms, others with writings, others again with money, troops and supplies, so that the excellent work of liberty, already begun, may be brought to its desired completion. A knowledge of the justice of the cause which we defend may be of no small assistance, because our Catholic leaders and soldiers will then be prepared to fight for our true and just cause with uninhibited vigour. For justice adds warlike valour to the cause, while injustice subtracts it, as the pagan poet Propertius, guided solely by the light of nature, brilliantly sang:

Frangit et attollit vires in milite causa,
Quae nisi iusta subest, excutit arma pudor.

What breaks or sustains the soldier's strength is the cause,
for unless it is seen to be just, shame robs him of his arms.

FOREWORD TO CATHOLIC READERS

The pagans, for whom the star that gives true light has not yet risen, walk miserably in darkness and in the shadow of death. The Jews, with their hearts permanently sealed, are blind to this present day. The heretics, led astray by devious error, rave deliriously. Some Catholics also are apathetic, because charity has grown cold in their worldly hearts and so they do not practise good works or demonstrate zeal. They are ignorant of how the right of their kingdom has long ago been usurped by alien heretics, bringing shame to their country, injury to the Catholic religion and offence to God.

I have therefore drawn up the following argument, so as to instruct some of the Catholics of Ireland about the true right of our kingdom. I know that many are ignorant of it and others, to preserve their fragile temporal comfort, do not defend it as they should. I also wish to refute some English heretics who attack this right of ours, more by violence of language than by weight of reasons, and strive to overthrow it; but helpless as they are in the light of truth, they are not successful, nor shall they succeed in the future. Finally, then, I propose to give a clear vindication of the truth and justice of our cause from their attacks.

If I accomplish the work rightly, I think it will be no small service to my Irish fellow-countrymen. If I fall short, my good intention should be accounted in place of the fact, until such time as other doctors with a greater abundance of learning (and perhaps more leisure) can finish the task I have begun. In the meantime I present this little work. The style will be clear and scholastic; this I consider more suitable than a flowery rhetoric for the purpose of winning intellectual assent, destroying my opponents' arguments and making what I have to say comprehensible.

If certain people should happen to take offence at what I say here, or should suffer unmerited scandal, I counter their objections with the considered judgment of St. Augustine: *"If a scandal arises in connection with the truth, it is better to let the scandal emerge than to abandon the truth."* Which is all the more valid when someone is defending his right or his people's right against unjust aggression, repelling force with force, as every law and all forms of right permit. Apart from which: *"He who avails of his own right does no one any injury".* And Englishmen need not be surprised that I, a Catholic Irishman, am fighting against the injustice of the English heretics. In fact, there are many orthodox English writers who have fiercely condemned the sectaries of England, rebuking their morals, arguing against their errors and refuting their heresies. One can find numerous English writers who are engaged in polemic on the side of the Catholic Church in England, and Phillipus Alegambis has edited not a few of their works in the *Biblioteca Scriptorum Societatis IESU* (Library of Jesuit Writers). This is not to mention the many Italians, Germans, French, Spanish, Portuguese, Irish, Scots, and men of other nations besides, who have written most learnedly against the heretical errors of the English after their defection from the Catholic, Apostolic and Roman faith.

A Factual Basis Admissible by both Irish and English

1. The island of Ireland, which was once in a flourishing state and quite an opulent kingdom, was first inhabited by human beings 300 years after the universal deluge. Its first inhabitants were Bartolanus, son of Sera, of the stock of Japhet son of Noah, and his three sons Languinus, Salanus and Returургus with their wives, and a few other allies of theirs, who reached the shores of Ireland whether by enterprise or chance. These settlers began to prosper considerably, as events unfolded and generations succeeded one another. Within 300 years of their arrival the numbers of their descendants are said to have grown to as many as 9,000. At length a particular clan won a great victory in battle against the Giants and succeeded in overthrowing their enemies. But a sudden plague, arising from the severe contamination of the air by the bodies of the fallen Giants, destroyed the entire generation, with only a few people being spared. When the said Bartolanus with all his descendants had succumbed to this bitter plague, the land remained bare of any cultivator for some time.

However, Nemedus son of Agnominius, of the Scythian nation, with his four sons Starius, Gerbal, Anninus and Fergusius, was transported to the shores of this desolate land in the year 2317 from the world's foundation. The descendants of this Nemedus, his sons and grandsons and their successors, became so numerous that they came to fill almost the entire island. But the greater number of them perished in the wars that they waged with the Giants, who at that time remained in the island, and because of various other difficulties and misfortunes. The remnant found themselves unfavourably circumstanced and in decline; some of them sailed for Scythia, others headed for Greece. For 215 years, then, the Nemedian race held Ireland, and afterwards it was empty for a further 200.

At length five highly celebrated men, Gandius, Genandius, Sagandus, Rutheragus and Slanius, all brothers, sons of Dela of the posterity of Nemedus already mentioned, came to Ireland in the year of the world 2535, and finding it almost empty divided it into five provinces, each of them taking one part for themselves. These five brothers maintained their occupancy for a number of years in the greatest mutual concord. But afterwards when they had multiplied and increased in strength, blind ambition induced them to begin using the sword against one another. It was Slanius, the youngest in birth, who emerged victorious from this conflict (with part of the the others banished and the other part exterminated) and took all of Ireland under his sovereignty. He is therefore named as the first king of that country. There were nine kings in all from these brothers and their descendants; they reigned only briefly, for a period of thirty years. (Slanius is buried in a certain hill in Meath which has taken its name from him, the hill of Slane.) To a great extent, therefore, that nation was weakened to extinction by its various internecine conflicts, but most of all by the very costly war which it waged with another branch of the Nemedian posterity which had come across from Scythia.

Eventually five illustrious brothers, sons of king Milesius, came to Ireland out of Spain. They sailed in a fleet of sixty ships in the year 3342 from the world's foundations and before Christ's birth, 4987 years before this present year of 1645 AD (which is year 5594 from the world's foundation as reckoned by most computists). Straightaway they took over the entire island, with no one resisting. In the course of time the two most outstanding of these men, named Hiberus and Herimon, divided the island between them into two equal parts. The southern part was given to Herimon, the northern to Hiberus. For some time they reigned together prosperously enough. But there is no faith between allies in a kingdom; it is normal with all power that it tends to be intolerant of partnership. Ambition, the blind mother of evils, progressively dissolved the bonds of their brotherhood and stirred up discord of all sorts. The various conflicts between the brothers produced inconclusive military results, until in the end victory went to Herimon. Hiberus was killed in battle and Herimon obtained the entire kingdom of Ireland for his own.

Therefore Herimon was the first monarch or sovereign king of that people, and his posterity has survived in Ireland to this very year and day when I am writing these words. The island had 131 monarchical kings down to Saint Patrick, the apostle of this land, who was sent by Celestine, the Supreme Pontiff of Rome, in 431 AD. Arriving in Ireland, where he found only a few Christians, Saint Patrick converted all the other inhabitants to orthodoxy, reconciling them to Christ. Afterwards Ireland had 50 other monarchical kings of the same Milesian race and bloodline (leaving out the petty kings of the provinces, who were numerous). Altogether there were 181 High Kings. If we add to these the 9 mentioned above of the family of Dela and the 21 English kings, there are 211 in all. However, the last 21 English kings are intruders and tyrants and should not be reputed true and legitimate kings, as will be shown in this argument.

This brief narration and historical basis is collected not only from the abiding tradition of Ireland but also from English and Irish historians. Of those one may consult Sylvester Giraldus Cambrensis in *Appendix to the Topography of Ireland* Ch. 12 and following; Richard Stanihurst, *On the History of Ireland*, Bk. 1; Don Philip Sullivan in *Compendium of the History of Catholic Ireland* Vol. 1 Bk. 3 Ch. 1, and in the *Life of Patrick* Bk. 1 Ch. 2; William Camden in his *Britannia* and *Descriptio Hiberniae*; Lord Peter Lombard, Archbishop of Armagh and Primate of All Ireland, in *Commentary on the Kingdom of Ireland, Island of Saints* Ch. 1, and many others.

However, here I must point out that the above-mentioned historians and others do not always agree with one another, either concerning the names of those who occupied Ireland or the lengths of their occupations, and in various other details. I have written what seemed, in antiquity's dim confusion, most likely to be true, but if unintentionally I have committed some errors I am ready to learn from others. At all times I submit what I write and say to the censure and correction of the Holy Roman Catholic Church.

***

First Section

Setting forth the issue, the right which is claimed, and the opponents' arguments

2. Some Englishmen, especially the heretics and their supporters, with their typical deceitfulness and obstinacy deny many truths of the divine faith and affirm blatant lies against the revealed doctrines of divinity. Likewise, they unscrupulously misrepresent many human truths and construe opposing and false propositions. Of these there is one claim of theirs which is notorious: that the right and total dominion of the Kingdom of Ireland has belonged to the kings of England from 1172 AD to this year 1645, when I am writing; and that we Irishmen are barbarous, bestial reprobates, profligates, rebels, public enemies, and criminal outlaws, as long as we deny this royal right and oppose it whether by diplomacy, arms, or stratagem. They molest us with these and other calumnies and insults. Nevertheless, it is best for me now to give them a patient hearing, lest when a cause has been indicted I should seem to be condemning individual men. But afterwards they will hear me speaking more truthfully, whether they wish to or not, so that they may learn this much at least: *"He who says what he likes hears what he doesn't like."*

3. So then, their first objection is the following. Henry II, King of England, occupied Ireland in a just war; therefore he and his successor kings retain that land rightfully and have all right and dominion over it and in it.

4. Their second objection. In 1156 AD the said King Henry obtained an Apostolic Bull from the Supreme Pontiff Adrian IV constituting him Lord of Ireland, as is clear from that bull which is quoted verbatim by some English and Irish writers, e.g. the Englishman Matthew Paris in *Historia Anglica* p. 91 in the Tigurina edition of 1589; Lord Peter Lombard, Archbishop of Armagh and Primate of All Ireland, in his *Commentary* on that kingdom, ch. 17 p. 245; Don Philip Sullivan in tome 2 of the *History of Catholic Ireland*, bk. 1 ch. 4 p. 59, and others. The bull is as follows.

"Adrian, bishop, servant of the servants of God, to my very dear son in Christ the illustrious king of England, greetings and apostolic blessing.

5. Laudably and beneficially Your Majesty is proposing to spread the glory of your name on earth and lay up a reward of eternal happiness in Heaven, and fittingly for a Christian prince your intention is to expand the bounds of the Church, to declare the truth of the Christian religion to an ignorant and uncivilised people, and to eradicate the weeds of vice from the field of the Lord; and in order to achieve this purpose more adequately you seek our advice and goodwill. And insofar as you proceed in high partnership and with great forethought, so much the easier with the help of God will your progress be, since it is usual that projects which are motivated by the zeal of faith and the love of religion have a good end and outcome.

As Your Majesty acknowledges, Ireland and all the islands upon which Christ, the son of justice, has shone and which have accepted the teachings of the Christian religion, rightfully belong without any doubt to Blessed Peter and the Holy Roman Church. And therefore we are all the more willing to plant the faith in them and introduce a government pleasing to God, because from examination of conscience we foresee that a stricter reckoning will be demanded of us on their account. Dearest son in Christ, you have indicated that you wish to enter the island of Ireland to subdue that people to laws and eradicate the weeds of vice there, and that you will pay a tribute of one penny yearly for each individual house there to Blessed Peter and will keep the rights of the Church in that land inviolate and entire.

Responding to your pious and praiseworthy desire with appropriate goodwill, we kindly assent to your petitions, and we gladly consent that in order to expand the bounds of the Church, restrain the decadence of vice, reform the people's way of life, and strengthen the Christian religion, you shall enter that island and do whatever tends to the honour of God and the welfare of that land; and that the people of that land shall receive you with honour and reverence as their Lord, provided that the right of the Church remains inviolate and entire and that a tribute of one penny yearly for every house is duly paid to Blessed Peter and the Holy Roman Church. If then you bring what you have mentally conceived to practical fruition, you should strive to educate that people in good ways of life, and through your efforts and the efforts of those followers of yours whom you find to be suitable in faith, word and deed, you will cause the Church there to be adorned and the Christian religion to take root and grow, and all that pertains to the honour of God and the well-being of souls will be so ordained by you that you will merit from God his highest eternal reward, and on earth you will have a glorious name throughout the ages. *Given in Rome in the year of salvation 1156."*

6. Their third objection. The said King Henry was received with acclamation by the three estates of the kingdom, clergy, nobility and people, and consequently also those kings of England who succeeded him, even the heretics.

7. Their fourth objection. Those same kings of England – there were many of them, as I will immediately show – have ruled for so many years in the peaceful possession of Ireland from Henry II to the Charles now reigning, and from 1172 AD to 1641 (when the Catholic Irish assembled in arms to defend the faith of Christ and their own liberty) that they have become, are now and shall be legitimate lords and kings. And here we may call the roll of those monarchs of England: Henry II, Richard I, John I, Henry III, Edward I, Edward II, Edward III, Richard II, Henry IV, Henry V, Henry VI, Edward IV, Edward V, Richard III, Henry VII, Henry VIII, heretic, Edward VI, heretic, Queen Mary, Catholic, Queen Elizabeth, heretic, James, heretic, and Charles I, heretic. The studious reader, if he wishes, may find their lives, acts and the years when they were born, died, began to reign and ceased reigning, in Polydore Virgil's *Historia Angliae* and the Briton or Englishman George Lily's *Epitome Chronices Regum Anglorum*, and other historians' works; but it is not to my present purpose to explore these matters further.

So then, those are our opponents' principal objections. When considering them, I am immediately reminded of that saying in Psalm 118, *"The wicked have told me fables."* Such objections are fables indeed, as I will demonstrate below, replying to them one by one.

SECOND SECTION

The opponents' first objection is refuted and our own right is more extensively stated and proved

8. To the first objection, I reply that the war in which Henry the Second occupied Ireland was not just, rather it was unjust and thoroughly evil. To make this plainly apparent we must briefly go over the true history of the occupation, which our opponents do not deny – in fact they affirm it, and not a few historians, both English and Irish, put it down on record. One may consult Richard Stanihurst, bk. 2 *On the History of the English in Ireland*, p. 59ff.; Philip Sullivan, Tome 2 Bk. 1 Ch. 3 of the *History of Catholic Ireland*; Peter Lombard, Archbishop of Armagh and Primate of All Ireland, in *Commentary on Ireland* Ch. 17; William Newbridge, *Rerum Anglicarum* Bk. 2 Ch. 26 and Bk. 3 Ch. 9; William Camden in his *Britania* p. 685 (Third Edition); Sylvester Giraldus Cambrensis, and others.

9. About 1168 AD the five provinces of Ireland, i.e. Munster, Leinster, Connacht, Ulster and Meath, were ruled by five or more sub-kings under the overlordship of Roderick of Connacht, who was High King and Monarch of all Ireland at that time. The entire kingdom was living in peace and contentment; its inhabitants were leading quiet and tranquil lives. But then one of those sub-kings named Dermot MacMurrough, or as others write it Diarmaid son of Murchadh, King of Leinster, abducted the wife of Roderick, or O'Rourke, king of Meath. She was the daughter of a certain family derived from Malachy (Ó Maoilsheachlainn, as we say in Irish), highly-born and beautiful and a queen by destiny. When asked to restore her the abductor was unwilling. The grave news of this evil was brought to the absent husband, and when he heard it some time elapsed when his spirit was quite exhausted by sadness and grief.

Afterwards, when sorrow had somewhat receded and anger had become intense, he wrote letters to Roderick the High King of Ireland, in which he made plain the atrocity of the crime and the magnitude of the injury that he had suffered. Roderick, having ascertained that the crime had indeed been committed, supported by the other great lords and with a powerful army launched an attack on Dermot, who, preparing to resist, suddenly found himself abandoned by his supporters, and fled to England. From there he proceeded to Aquitaine to Henry II, King of England, and explained to him how he had been pursued by the kings of the united provinces and militarily overwhelmed, and so he had fled to King Henry's mercy and offered himself to his protection, and would confer on him the right to recover and reoccupy his province. Henry most willingly accepted this offer, because he saw it as opening a way towards the occupation of Ireland, which he had long desired and hoped for. The justice or rather injustice of the cause being the least of his considerations, he gave Dermot the following letters patent to all of his imperial subjects.

> "Henry, King of England, Duke of Normandy and Aquitaine and Count of Anjou, to all of his faithful subjects, English, Norman, Welsh, Scottish, and of whatever other nations, greetings.
>
> **10.** Dermot, prince of Leinster, having been most unjustly expelled from his kingdom, has implored our aid. We have accepted him in faith and friendship, and we ourselves hold dear the desire of this most friendly king who is kindly disposed towards our own dignity. To all who are under our own power, we give license freely to associate with him and to employ men and arms for the purpose of avenging his injuries. Whoever shows zeal in the restoration of this prince, let him know that he will have our highest approval and that Dermot himself will show him the utmost gratitude."

11. This letter is quoted verbatim by Richard Stanihurst in *On the History of Ireland*, Bk. 2 p. 66, and by Peter Lombard, Archbishop of Armagh and Primate of the Kingdom of Ireland, in his *Account* ch. 17 p. 250. They do not give the year when it was written and delivered to Dermot, but it was obviously in that same year 1168 when he fled to England, as related above.

12. Now there are three things in King Henry's letter that conform to reason and justice in the least possible degree. The first is that Dermot was most unjustly expelled from his kingdom. Which is false, because that adulterer had been expelled most justly, since he had abducted another man's wife and refused to restore her, as already said. Secondly, the licence given by Henry to all his subjects to commit themselves to Dermot and render him aid and assistance in such an unjust cause. Thirdly, this aid, which was to be unjustly given, would gain King Henry's favour.

13. The exiled Dermot, accepting this letter from Henry, sailed for England with a fair wind.

"Oh, if only then, as he sailed for the English realms,
the adulterer had drowned in the raging waters!"

He arrived in the city of Bristol, where he had Henry's letters, with the guarantee of his own generous reward, read out to a great crowd of men, and he had copies put up on doors and pillars plainly for all to see. Some prominent men were attracted, and they offered their services and contracted to help in his restoration. Dermot continued onwards to Cambria or Wales, the province of the ancient Britons, where many came forward and likewise promised on certain conditions to be his auxiliaries and allies. Overjoyed by all of this and burning with the desire to see his native land again, Dermot sailed for Ireland as an ordinary traveler, incognito. Throughout the winter he remained among those who were faithful to him, waiting for his cohorts to come over from Britain or England with the arrival of Spring. On hearing that they had landed he emerged from his hiding-place and received them with all possible liberality and magnificence.

When the news went round that Dermot had returned to the region with innumerable

British or English soldiers, many of the Leinstermen spontaneously assembed to help their returning king. With these and the Britons massed in attendance, Dermot besieged and attacked Dublin, Wexford and other cities and captured them by force or guile, and he made armed onslaughts on the Irish elsewhere, depopulating, devastating and razing all before him. King Roderick, accompanied by the other great lords and with a powerful army (more than the equal of Dermot's) confronted him, and in the series of battles which followed he suppressed Dermot's fury, slowed his advance and forced him to offer his son Cornelius as a hostage. Immediately after this Roderick and Dermot entered into a formal treaty and delegations were sent a number of times to negotiate honourable terms of peace for Dermot, and principally that he should be allowed the peaceful and entire rule of his kingdom of Leinster, on the same basis as before, and that the crime of abduction should be condoned provided he was willing to desist from war.

14. While these talks were continuing, Dermot, being a perfidious, restive man, born for contentions and disturbances, began a new military action, invading the principality of Ossory. Then he made his way towards Thomond, but Domhnall O'Brien, the prince of Thomond, repulsed him powerfully. But a terrible war blazed up suddenly (I do not know the reason) between Domhnall and King Roderick. Having weighed this situation, Dermot joined forces with Domhnall, aiming to break Roderick's power and seize the sovereignty of the whole of Ireland. Time and again he was warned and called upon, both by Roderick and by other great lords and friends, to desist from what he had begun and be mindful of his treaty and the son he had given as hostage, but he would not. The infuriated Roderick then had Dermot's son, his hostage, put to death. Afterwards war continued between the English and the Irish, and indeed among the Irish themselves, because more than a few of them gave strong support to Dermot and the English.

15. With the fighting in progress King Dermot of Leinster, full of years and empty of merits, died at Ferns in 1171. The historians tell us much about his faults and evil habits, but there is no record of his final repentance and the satisfaction which he should have given to God and man. His obituary is briefly written by Richard Stanihurst, *On the History of Ireland,*, Bk. 2, pp. 59ff. and Bk. 3 p. 111; Peter Lombard, Archbishop of Armagh, in *Commentary on the Kingdom of Ireland* ch. 17 pp. 248ff.; Philip Sullivan, *History of Catholic Ireland* Bk. 1 Ch. 3, and others.

16. While all this was occurring, King Henry II of England came to Ireland with a huge fleet and a numerous army, landing at Waterford on October 18, 1172. There he was politely received by the other great lords of Ireland, not as king or lord of Ireland, but as Prefect or Commissioner sent by the Supreme Pontiff, and in hopes he would settle all strife between the English and the Irish – as indeed he did, whereupon the following year he returned to England. However, the English were not content to retain the lands and possessions they had received from King Dermot and try to possess those peacefully, but (to anticipate my later account) they frequently attacked other holdings of the Irish, while all the time auxiliary soldiers were pouring in from England. For this reason war broke out immediately after King Henry's departure and continued for a long time.

17. This, then, is the true history, which shows us the manner in which the English first entered Ireland and occupied part of it, while always coveting the entire kingdom. Now, to argue about the justice of the case, I say in a few words that the English had no right or justice in the invasion or occupation of Ireland. Firstly, because they took up the defence of an adulterer's base and unjust cause (a man who had violated another's marriage-bed, carrying off a Queen who was another man's wife and refusing to restore her when called upon, and also committed other crimes against the commonwealth). Secondly, because they did not merely lead the exile back to his vacated seat, restore his possessions and take the prize or payment received from him. On the contrary, they did not hesitate to invade the estates of others, nor did they spare what belonged to the Church; and therefore the assumption in the first objection is entirely false, that King Henry II of England occupied Ireland by just war. I have shown that that war was iniquitous, founded on a despicable cause, and entirely unjust. Thirdly, because all who unjustly bring harm upon others in any of the nine ways which I am about to quote, commit sin and are bound to restitution, as the Doctors in general consensus declare. But the English by aiding the banished Dermot brought most serious injury upon the Irish, both in religious and secular affairs: therefore they had sinned, and they abhorred all thought of restitution. The nine ways are these:

"Order, counsel, agreement, enticement, recourse, participating, keeping silent, not opposing, not making known."

That is what the doctors say on the matter of justice and restitution, where they present these verses and expound on the nine modes which incur an obligation to restitution. One can consult *Molina t. 3 de Iust. disp. 229*ff. *Satyrus in Clavi Regia l. 10 tract. 2 c. 4*ff. *Lessius lib. 2 de Iustitia c. 13. Fillucius tom. 2 tract. 32 ch. 5 questione 9. Azorius tom. 3 libro 8 cap. 39. Rebellus 1. parte de obligationibus Iustitiae lib. 2 quaest. 18. Cardinalis Ioannes de Lugo tom. 1 de Iustitia disp.* 19. *Bonacina tom. 2 disp. 1 puncto 3. de restitutione ingenere quaest.* 2ff., and many other authors.

THIRD SECTION

The opponents' second objection is refuted.

18. Now to the second objection, which asserted that King Henry II of England had obtained an Apostolic Bull from the Supreme Pontiff Adrian IV, constituting him and his successors lords and kings of Ireland. I reply that the bull or rescript with which the English try to shield themselves, and on which they largely base the justice of their case, was acquired on false pretences and was void, and consequently their objection has no force or efficacy. That the bull was acquired on false pretences is clear from the fact that all rescripts, whether they are concerned with justice or with favour, are judged to be falsely gained and void when falsehood is told in their petition or when there is a silencing of essential truth which must rightfully be told. (All theologians and legal experts who address the question affirm this as regards a final cause, and many say the same regarding an impulsive cause.)

19. But what is a rescript of favour and a rescript of justice? And what is the difference between a final cause and an impulsive non-subjected cause? Here are brief definitions from Catholic theologians and jurists (we take no account of heretics, who are destitute of divine and human faith), so that you may understand my refutation. Rescripts of favour are those by which benefits, pensions or other favours are conceded. Rescripts of justice are those which are directed towards legal disputes and similar cases to bring them to a just conclusion or to explain the right involved, etc. One may consult *Suarez lib. 8 de Legibus cap. 2 n. 8 & 9 Sanchez tomo 3. de Matrimonio libro. 8. disp. 21. n. 1. Menochius de Arbitriis lib. 2. centuria 3. casu 201. Garcia de Beneficiis part. 8. cap. 3. num. 1. Salaz. disp. 20. de Legibus, sectione 15. n. 110. Fillucius tract. 10. part. 2. quaest. 7. pagin. 385. num. 323. Bonacina tomo 2. disp. 1. de Legibus quaest. 2. puncto 4. n. 1. Laymanus libro 1. tract. 4. caap. 22 n. 12. Aegidius de Conink in tomo de Sacramentis disp. 33. dub. 6. n. 56*, and others passim.

20. A final cause is that which the rescriptor or conceding party has in view principally and whereby he is moved rationally to concede what is asked for, and without which he would by no means concede it, or not without certain conditions and limitations. An impulsive cause is that by which the rescriptor or conceding party is more easily moved to grant the petition, but nevertheless even without it he would concede the petition according to right reason and on the merits of the case. Thus *Aegidius*, cited above, *n. 58 Sanchez in Summa lib. 4. cap. 2. num. 38 et cap. 47. n. 11. et tomo 3. de Matrimonio lib. 8. disp. 21. n. 8. ff. Covarruvias lib. 1. variarum resolutionum cap. ultimo Vasquez tomo 1. in l. 2. disputatione 70. cap. 3. et in opusculis moralibus tract. de Beneficiis, et praebendis cap. 3. §. 4. dubio 3. Tiraquellus tractatu cessante causa, limitatione 1. Suarez tom. 1. de Religione lib. 6. de voto, c. 27. n. 9.* and many other theologians and legal experts.

21. Bearing these points in mind, my solution and conclusion, taken from law, reason, and the authority of Doctors, may easily be proved valid. For the laws acknowledge that favour and concession obtained by fraudulent means are void. See the heading *Postulasti: De Rescriptis. "(The petitioner) should not gain advantage by letters of this kind where it is likely that they were acquired through concealment of the truth."* And in the chapter *Constitutus: eodem.* it is said that whatever is done by virtue of letters obtained in this way is null and void. And see the final heading *De filiis Praesbiterorum in 6.* where the concluding text holds that a dispensation obtained by an illegitimate to acquire a particular benefice is not valid if he acquired it before mentioning his prior defect. The justification is given as follows: *"Since it is not likely that the dispensation of that benefice would have been desired, with the person in question suffering the aforesaid defect, if that had been declared."* See also the heading *Quod super his. De fide instrumentorum in 6.*

22. There are a number of good reasons for this rule. Firstly, since ignorance of what is true or false causes a prince or prelate to do what is involuntary or not voluntary. But a dispensation or concession, if it is not sufficiently voluntary, is null, because without voluntariness it is not valid, as is evident; therefore, etc. Secondly, since a concession or dispensation is a human act: therefore it should proceed from the free will of the man who intends that some thing should be done; but whoever is ignorant or in error does not wish to concede the unknown thing that is asked from him unless he is told the truth, or only on the tacit or express condition that the matter is so and nothing false is added or concealed, etc. Thirdly, the actions of agents are not operative beyond their intentions. *L. non omnis ff. si certum petatur:* therefore if the intention is absent in the person conceding or dispensing, it has no effect: but if the will is lacking, the intention is lacking; therefore, etc. Fourthly, a general concession does not include things which it is improbable that the person would have conceded, according to Rule 81 of the Rules of Law in 6.

23. In conclusion I might quote many doctors, but so as not to weary you, reader, a few good ones may suffice; read, if you please, *Suarez de Religione tom. 2 lib. 6 de voto, ch. 27,* and *de Legibus, lib. 6 ch. 21 Sanchez tomo 3. de Matrimonio libro 8. disp. 21. et in Summa lib. 4. cap. 47. Rebellus 2. parte de obligationibus iustitiae libro 3. quaestione 5. section. 4. Aegidius Conichus in tomo de Sacramentis disp. 33., de dispensatione impedimentorum matrimonii dubio 6. Reginaldus in Praxi libro 31. cap. 26. num. 198. Vasquez loco citato de beneficiis,* and many others. Hence in order to be secure in conscience, anyone who seeks a favour from prince or prelate should not knowingly express any falsehood or suppress any truth, at any rate on matters which are grave and concern the final cause of what is sought and conceded, as the above-named doctors and others generally teach.

24. Nor does the concession count as valid if it was through the ignorance or simplicity of the petitioner or the malice of somebody else that this taciturnity or expression of falsehood came about, or that truth was suppressed or falsehood expressed concerning the intrinsic qualities of the concession. Rather, the concession, whatever it may be, always ceases to stand. This is established under the heading on letters of rescripts, as follows: *"If it was through an expression of falsehood of this kind, or through such a suppression of truth that the letters were acquired, whereas if the falsehood had been omitted or the truth expressed we would not have granted letters at all, the authorities should not act on them in any way."* This is the commonly-held position of doctors, theologians and jurists. See Sanchez, *op. cit., lib. 8 disp. 21 nn. 56, 57* and *72,* where he cites many, *et lib. 4. Summae c. 47. n. 15. Bonacina op. cit. puncto 4. n. 8. Panormitanus, Decius Felinus,* and other legal experts on the paragraph on rescripts cited above.

25. King Henry II in his petition for this rescript made false statements. He said that Ireland at that time was not within the domain of the Catholic Church, and that the Irish were uninstructed and uncivilised, and that it was necessary to declare the truth of Christ's faith to them and subject them to law. This false declaration is to be found in the Apostolic letter quoted above in section 4. There the Pope, referring to King Henry's petition, expresses himself as follows:

> "Laudably and beneficially Your Majesty is proposing to spread the glory of your name on earth and lay up a reward of eternal happiness in Heaven, and fittingly for a Christian prince your intention is to expand the bounds of the Church, to declare the truth of the Christian religion to an ignorant and uncivilised people, and to eradicate the weeds of vice from the field of the Lord," etc.

And later on: *"to subject that people to laws,"* etc.

26. So then, the king said that he wished to invade Ireland in order to extend the bounds of the Church. I ask, was not the whole of Ireland Catholic at that time, with all of its inhabitants? Indeed it was, nor did it ever defect from the Catholic faith once it had received it from Saint Patrick, its apostle, who began to preach there in AD 431 or 432 or 441, according to the differing opinions of authors (let us omit the more ancient mission in Ireland of Saint James the Apostle, son of Zebedee) down to the present time, the year 1645 when I am writing. Therefore it belonged to the domain of the Church. Therefore King Henry lied in declaring that it did not so belong, or was deceived in supposing this.

27. Henry continued his petition with the words, *"to declare the truth of the Christian religion to an ignorant and uncivilised people."* But Ireland at that time had bishops and masters more learned than those who could have come from England, nor in fact did any arrive for the purpose of preaching and teaching; though afterwards some did indeed come, not to preach but to take possession of fat benefices. One of those was Richard FitzRalph from the Chancery of Oxford, promoted to Archbishop of Armagh, who perhaps did more harm than good to Catholics by his writings, since many errors can be found there against sound Catholic doctrine; those are dealt with by Antonius Possevinus, *tom. 3 apparatus sacri pag. 131. litera R. Thomas Vualdensis to. 2. et 3. Bellarminus in lib. de Scriptoribus Ecclesiasticis, et in tomo 1. controversarium lib. 2. de Monachis cap. 45 et 46.*

But on the other hand, in earlier times Irish bishops and priests had gone to England and preached the faith there, and had instructed the English and brought them over to the orthodox faith. Read Bede in his books on the *Ecclesiastical History of the English People* in Vol. 3 of his works, and Philip Sullivan in the *Compendium of Catholic History*, vol. 2 bk. 1 ch. 1 and *The Life of Saint Patrick*, bk. 1 ch. 5 fol. 66ff. And those people were not afterwards so uncivilised and uninstructed that they needed new masters from England (whose language they did not understand) to comprehend the Catholic faith, since they had native masters, and better ones, at home. There were 34 or 35 bishoprics in Ireland in King Henry's time with as many bishops, of whom four were archbishops, in Armagh, Dublin, Cashel and Tuam. There were many secular priests and monks of diverse religious orders. Albertus Miraeus of Brussels writes extensively on the archbishoprics and other bishoprics of the kingdom of Ireland in the work entitled *Notitiae Episcopatum orbis Christiani, lib.1 cap. 7 pag. 13, 14* and *lib. 4 cap. 22 pag. 219, 220*, where he names all of them in a lengthy catalogue; and in *lib. 5 pag. 341* he says that those four archbishoprics were instituted on the authority of Pope Eugenius III in 1151 AD by the Papal Legate Ioannes Papiro, as Caesar Baronius and Henricus Spondanus record in their annals for that year. Giraldus Cambrensis states the same in *Appendix to the Topography of Ireland* ch. 20, Rogerius in his annals, and others. William Camden, however, in his *Britanica* relates (from Philip Flatbury) that they were instituted by Papal authority in 1152 by Christian, bishop of Lismore, as Legate of Ireland. See also Sullivan, *History of Catholic Ireland*, tom. 2 bk. 1 ch. 7 and Augustinus Barbosa in *de Officio et potestate Episcopi, part 1 tit. 1 cap. 7*, where he presents a catalogue of the bishoprics of Ireland, and the other kingdoms of the entire Christian world.

28. Henry proceeds in his petition: *"To subject that people to laws."* I ask: what laws are those, to which Henry wished to subject our Irish people? If ecclesiastical – the Irish were always more observant of those than the English and than Henry himself, for Ireland and its people never defected from the Catholic faith once adopted, but England and its people frequently did, as I shall demonstrate below. Or were those the laws which Henry had established in England and wished to introduce against the liberty and dignity of the Catholic Church? They were abominable and damnable to us, as they were to St. Thomas Archbishop of Canterbury, who opposed them as sacrilegious even to his death. Concerning those heinous laws, one may consult Matthew Paris in *Historia Anglicana pag. 96, 97*; Petrus de Ribadeneira in *Vita Sancti Thomae Cantuariensis*; Bernardus de Britto in *Chronica Cisterciensis ordinis prima part. lib. 6 cap. 5*, and others. If it was other more civil laws that he wanted, we stood in no need of them, since those which we had in our own kingdom were better, or certainly sufficient. From all of this it is clear that King Henry made false statements and kept silent about the truth, and in consequence the Papal Bull was fraudulently obtained and of no validity or force in law, or for conferring any dominion whatever in Ireland upon the English kings: hence the second objection counts for nothing. Added to this is the fact that it is not usual or even possible for the Pope to deprive particular Catholic kings of their kingdoms and grant them to others. For the Pope is not the temporal lord of kingdoms, as the better and more general opinion of theologians and legal experts teaches. See Bellarmine *tom. 1 controversariarum lib. 5 de Romano Pontifice cap. 2 et sequentibus*, Suarez in *de legibus lib. 3 cap. 6* and in *Defence of the Faith Against the Errors of the English Sect bk. 3 ch. 5* and Molina *tom. 1. de Iustitia.* These authors cite many others.

If certain Popes in certain cases deposed kings, they were using their supreme power,which is spiritual directly and temporal indirectly, on account of heresy or other very grave crimes committed by these kings. Following that, I put the question to the English: did Henry II, on his own behalf and that of his successors, accept Ireland from the Pope by feudal right or not? If they deny it, what is the point of citing that bull in their favour? If they affirm it, consequently the kings of England are feudatories and vassals of the Pope, whose power as regards the conferring of the kingdom they recognise and in every other respect deny. To my mind, people should write and speak more coherently and truthfully, if they are not to be seen contradicting themselves and become a laughing-stock! But this much by the way.

29. Even supposing for the sake of argument that the Apostolic Bull of Pope Adrian IV, which the English employ to protect their position, and on which they mainly base the justice of their case, was a true and legitimate bull, not affected in any way by the evil of fraud; even then their objection would not be convincing. Firstly, because the conditions laid down in that indult or bull were not implemented by King Henry nor by his successor kings, much less by the last five heretical monarchs, namely Henry VIII, Edward VI, Elizabeth, James and Charles, as I am about to demonstrate. Secondly, because there are other indults or bulls by later Popes which exempt Ireland and the Irish from all English dominion, and exhort the Irish themselves to undertake and sustain a just war against the English, as I shall also substantiate below.

30. The principal conditions which are demanded in that bull of Adrian IV are the following: firstly, *that the limits or bounds of the Church be extended.* Secondly, *that the incidence of vice be restrained.* Thirdly, *that vicious customs be corrected.* Fourthly, *that the Christian religion be strengthened.* Fifthly, *that the worship and honour of God and the salvation of souls be accomplished to the greatest extent.* Sixthly, *that ecclesiastical law be entirely observed.* Seventhly, *that the annual tax of one penny from each single house in the kingdom should not be discontinued but rather should be paid.* All of these conditions are unambiguously taken from the words of Pope Adrian IV contained in that bull quoted above, where he addresses Henry II of England as follows:

> "Responding to your pious and praiseworthy desire with appropriate goodwill, we kindly assent to your petitions, and we gladly consent that in order to expand the bounds of the Church, restrain the decadence of vice and reform the people's way of life, and strengthen the Christian religion, you shall enter that island and do whatever tends to the honour of God and the welfare of that land; and that the people of that land shall receive you with honour and reverence as their Lord, provided that the right of the Church remains inviolate and entire and that a tribute of one penny yearly for every house is duly paid to Blessed Peter and the Holy Roman Church, etc."

31. These, then, are the conditions which Pope Adrian IV imposed upon King Henry II. Let us see how his successor monarchs and their English ministers complied with, or rather spurned those conditions and wished to bring about – and actually did bring about, to the best of their ability – the direct contrary. Firstly, they did not expand the domain of the Church but contracted it as far as they could. Secondly, they did not restrain vice but increased it. Thirdly, they did not correct customs but rather depraved and in every way corrupted them. Fourthly, they did not promote or conserve, but made every effort to extinguish, the Christian religion. Fifthly, they neglected the worship and honour of God and the salvation of souls, and above all they attacked it by introducing heretical sects, after Henry VIII's defection from the Holy Roman Catholic Church about 1535 AD. Sixthly, they diminished and plundered ecclesiastical holdings. Seventhly, they did not pay but retained Blessed Peter's Pence. They have sought and seek to this day to destroy the Catholic faith and by all means to wipe it out: they have mixed sacred and profane and laid impious hands on sacred images and other sacred things; far from establishing any definite religion or any firm faith, they have introduced diverse heretical sects, at variance both with one another and with the true Catholic faith, above all during the reigns of those five heretical monarchs of recent times, Henry VIII, Edward VI, Elizabeth, James and Charles.

32. Now take the next step along with me, Catholic reader. When someone concedes something to someone else under some definite, just condition or conditions, if some licit contract is made between them, especially one of obligation which is transactional or coming under a transaction (such as purchase, sale, barter, exchange, loan, rent, hire, feud, emphyteusis etc.), or non-transactional or not coming under a special transaction but generically of that kind (such as *do ut des, do ut facias, facio ut des, facio ut facias* – "I give so that you give, I give so that you do, I do so that you give, I do so that you do"), is it not true that if some just and honest condition, or number of conditions, are lacking, particularly on the recipient's part, the concession becomes null and the contract is rescinded, or certainly can be rescinded, annulled and made void?

All theologians and law experts by unanimous consensus teach this. But if it is the case that Pope Adrian the Fourth conceded the dominion of Ireland (if what the English argue is true) to King Henry the Second of England and his successor kings under the definite, honest conditions set out above, it follows that if any of those kings was unwilling to implement those conditions or to stand by his promises and undertakings, such a contract is null and rescinded, or ought to be rescinded. Especially when this is desired by some other Pope, successor of Adrian the Fourth, and the people of Ireland, no faith need be kept with the faith-breaker, at least in that particular matter.

"It is vain for anyone to demand that another keep faith with him, if he himself refuses to keep the faith that he himself has pledged to that other." Rule 75 de regulis iuris in 6. Now, the monarchs of England, especially the five recent heretics, have not implemented the conditions in Pope Adrian's bull; therefore any of Adrian's papal successors and the Irish people could justly deprive of all dominion and pretended right any English monarch who had not been willing to implement the aforesaid conditions – since now he was not a true king and lord, but rather a usurper and a tyrant in possession of the kingdom's government, and in

consequence he was deprived of that right, or certainly he ought to be deprived of all title of king and lord, as having possession in bad faith and unjustly. These things are so clear that they scarcely need supporting reference to Doctors or texts, since no one except an obdurate heretic or an utterly foolish man would be capable of denying them or by any means getting round them.

33. I come to the second matter which I raised in section 29 above, where I said that other documents existed – indults, diplomatic letters, rescripts or bills by the later Popes – which exempt Ireland and the Irish from all dominion by the English, and call on the Irish themselves to undertake and sustain a just war against the English. And that is to omit the story of St. Lawrence, Archbishop of Dublin, which many relate verbally and a few have put in writing, one of those being Philip O'Sullivan in the *History of Catholic Ireland*, tom. 2 bk. 1 ch. 7 fol. 62. That saint and prelate, grieved by the unjust administration of Ireland by King Henry II and the English, went to the Pope who was then governing the Church (by computation of time he was evidently Lucius III) and obtained from him a diplomatic letter depriving the English and the said King Henry of Ireland's administration. But before reaching Ireland he ended his life in the French town of Eu, in the church of Saint Mary in the diocese of Rothomages. The reader will find an extensive account of his life, replete with piety, good works and miracles, by a very old writer, in Laurentius Surius, Vol. 6, November 14. Caesar Baronius records his passing in the *Roman Martyrology* of that day and in his notes to the same. Richard Stanihurst has written an elegant, brief memorial of that saint's life and glorious death in *On the History of Ireland,* bk. 4, p. 194ff., indicating that the year of his death was 1184. Readers may also, if they wish, see what Stanihurst has to say about him in bk. 3 p. 106. Honorius III, Supreme Prelate of the Church, placed him among the number of the Holy Confessors in the tenth year of his pontificate (1226 AD). See his bull of canonisation dated December 11 of the same year, which is in the *Bullarium Romanum,* Vol. 1, pp. 82-83.

Nor does it seem irrelevant that King Henry was an impious, tyrannical and cruel man. Among his crimes, which were many, he was responsible for hounding two outstanding prelates to their deaths, Thomas, the Archbishop and glorious martyr of Canterbury, and Lawrence, Archbishop and Holy Confessor of Dublin, son of an Irish king and queen (so described in the above-mentioned life in Surius, Cologne Agripina edition of 1575, ch. 31 p. 322, and in another Cologne edition of 1581, p. 354). *"A grave dissension arose between King Henry of England, under whom Saint Thomas had suffered his grievous martyrdom, and Roderick, the most powerful king of Ireland. Wishing to compose this quarrel, Blessed Lawrence intervened. He came to England bringing with him a relation of his, an elegant youth, who was to be given to King Henry as a hostage, if it were possible on any terms to make peace with him. But the king of England repudiated peace and showed himself rather a cruel tyrant. By a royal edict he prevented the man of God from returning home, demanding that all ports which faced towards Ireland should be closed to him, and so he compelled the holy man to go into exile etc."* The result was that he was forced to sail for France, where he died (ibid., and in the following chapters).

I leave out of account also the letters of Pope John XXII to King Edward II of England, in which he warned him about the unjust administration of Ireland and the vexations and oppressions with which the English of that time were afflicting the Irish, who were consequently thinking of choosing another king for themselves. This letter of Pope John XXII is recorded by O'Sullivan in the *History of Catholic Ireland*, tom. 2 bk. 1 ch. 9 pp. 64-65; it is found also in the *Bullarium Romanum* Vol. 1 p. 172. Although the year when it was sent is not noted, the distinguished English Catholic Doctor Nicholas Sanders, referring to it in *Rise and Growth of the English Schism*, Bk. 1, pp. 222-223, says it was written about 1320 AD. It happens that the same King Edward, on account of his lethargy, was deprived of his kingdom and his life by his own English subjects in 1326, as I mention later on in section 91.

34. Pope Paul III's Bull which begins *Eius, qui immobile permanens*, is contained in *Bullarium Romanum* Vol. 1 pp. 514ff., published in Rome at Saint Mark in 1535, August 30. Section 9 of that Bull declares that all of the children of King Henry VIII of England by Anne Boleyn, and the children of the said king's accomplices, partisans, adherents, counsellors and followers, are infamous and incapable of all lordship or any temporal or ecclesiastical benefice, etc., as is clear from the words of that Pope in the place cited, as follows.

> "And the children of King Henry and of his accomplices, partisans, adherents, counsellors, followers, and other culpable parties already mentioned suffer the same penalties, as is appropriate in this case. And we declare our decision that all the children born to King Henry

of the said Anna and the children of those previously mentioned, already born or yet to be born, and their descendants down to that degree to which the laws in such cases extend the penalties (with no exceptions concerning minority of age, sex, ignorance, or any other reason whatsoever) are deprived of the dignities and honours which are theirs, however established, or which they enjoy, use, control or have vested interest in, and likewise of their privileges, concessions, graces, indulgences, immunities, remissions, liberties and indults and dominions, cities, camps, lands, villas, towns, and places commended or conceded to their governance, and whatever they have, hold or possess in feud or emphyteusis or otherwise from the Roman or other churches, monasteries, and ecclesiastical places, and secular princes, lords, potentates, even kings and emperors, or other private or public persons. And the said feudal goods or emphyteutica, and all which they have obtained by whatever means from others, are devolved to those other owners, so that they may freely dispose of those goods. And we also decree and declare that those clergy and monks who have acquired from those people in whatever manner cathedrals and metropolitans, as well as monasteries, priories, praepostorships, prefectures, dignities, personalities, offices, canonries and prebends, or other ecclesiastical benefices, are deprived of those, and we decree and declare that they are likewise ineligible to obtain these or other positions in the future, and so with due authority, knowingly and entirely we debar those deprived from acquiring anything else of a sinilar kind, or any dignities, honours, administrations and offices, lands and feuds, in the future."

– These are the Pope's words, formally expressed in Section 9, as already mentioned.

35. And in the same Bull, Section 10, this same Pope continues as follows against King Henry VIII:

"The magistrates, judges, counsellors, guardians, and all officials of King Henry, his kingdom, and all other dominions, cities, lands, castles, villas, fortresses, citadels, towns, and their own seats, including those obtained de facto, and the communities, universities, colleges, feudatories, subject vassals, citizens, inhabitants, and commercial dwellers, laymen in de facto obedience to the said king, and those clergy who on account of some church living acknowledge King Henry as their superior, or his supporters, adherents, counsellors and followers mentioned above, are hereby absolved and entirely freed from their oaths of loyalty, oaths of vassalage and all subjection to the said king and the others mentioned. This notwithstanding, we order the aforesaid people on pain of excommunication to withdraw their obedience thoroughly and entirely from the said King Henry and his officials, judges, and magistrates, not recognising them as superiors or obeying their laws."

– These are the Pope's words, Section 10.

36. And in another Bull, which begins *Cum Redemptor Noster* (given at Rome at Saint Peter's on December 17, 1538 in the fourth year of Paul III's Pontificate, as contained in the *Bullarium* Vol. 1 p. 517), the Pope confirms the penalties in the previously-mentioned Bull despatched on August 30, 1535, against King Henry and his accomplices, partisans, etc. In Section 1 of this second Bull the Pope speaks as follows:

37. "When we were told that King Henry of England, apart from recklessly contracting a marriage against the Church's prohibition, had issued certain laws, or general regulations and constiutions, which would draw his subjects into heresy and schism, and that he had caused Cardinal John of Rochester of happy memory, Priest of Saint Vitalis, to be publicly condemned and capitally punished, and many other prelates and clergy to be imprisoned, because they were not willing to adhere to this heresy – even though these things were reported to us by people of whose truthfulness there could be no possible doubt, nonetheless out of respect for King Henry, whom we had held in special affection before he fell into this insanity, we hoped to discover that the foregoing reports were false and took pains to acquire independent information regarding these affairs. Finding that the complaints which had reached us were indeed true, so as not to be remiss in our office we decided to proceed against him according to the form of certain letters of ours, etc."

– as above in the first Bull of 1535.

38. And Section 3 of the above-mentioned second Bull of 1538 is as follows (the same Pope is referring to the same King Henry):

"King Henry has not only not returned to his senses and amended his conduct, as we have been expecting for almost three years, but on the contrary becomes daily more and more confirmed in his cruelty and recklessness, breaking out into new crimes. Not content with the brutal slaughter of living priests and prelates, he has not shrunk from exercising his cruelty against the dead, including those whom the

Church has received among its saints and venerated for many centuries. They include Thomas, the godly archbishop of Canterbury, whose bones, on account of innumerable miracles worked by Almighty God in the kingdom of England, were kept with the highest reverence in a golden casket in the town of Canterbury. King Henry had him called to judgement and damned as a rebel, pronounced a traitor, exhumed and burnt, and ordered his ashes to be scattered in the wind, plainly surpassing the brutality practised among peoples anywhere, since even in war it has not been normal for the victorious enemy to savage the corpses of the dead. In addition to that, he seized for himself the gifts that had been given by diverse kings of England and other princes, appended to the casket, which were many and very precious, and as if he had not done enough injury to religion by this, he plundered the monastery of the Holy Augustine, from whom the English received the Christian faith, a consecrated place in that same town with its treasures which were many and great. It was as if he were transformed into a wild beast, and indeed the men whom he was willing to honour as his associates were wild beasts too. They were like savage animals in that monastery; the monks were expelled and an abominable kind of criminality introduced there which is unheard-of not only among faithful Christians but even among the Turks."

– These are the words of the Pope.

39. And Pope Pius V in the Bull beginning *Regnans in excelsis* (given at Rome in Saint Peter's on February 25, 1569, the fifth year of his Pontificate; contained in the *Bullarium Romanum*, Vol. 2, p. 229, in the Roman edition of 1638; Nicholas Sanders also refers to this Bull in *Rise and Growth of the English Schism*, Bk. 3, p. 423, in the Roman edition above, and Peter Lombard in his *Commentary on the Kingdom of Ireland,* ch. 25, p. 475) expresses himself as follows:

"He who reigns on high, to Whom is given all power in Heaven and earth, has entrusted the one holy Catholic and Apostolic Church, outside of which there is no salvation, to one alone upon earth, namely to Peter, first of the Apostles, and Peter's successor the Roman Pontiff, to be governed in the fulness of power. God has placed him over all peoples and all kingdoms, to uproot, destroy, scatter, disperse, plant and build, so that he may present the faithful people, held together by the bond of charity, in the unity of the spirit, safe and spotless to their saviour etc. But the number of the wicked has so much increased in power that there is no place left on earth which they have not tried to corrupt with their vicious doctrines.

Active among them is Elizabeth, pretended Queen of England and serving-maid of crime, to whom the most wicked of all have made their way and with her found refuge. Having occupied the throne, she usurped the place of the supreme head of the Church in all England and monstrously claimed his authority and jurisdiction as her own, and once more she has brought that kingdom to miserable ruin, though previously it had been restored to fruitfulness in the Catholic faith. Employing her power to prevent the practice of the true religion (which was overthrown by the deserter Henry VIII but restored with the help of this See by the legitimate Queen Mary of radiant memory), she has followed and embraced heretical errors; dissolved the Royal Council composed of members of the English nobility and filled it with obscure heretics; oppressed those who practice the Catholic faith and given places to vile preachers and ministers of impiety. She has abolished the sacrifice of the Mass, prayers, fasts, distinction of foods, celibacy and Catholic rites; she has ordered that books containing manifest heresy be propounded to the whole kingdom, and that her subjects also should observe the impious rites and customs prescribed by Calvin, which she herself has accepted. She has expelled bishops, church rectors and other Catholic priests from their churches and livings; she has dared to give heretics the disposal of these and other Church affairs and to decide on cases of ecclesiastical law. She has forbidden the prelates, clergy and people to recognise the Roman Church or to obey its precepts and canonical sanctions. She has compelled many to conform to her wicked laws and to abjure the authority of the Roman Pontiff and the obedience due to him. She has forced them to recognise on oath that she is their sole overlord in temporal and spiritual affairs. She has imposed penalties and physical punishments on those who would not conform, and demanded that all who persevere in the unity of the faith and in obedience to the Pope shall be punished likewise. She has had Catholic bishops and church rectors incarcerated in chains, where many of them, worn out by long enfeeblement and sorrow, have ended their days miserably.

All of this is plain and notorious among the nations, and it is so well established by the testimony of many people of the gravest character that there is no place left for excuse, defence or evasion. Her impieties and crimes are multiplying more and more, and the persecution of the faithful and affliction of religion becomes daily harsher through the initiative and energy of Elizabeth herself. We understand her mind to be so resolved and hardened that she has not only spurned the pious prayers and admonishments of Catholic princes who have attempted to cure her and convert her, but she has not even permitted the envoys which this See despatched in connection with these matters to land in England.

Of necessity we have taken up the arms of justice against her, though we cannot but feel sorrow that we are forced to punish somebody whose forbears deserved so well of the Christian commonwealth. Therefore, sustained by that authority whose will it was to place us on this supreme throne of justice (unequal though we are to the burden), in the fulness of Apostolic power we declare that the said Elizabeth, being a heretic and partisan of heretics, along with her adherents in heresy has incurred the sentence of anathema and is cut off from the unity of the Body of Christ. Furthermore, she is deprived of her pretended right to the kingdom and of all lordship, dignity and privilege, and the nobility, subjects and people of the said kingdom, and all others who have sworn oaths to her of whatever kind, are absolved perpetually from such oaths and from all duties arising from lordship, fidelity and obedience. By the authority of this letter we absolve them as aforesaid, and we deprive the said Elizabeth of her pretended right to the kingdom, and we command all the others named above and warn all and sundry nobles, subjects, people, and others aforesaid, that they are forbidden to obey her edicts, commands and laws; and those who act otherwise are included in the same bond of excommunication. etc."

– These are the words of Pope Pius V in his Bull.

40. Those are the indults, diplomatic briefs, rescripts, bulls, or letters of the Popes who exempted Ireland and the Irish from all dominion and jurisdiction of the heretical monarchs of England. It only remains to give due place to other indults or bulls by other Popes, where the same Irish Catholics are urged to wage and maintain just war against the English heretics, as I said in No. 29 above.

41. Pope Gregory XIII more than once urged the Catholics of Ireland to wage war against the English heretics, providing plenary indulgence, forgiveness and remission of sins to all who would follow James and John FitzGerald, the stalwart Irish Catholic leaders, and join with them, whether by giving counsel, favour, supplies, arms or other war materials, or in any degree giving aid in the war against the heretical English. This is clearly apparent in the Bull issued by him in Rome at Saint Peter's on May 13, 1580, in the eighth year of his Ponificate, recorded by Philip O'Sullivan in the *History of Catholic Ireland*, tom. 2 ch. 17 fol. 100-101, which we transcribe here word for word.

POPE GREGORY XIII

to all archbishops, bishops and other prelates, as well as princes, counts, barons, clergy, nobility and people of the kingdom of Ireland, greetings and apostolic blessing.

42. "In recent years we have addressed you in our letters, urging you to recover, guard and preserve your liberty against the heretics, and to support James FitzGerald, who in high ardour of spirit was planning to remove the yoke of servitude imposed on you by the English deserters from the Holy Roman Church. We called on you to give him prompt and vigorous assistance, as he prepared to confront God's enemies and yours. So that you might do this with more alacrity, we allowed a plenary pardon and remission of all their sins (of the kind usually given by the Roman Pontiffs to those going to war against the Turks or for the recovery of the Holy Land) to all those contrite and confessed people who acknowledged James as leader and his army as defender and champion of the Catholic faith, and joined with him or gave him favour, supplies, arms and other war materials, or who helped in this expedition to whatever degree. But lately we have heard with great sorrow that James, while fighting bravely against the enemy, was killed (as God willed it), and our dear son John FitzGerald, his relative, who had already merited well of the Catholic faith by his exceptional deeds, with piety and greatness of mind has succeeded him as leader of this expedition (thanks be to God, Whose cause is at issue). We ask you, therefore, with the greatest urgency at our command, to assist John as leader and his army against the aforesaid heretics with all the aid that you gave to James when alive. To all who have confessed and received Communion and who do for John and his army what is contained in the said letters, and who after his death, if that should happen (which may God prevent) adhere and give support to his brother James, we give the same plenary indulgence and remission of sins which those fighting against the Turks and for the recovery of the Holy Land receive, through the mercy of Almighty God and the authority of Blessed Peter and Paul his Apostles, by this present letter which shall be valid as long as the said brothers John and James shall live, etc."

43. Pope Clement VIII in 1603 sent Friar Matthew de Oviedo, a Spaniard, to Ireland as his Papal Legate and Archbishop of Dublin with a bull of indulgence to all who took arms against the English for the Catholic faith, as O'Sullivan relates in tom. 3 bk. 5 ch. 12 fol. 167. The interested reader may also find Paul V's letter of consolation and exhortation to the Catholic Irish in O'Sullivan's *Life of St. Patrick*, bk. 10 ch. 9 fol. 169.

44. Finally, Pope Urban VIII gave the following bull and indulgence to Eoghan O'Neill, that most stalwart and noble Irish commander, and the other Catholics who were waging a sustained war against the English heretics.

To Our Dear Son Eoghan O'Neill

> **45.** "Greetings to our dear son. You are accustomed to let no opportunity pass where you may follow in your ancestors' footsteps and demonstrate your zeal and energy in promoting the interests of the Church, and you have shown this splendidly on the present occasion, planning to set out for Ireland to assist the Catholic cause. In connection with this we have received your most welcome letters, where you announce the journey you are contemplating, and knowing that the auspices are best for the project's success if it is begun with celestial aid, in a humble and religious spirit you request our Apostolic blessing. We give high praise to this excellent ardour of yours and your constancy against the heretics and spirit of true faith: already aware, as we were, of your piety, we expect from you proofs of that stalwart strength which in earlier times established the fame of your family name. We likewise commend the decision of those you have mentioned, whom you inspire by example. We hope therefore that the Almighty will be favourable to your cause and that its power may be made known among the peoples. Meanwhile, so that you may the more confidently commence everything, we unceasingly pray the divine mercy to bring the enemy's efforts to naught; to you and to the other Catholics undertaking the work in the kingdom of Ireland we freely impart our blessing, and to all and each who have penitently made confession and duly received Holy Communion (if they had means of doing so) we grant a plenary pardon and remission of all their sins; and we also extend a plenary indulgence at the moment of death. Given in Rome under the Fisherman's Ring on October 8, 1642, in the 20th year of our Pontificate."

– These are the Pope's words.

46. No Catholic has ever been able to doubt with any semblance of plausibility – after the defection and apostasy from the Catholic faith of

King Henry VIII of England, Edward VI, Elizabeth, and other heretical monarchs of the English – that the war of the Catholic Irish is a just one. In this regard see also the learned and grave judgement of the Doctors of the Academies of Salamanca and Valladolid in Spain in Philip O'Sullivan's *History of Catholic Ireland*, tom. 3 bk. 8 ch. 7, fol. 202ff.

One must add here, as an absolutely certain fact, that all Irishmen are bound by human, divine and natural precept to combine with one another so as to expel the heretics, and to avoid communication with them; and still more they are obliged not to offer them any kind of aid, counsel, furtherance, arms or supplies etc. against the Catholics. The human precept, as expressed by the Church, consists not only in the Papal constitutions cited above and many other legal texts which for brevity's sake we omit, but also in the Bull which is read and proclaimed on Holy Thursday at the feast of the Lord's Supper, where the Pope speaks as follows in the first clause.

> "On behalf of Almighty God, Father, Son and Holy Ghost, on His authority and on that of the Blessed Apostles Peter and Paul, we excommunicate and anathematise all Hussites, Wycliffists, Lutherans, Zwinglians, Calvinists, Huguenots, Anabaptists, Trinitarians, and apostates from the Christian faith and all other heretics, by whatever name they may be known and to whatever sect they may belong, and their believers, harbourers, supporters, and generally all defenders of theirs whatsoever, and their books which contain heresy or treat of religion, and those who without our authority and that of the Holy See read them or retain them, print them, or in any way defend them for whatever reason, publicly or secretly, with whatever art or on whatever pretext; and the schismatics and those who persistently withdraw themselves from obedience to us or to whichever Roman Pontiff holds office at the given time."

The divine precept may clearly be gathered from the words of the Holy Apostles Paul and John quoted immediately below, and indeed from the words of Christ Our Lord, hence the Catholic reader should see that the obligation on Catholic Irishmen in this regard is of the strictest and most urgent kind. Saint Paul, then, in his *Epistle to Titus*, 3, 10, speaks as follows. "A *man that is a heretic, after the first and second admonition, avoid: Knowing that he, that is such an one, is subverted, and sinneth, being condemned by his own judgment."*

Here the apostle forbids communication with an obstinate heretic who has had sufficient warning. Saint Bernard, referring to heretics in

Cantica, Sermon 66, gives excellent justification for this course of action: *"They are not convinced by reasoning, because they do not understand it; they are not corrected by authority, because they do not accept it; they are not moved by persuasion, because they are warped."*

Saint John the Apostle, *Epistle* 2, 9/ 10 / 11, speaking of heretics, says:

> "Whosoever revolteth, and continueth not in the doctrine of Christ, hath not God. He that continueth in the doctrine, the same hath both the Father and the Son. If any man come to you, and bring not this doctrine, receive him not into the house nor say to him, God speed you. For he that saith unto him, God speed you, communicateth with his wicked works." And Saint Jerome in Epistle 5 to the Galatians compares heresy to idolatry: "The heretical dogmas are idols, which the heretics would have the faithful adore."

Finally, Christ Our Lord has commanded us to avoid any man who refuses to hear the Catholic Church as if he were a heathen or a publican. *"And if he will not hear the church, let him be to thee as the heathen and publican"* (Matthew 18, 70). But the heretics do not wish to hear the Catholic Church of the living God, which is the pillar and the ground of truth as Saint Paul affirms (*Epistle 1 to Timothy, 3, 15*). Therefore we should regard them as heathens and publicans, and consequently we should avoid all communication with them. It is certain that on one occasion when Saint Polycarp (Bishop of Smyrna and a celebrated martyr at Rome) saw the heresiarch Marcion coming towards him, he refused to speak to him. When Marcion came up to him he said, *"Do you recognise me?"*, to which Polycarp replied, *"I recognise the firstborn son of the Devil!"* In imitation of this saint we too can regard all heretics as he did and call them sons of the Devil.

Precept and natural law both dictate that we should defend our country and our Catholic neighbours from heretics unjustly invading our temporal and spiritual goods; but the English heretics have invaded us, our country, our neighbours and our goods; therefore we are bound to defend these, and all laws prescribe or permit that force may be repelled with force. Apart from that, it is necessary to be fully on guard against the danger of perversion which derives from communication with heretics, as law and natural intelligence dictate. Hence not only should you expel the English and Scottish heretics, but you should even remove from your midst, as traitors and enemies of their country, those

Irishmen who give aid to heretics or further them in any way; you are not unaware of the punishments which heretics and their supporters incur according to law. Read chapter 32 of *Exodus*, and you will find that the Holy Patriarch Moses ordered 23,000 Hebrews to be killed on account of the sin of idolatry. Likewise, read chapter 25 of the *Book of Numbers*, where again on account of the sin of infidelity and idolatry God commanded that all the leaders of the people be removed and hanged on gibbets. And on that day 24,000 Israelites were killed. I have already said above that heresy is to be compared with idolatry and heretics are similar to idolaters; for they are unfaithful to God and men. So that evil may be removed from you, therefore, strike the heretics and their supporters from your midst, even if otherwise they are your brothers and your neighbours – as God commanded and Moses put into practice.

FOURTH SECTION

The opponents' third objection is met

47. To the third objection, which asserted that King Henry II of England had been received and acclaimed or greeted as king and lord of Ireland by the three estates of the kingdom: I reply first of all by denying that he was received as such by the Irish. For to begin with, many princes, nobles and peoples in Ireland were not willing to receive him or ever to obey him, as even the older English writers who lived at that time admit openly, and still more so the writers of Ireland. Certainly Sylvester Giraldus Cambrensis, a writer of that time and the king's own secretary, whom Richard Stanihurst cites approvingly in *On the History of Ireland*, bk. 3, admits that the princes and inhabitants of the entire province of Ulster did not receive Henry or swear acceptance of his sovereignty. Matthew Paris, also an Englishman and a very old writer, in his *Historia Anglica*, p. 121, No. 10, clearly says that Roderick, prince of Connacht and king of Ireland, had omitted to come to meet King Henry and did not wish to acknowledge him as lord. So then, there were two portions or provinces of Ireland, namely Ulster and Connacht, which were unwilling to receive King Henry. O'Sullivan in his *Catholic History*, tom. 2, bk. 1, ch. 5, says that Henry had not been received as lord or king, but rather as a prefect or commissary sent by the Pope. Archbishop Lombard, already mentioned, in his *Commentary*, ch. 17, p.

253, says that some of the Irish who received Henry were subjected by force and others by fear. Finally, in the book which he gave to the press in 1612 King James's Attorney General admits that Ireland had never been totally subjected to the monarchs of England until the time of James, who began to reign in England after Elizabeth's death in 1603 and himself died in 1625. So our opponents' argument is of no value, insofar as it seeks to prove that Henry the Second was received as king and lord by the three estates of the kingdom of Ireland.

48. I respond secondly that even if purely for the sake of argument we grant that Henry was received, acclaimed and saluted by all estates of the kingdom, our opponents' argument gains no advantage by that, because it is a fact that the estates of the kingdom were coerced to receive him by grave fear. For Henry when he entered Ireland brought with him a huge fleet of 40 myoparones or large ships, full of soldiers and military supplies, and even previous to that he had a huge army in the land and many cities and towns had been reduced to his power. Hence his reception, acclamation and salutation by the Irish, who were compelled by grave fear, could not afford him any right. For all theologians and legal experts plainly declare that acts and contracts which are enacted under grave fear and unjust compulsion, are *ipso facto* and by positive human and canon law invalid, or certainly they ought to be made invalid. And in either of the laws one may easily find and demonstrate a leading opinion which asserts that they are in fact invalid.

So then, this is proved and demonstrated first of all from l. 1 cap. *de rescindenda venditione* (on rescinding sale) where it says *Irrita est* ("It is invalid"). These words, being in the present tense, cancel the arrangement ipso facto and by law according to the doctrine of the gloss. *L. Iubemus 14 §. oeconomicus Verbo. Privetur. C. de Sacrosanctis Ecclesiis, et l. 5. verbo. Habeas. Cap. de iurisdictione omnium Iudicum, testaturque Cremensis singul. 7. Iasson. l. 2. num. 13. et 15. Cap. de iure emphyt. Tiraquel. cum multis, l. si unquam Verbo (Revertatur) num. 21. et sequentibus. Cap. de revoc. donat.*

Secondly, from l. *Qui in aliena, §. Celsus, ff. de acquiren. haered.* where it says, *"Whoever by verbal intimidation, or under the compulsion of fear of whatever kind, has falsely assumed an inheritance, or becomes free, is not regarded as an heir if he is a freeman, or his master is not regarded as making him an heir if he is a slave."* Therefore things which are done through fear are null by virtue of the law.

Thirdly, from l. *Qui in carcerem 22. ff. de eo quod metus causa* where it says, *"When someone has put another person in prison in order to extort something, whatever is done for that reason is of no account."* Here it is clear that an act and contract concluded through fear is null by virtue of the law. The phrase *nullius momenti est* means the same as "of no consequence or worth", *cap. ordinar. in fine de officio ordinarii in sexto*, and there the Archdeacon has an annotation: and many others whom he cites understand that text similarly, and Rolandus follows, *cons. 2. num. 83. limitat. 1.*

Fourthly, from *l. 2. ff. de iudiciis, vers. ac si restituisset,* where if someone has been compelled by a magistrate to consent to his jurisdiction, such jurisdiction is null according to the law.

Fifthly, when false dealing gives rise to a contract entered into in good faith, that contract is null by virtue of the law. *L. et Eleganter §. 1. ff. de dolo.* But fear has false dealing inherent in it. *L. si cum exceptione, §. eum, qui ff. de eo quod metuis causa, et l. 2 §. doli mali ff. de vi bonorum raptorum.* And so false dealing and fear are commonly equated, *cap. cum contingat. Fine. De iure iurando, et cap. 2. de pactis in sexto cum aliis iuribus*. Hence a contract and act concluded through fear is null.

Sixthly, without agreement the contract is null, for its substance consists in agreement. *L. obligationum ff. de actibus, et obligationibus*; but where fear is present agreement is lacking, according to the rule *Nihil consensui 117. ff. de regulis iuris*, where it says *"Nothing is so contrary to agreement as force and intimidation"*, and *cap. cum locum desponsalibus*, where it says, *"Since there is no room for agreement where fear or compulsion interpose themselves"*, etc.

Seventhly, since whoever brings force to bear and extorts things by fear is guilty of theft and rapine: therefore, just like the common thief, he acquires no dominion over the thing taken and its acceptance is not valid. Finally, since fear contains in itself ignorance. *L. cum exceptione 14 §. in hac actione ff. de eo quod metus causa,* where it says, *"For since fear contains in itself ignorance"*: but ignorance is contrary to agreement. *L. si per errorem ff. de iurisdictione omnium Iudicum*; therefore a contract entered into is ipso facto null insofar as it lacks consent. Bartolus is of this opinion. *L. metum autem presentem 9. §. volenti numer. 387.* and following, and so are many other legal experts, and among the theologians Dominicus Sotus *libro 8. de Iustitia quest. 1. art. 7. in solut. ad tertium vers. seriosus tamen argumentum. Ludovicus*

Carbo de restit. q. 46. concl. 5. Ludovicus Molina tomo 2. de Iustitia tract. 2. disput. 326 in solut. ad secundum Michael Palacius libro 4 de Contractibus cap. 9 § dixerim igitur, and others cited by Sancez and by Gutierres *libro 3. capit. 76 num. 1 et alios. Item Bonacina tomo 2. disputat. 3. de Contractibus quaest. 1. puncto 3. § 3.*

49. A second opinion, held by other doctors, is that contracts entered into in grave fear are valid, but may however be invalidated. This opinion is proved firstly from *l. 1. ff. de eo quo metus causa*, where it says, *"The office-holder says, I will not ratify what has been done through the agency of fear."* Here the verb in the future tense does not signify that it is invalid by virtue of the law, but rather that it ought to be invalidated, as Tiraquellus (with many others) teaches, *l. si unquam. Verbo. Revertitur. num. 39. cap. de revocanda donat.* And since the office-holder has promised action, or exception, so as to rescind what was done through fear.

Secondly, from *l. finali capit. de bis quae vi*, where it says, *"We command that purchases, donations and transactions which have been extorted by the use of power shall be invalidated"*; therefore although they are valid, nonetheless by legal remedy they are to be invalidated.

Thirdly, from *cap. Abbas de his, quae vi, in fine*, where it says, *"According to the law whatever is done through fear and by force should be revoked and made invalid."* I omit other laws, proofs, and the many Doctors whom Sanchez cites in support of this opinion, which he himself follows, *tom. 1. de Matrimonio disp. 8 n. 4. Gutierres citatus numero 2. Lessius libro 2. de Iustitia cap. 17. dubitatione 6.,* speaking with qualifications regarding certain contracts.

50. But when we come to speak of the divine and natural law, the true opinion teaches that contracts concluded through grave fear are invalid by virtue of divine and natural law. Firstly, because any contract violently concluded cannot be lasting and firm, in the light of the statement *"Nothing violent is lasting"*: therefore compulsion is repugnant to the nature of the contract and consequently will invalidate it. Secondly, since every transferral by which dominion is handed over must be fully free, as is clear from many examples, e.g. donation means free donation, and if it is extorted through fear it imposes an obligation of restitution; this is equally true in purchase, sale, rent, loan, marriage, etc. Thirdly, since in all natural and divine law there should be provision for all injury to be repaired, otherwise the natural law would be deficient in essentials; but the injury inflicted upon a contract through its being compelled cannot otherwise be repaired than by the invalidation of such a contract, since if once it is valid it cannot be rescinded: therefore the law of nature de facto will invalidate every contract concluded or extorted by grave fear and coercion. I omit other proofs of this opinion given by authors; many of the weightiest among them support it, some of them speaking of one, others of another contract, while yet others speak of all contracts. Saint Thomas Aquinas holds this opinion in *4 distinctione 29. quaestione unica, articulo 3. quaestiuncula 1. in corpore. Scotus ibi, distinctione 39. quaestione unica, § de secundo dico. S. Bonaventura ibi, quaestione 1 num. 5. S. Antonius 3. part. tit. cap. 7.* These leading authors are followed by very many more of ancient and modern times, such as *Dominicus Sotus in 4. distinctione 29. quaest. 1. art. 3. vers. 7. arguitur. Victoria in summa loquens de matrimonio, et Martinus de Ledesma, 2. parte quarti, quaest. 49. art. 3. Ludovicus Molina tom. 2. de Iustitia, disput. 326*, citing others. *Altisiodorensis, Ricardus, Gabriel Turrecremata, Bartholomaeus de Ledesma,* and many other theologians and legal experts, whom Sanchez cites, *op. cit. libro 4. disputatione 14. numero. 4. Aragon secunda secundae quaest. 89. art 7. indubio circa solutionem ad tertium, conclusione 1. Rebellus part. 2. libro 1. quaestione 5. num. 15.* citing many, *Lessius libro 2. de iustitia cap. 17. dub. 6.* citing laws and Doctors, *Basilius Poncius lib. 4 de matrimonio, cap. 6 and 8. Antoninus Diana 3. part. tract. 5. resol. 118 and 119 pagin. 240 et 241. Ioannes Gutierres lib. 3. quaestionum Canonicarum cap. 76. num. 3. et 4* selecting certain cases: even a contract made through mild fear is not valid in conscience according to many Doctors, namely *Sanchez tom. 1. de matrimonio lib. 4. disp. 9. num. 4. citing many. Rellus 2. parte libro 1. q. 5. n. 9. et 16. Lessius lib. 2. cap. 17 dub. 6. n. 46. Navarrus cap. 17. num. 15 et cap. 22. num. 51. §. 7, Gutierres citatus n. 7.* and others.

51. With any one of these three opinions we have a firm position against our opponents, since it is established that contracts and acts which are entered into in grave fear are invalid *ipso facto* by positive human law, or by divine natural law, or they should be immediately rescinded. This being so, we have no reason to spend any further time in refuting this objection.

FIFTH SECTION

Our opponents' fourth objection is met

52. To our opponents' fourth and final objection, which asserted that the kings of England had acquired prescriptive right of dominion in the possession of Ireland during so many years: I reply by denying that they could have acquired prescriptive right in the absence of those conditions which are altogether necessary for prescription of the property of others. So that my response may be well understood and rightly grasped, it will be useful first of all to set out what prescription is, according to the law and the legal experts, and what conditions it must fulfil to be true and valid. We may omit the various meanings of the word prescription and their agreement with and difference from the concept of *usucaption*. The Doctors of theology and legal experts deal with these matters in numerous places. Here I accept the word *prescription* as it is most commonly used in Canon Law and among theologians and interpreters of the two laws, and in the sense pertinent to our opponents' objection, namely acquisition of dominion from possession, time and the requisite conditions, for which *Sylvester verbo, praescriptio, Ludovicus Molina tomo primo de Iustitia disp. 60 et sequentibus, Leonardus Lessius libro 2. de Iustitia cap. 6. Vincentius Fillucius tomo 2. de Christianis officiis tract. 31. cap. 8. Martinus Bonacina tomo 2. disputatione 1. de restitutione in genere quaestione ultima, puncto 2. §. 2. Dominicus Sotus libro 4. de Iustitia quaest. 5. Paulus Laymanus in Theologia morali lib. 3. sect. 5. tract. 1. cap. 8. Didacus Covarruvias regula Possessor 3. p. §. 2. n. 3. Thomas Sanchez lib. 7. de Matrimonio disp. 37. num. 6. Ioannes Azorius tom. 3. institutionum moralium lib. 1. cap. 16. et sequentibus,* and many formulations by other theologians and legal experts. Acquired possession may therefore be defined with this meaning, as it commonly is in the law and by the Doctors.

53. *"Prescription is the acquisition or attainment of dominion over the property of another through continual possession in good faith over the space of time defined by the law."* It is thus defined in *Lege usu capis ff. de usu Capionibus* and in the teaching of theologians and legal experts generally. Even though some may differ from others by adding or subtracting some particle of this definition, they are nevertheless agreed upon its substance. See those cited above, who themselves cite others.

Prescription is said to be *acquisition* causally, since prescription is the cause of acquisition. It is said to be acquisition of *dominion*, meaning ownership or utility, since either may be prescribed. Dominion of ownership or direct dominion is when someone has the proper dominion of some thing, e.g. land, a vineyard, etc. Dominion of utility or useful dominion is when someone has the right to take the fruits of some thing, though the thing is someone else's. Prescription is said to be through *continuous possession*, since possession needs to be continuous and not interrupted, as will be clear from what is said below. It is said to be *in good faith*, since without good faith prescription cannot be given, as will also be demonstrated below. It is said to be *over the space of time, etc.*, since when one person loses the dominion of things and another acquires it, a certain time period is fixed by human law in order to avoid litigation and put an end to uncertainty about these things' dominion. This period will be legally determined according to the necessary conditions, which I am about to speak of now.

54. Four or five conditions are required for prescription to be true and valid. The first condition is *continual possession of the thing prescribed.* Second, *good faith*. Third, *a probable presumption of title.* Fourth, *the time defined by law.* Fifth, *active and passive capacity.* See the doctors cited above and others generally.

55. The first condition, then, which is possession, is so necessary that without it prescription cannot be given, according to the rule *sine possessione 3. de Regulis iuris in 6.* where it says, *"Without possession prescription does not proceed."* And the Doctors in general likewise. This possession, however, must be continuous, for if it should cease at any time, become dormant or be interrupted, it is not valid. So when are prescription and possession in progress, or not; when do they begin or not, cease, grow dormant; when are they interrupted, perpetuated or protected? Molina treats of this extensively in *tom. 1. de Iustitia tractatu 2. disputatione 78. et 79.,* where he cites laws and Doctors.

56. The second condition necessary for prescription is good faith. Without this prescription is never given, nor can it be given, as is clear from *regula secunda iuris in 6.* where it says, *"The possessor in bad faith does not prescribe in any length of time".* Didacus Covarruvias de Leina, bishop of Segovia, wrote a most learned commentary on this rule; see this Doctor and others too, if desired, and especially the oft-cited

Molina, disp. 63 and Lessius, also cited, cap. 6. dub. 2., and the same may be found in *cap. fin. de prescriptionibus*, which is taken from the great Lateran Council under Pope Innocent III, where this truth is dogmatically defined in the following words. *"Since all that is not from faith is sin, by synodal judgement we decree that no prescription, whether canonical or civil, shall be valid without good faith; since generally it is necessary to withdraw acceptance from all arrangements and customs which cannot be observed without mortal sin; therefore it is proper that he who prescribes should not at any time have knowledge that the thing is somebody else's."* Thus the Council. From its definition and that of the Doctors, it is evident what the good faith which we are dealing with here actually is. And I say that good faith is the belief whereby someone prudently persuades himself that the thing which he possesses is his, or at least he does not know it belongs to another. I have said *prudently*, for if his persuasion proceeds from crass or affected ignorance or inordinate cupidity, that will not be good faith, as is rightly noted by *Lessius op. cit. dub. 2. num. 9. Molina disp. 63. Fillucius tractatu 31. cap. 8. q. 3. n. 186. Sanchez in praeceptis Decalogi libro 2. cap. 23. n. 158. ff.*, citing many, and others passim; and it is clear from many laws, e.g. from *lex bona fidei 110. ff. de verborum significatione* where it says, *"That purchaser is seen to be of good faith who either does not know that the thing is somebody else's or has supposed that he who sold it had the right of sale"* ; and *cap. si Virgo 34 questione 2.* where it says, *"Somebody is rightly called a possessor in good faith so long as he is unaware of being in possession of what is someone else's"*. For brevity's sake I omit others.

57. The third condition is: a probable presumption of title. The title, however, must be believed and presumed to be true by the person who possesses the thing by that title. Such title, probably presumed, confers the condition of *usucaption* on that person by making him capable of prescription over the given time, so long as the other conditions are not lacking. I will make the matter clearer with examples of titles, since there are many titles of prescription, e.g. repayment, purchase, inheritance, donation, abandoned property, legacy, dowry, taking as one's own (*suum*), etc. The first title is for repayment, e.g. if you have promised me a horse and in order to pay it you deliver a horse which is not yours, but I have believed in good faith that it is yours, and I can prescribe it by title for repayment. The second is for the purchaser: if I have purchased something stolen by him who I thought in good faith was the true owner, I can prescribe it by purchaser's title. The third is for the heir: when someone is in reality not the heir but nonetheless has probable reason and cause for considering himself the heir, such a person can prescribe as the heir. The fourth is for something donated: when someone accepts some thing donated to him by a person who he believed in good faith, prior to acceptance, was the donated thing's owner. The fifth is for abandoned property, e.g. when a thing of mine is possessed by another, who is thought to be the true owner; but being abandoned by him, it is occupied by another and is prescribed in good faith. The sixth is for legacy, e.g. when something is bequeathed by the true owner in his will, but this bequest is cancelled in a codicil, which, however, is not known about. The seventh is for a dowry, as when someone has accepted as dowry a thing belonging to another, which he believed in good faith was the giver's or dowerer's. The eighth is for taking as one's own e.g. when someone takes someone else's deer believing that it is wild and not domesticated, he may prescribe it as his own. These titles and examples will suffice for now; others might be adduced if they were necessary for our purpose. See *Molina op. cit. disputatione 64. Lessius libro 2. capite 6. dub. 7. Fillucius capite 8. quaestione 4. Azorius op. cit. tomo 3. libro 1. capite 21* and others.

58. The fourth condition is: time defined by law. The civil and canon law, in order to avoid uncertainties in the ownership of things and to set a limit to legal disputes, have defined a certain time in which the possessor in good faith can prescribe and make his own of what he possesses. On this account the things which can be possessed are distinguished in two categories. Some are called movable things, which can be moved to a different place, such as clothes, arms, animals, ships etc. Others are called immovable, which cannot normally be moved, such as a house, a field; a city, a kingdom, etc. See *Molina disp. 68. Fillucius tract. 31. capit. 8. quaest. 5. Turrianus disp. 47. dubio. 4. Bonacina disp. 1. de restitutione in genere quaestione ultima, puncto 2. §. 2. num. 28. Lessius libro 2. cap. 6. dub. 7.* and others. This distinction is assumed henceforward.

59. The Doctors and the laws in general conclude that for prescription of movable things or goods (which is properly termed usucaption) a space of three years is required with title and good faith. *L. unica cap. de usucapionibus et institut de usucapionibus.*

60. This same time is sufficient, according to some Doctors, for prescription of the movable goods not only of laymen but also even of clerics and churches. Thus *Molina disp. 68. Sayrus in clavi Regia libro 9. capit. 12. numero 25. et Bonacina citatus num. 28.* citing others who assert that this is derived from *authentica (quas actiones) capit. de sacrosanctis Ecclesiis.* Azorius, however, *tomo 3. libro 1. capit. 22. questione 2.*, with others, denies that the space of three years is sufficient to prescribe the movable goods of churches, above all of the Roman Church. Firstly, because there is no text of the canon law where a three-year usucaption or prescription is approved as regards the movable goods of the Church. Secondly, since in *cap. 1 de prescriptionibus* it is said: *"The Roman Church does not accept a prescription of less than forty years against churches."* Here the Pope, speaking generally, makes no distinction of movable and immovable goods: therefore we should not make this distinction either. Thirdly, because usucaption does not come into effect against the state treasury, *institut. de usucapion §. res Fisci*: therefore neither should it be effective against the Church, which ought to enjoy not a lesser but a greater privilege.

61. For prescription of immovable goods a space of ten years is required against the persons deprived, in the case of those who are present with possession, title and good faith; in the case of those who are absentees, a space of twenty years is required. *Inst. de usucapionibus, et capit. Sanctorum de praescriptionibus*; and the Doctors in general. See *Molina disp. 69. Lessius lib. 2. cap. 6 dub. 8. Bonacina saepe citatum disp. 1. q. ult. p. 2. §. 2. n. 28. et 29.* Those present are said to be those who dwell in the same city or part of the kingdom. Absentees are those who live in different cities or parts of the kingdom, or territories, or the thing to be prescribed is there or elsewhere. Thus the doctors cited above and others in general.

62. An exception is made, however, for orphans. When they are deprived of properties, whether movable or immovable, no prescription is given against them while they remain in the age of orphanhood. *L. sicut rem 3. de prescriptione triginta annorum* (on thirty-year prescription). This provision is made for the benefit of those who are orphans in age and condition. There is also an exception for minors, those who have not yet reached the age of 25. The reason is that minors are not able to supervise their own affairs, especially since they do not hold the administration.

63. For prescription of immovable goods against a church, monastery, hospital or other religious interests a time of forty years is required with possession, title and good faith: against the church of Rome one hundred years are required, according to the *authentica cap. (Quas actiones) de sacrosanctis Ecclesiis*. There the time of prescription against the other churches and holy places is restricted to forty years (although previously it had been one hundred, as is clear from the immediately preceding law *ut inter divinum)*, and the privilege of one hundred years is restricted to the Church of Rome, alone among holy places.

64. For prescription against a kingdom or a sovereign the space of one hundred years is required, with possession, title and good faith: to prescribe even against towns that same space of time, one hundred years, is required. *L unica, cap. de sacrosanctis ecclesiis*. Hence similarly the same space of time is needed for prescribing a sovereign's goods and his kingdom, namely one hundred years. For the goods of the sovereign are considered as goods of the kingdom or principality. This is taught by Covarruvias: *ad regul. Possessor. parte 2. §. 2. n. 9.,* citing others; *Alvarus Velascus de iure Emphyteutico q. 17. n. 12; Molina tomo 1. de Iustitia disp. 74. n. 4. Lusius Turrianus in tomo de iustitia disput. 47. dubio 7. Bonacina tomo 2. disp. 1. de restitutione, quaest. ult. §. 2. num. 31. vers. respondeo secundo. Fillucius tomo 2. tract. 31. cap. 9. q. 5 n. 200.* And most recently Doctor Francisco Velasco de Gouveia in his analytical tractate *On the Just Acclamation of the Most Serene King of Portugal John IV*, pt. 3, sec. 2, no. 11, where he cites laws and doctors, especially *Felinus in cap. ad audientiam num. 22. Decius in cap. cum dilecta, num. 11, Franciscus Balbus de praescriptionibus*, and others, and responds fundamentally to another opinion which asserts that a time of forty years is sufficient for prescription of a kingdom. Finally, Doctor Antonio de Sousa in *Lusitania Liberata*, bk. 3 ch. 5, with his accustomed erudition, cites many authorities.

65. The fifth condition necessary for prescription is active capacity in respect of the one possessing and passive capacity in respect of the thing possessed, or in other words, that the possessor can possess and the thing can be possessed. Due to defect of this condition a professed monk cannot acquire prescription of anything, since he lacks active capacity. Nor can a layman prescribe the right of cognisance and judgement of law cases involving clergymen and churches, which has been the sacrilegious, wicked and tyrannical practice of certain kings of England, especially Henry II, Henry VIII, Elizabeth, James and Charles. See the authors who have written against these kings, such as Suarez, Bellarmine, Becanus, Sanders, Personius, Placenius, and others. See also *Molina disp. 79. Lessius libro 2. capite 6. dub. 2.* and the oft-cited Bonacina *disp. 1 q. ult. §. 2. n. 5 ff.*, where he cites other doctors.

66. Having laid down these conditions and explained them briefly, it remains to examine whether the pretended prescription of the English is deficient in any of them, because if even one is lacking, that pretended and imaginary prescription is without force and cannot possibly have force.

67. So let us begin at the beginning, which is continual possession of the kingdom. The English have never had this in Ireland. Firstly, since that pretended possession from the start was violent and invalid, and hence with the passage of time could not come into force. What was invalid from the beginning does not come into force with the passage of time. So it is said in Rule 25 of the civil law: *"An institution which was injurious from the beginning cannot come into force with the passage of time."* Secondly, even though they held this or that town, estate, stronghold, village or corner of the land, they did not hold many of the provinces, towns, estates and strongholds found in that kingdom, which had lords of their own. Thirdly, that pretended possession was often interrupted by Irishmen waging just war against the English, who were possessing unjustly: that much is clear from the historical accounts given by O'Sullivan in the *Compendium of the History of Catholic Ireland*, and it is confirmed by the Papal Bulls cited above in sections 33 to 46 inclusive. Fourthly, since the English did not have rightful possession of the movable and immovable goods which they afterwards obtained against law and equity: they took them in the manner of thieves who unjustly despoil the rightful owners of their goods. Hence robbers of this kind are never able to acquire prescriptive rights to goods so obtained, since the possessors are in bad faith regarding the same.

68. The second condition for prescriptive right of the English to the lordship of Ireland, i.e. good faith, is also lacking. Firstly, because the war they waged was unjust, as already proved. Secondly, since the Bull which they offer in justification was deceitfully gained and void.

Thirdly, even if it had been valid, it would have had no force without those conditions which the English have never fulfilled, as shown above. Fourthly, since the alleged acceptance by the people could have no force, given that it was under the duress of grave fear that some men accepted Henry II, as already mentioned. Because good faith was lacking they could never gain prescriptive right, since possessors in bad faith are unable to acquire prescription over any length of time, however long, according to Rule 2 of the law in 6: *"A possessor in bad faith does not obtain prescription over any length of time."* Here the doctors are in general agreement.

69. The third condition was, *A probable presumption of title*. This condition also could not be met by the English, who had a presumed title to Ireland not probably but improbably. We have already said enough about the injustice of this title (no. 8 above and following), where we proved that the English had acquired the dominion of Ireland by unjust war, etc. Otherwise let those people say that the Turks and Saracens justly possess the Holy Land, since by an unjust war they have occupied it: which would be an impious and ridiculous theorem.

70. The fourth condition was, *the time laid down by law*. Given that one hundred years are needed for the prescription of a kingdom, as we said above in No. 65, no English king met this condition, since none of them lived for a hundred years, and supposing one of them had done so, even then this length of time would not have sufficed, since it was not accompanied by good faith, which those kings have never had, as we have already proved. It is not sufficient that the first of them, Henry II, and his successors have had all this time and more. For when an heir accepts property from a possessor in bad faith, he cannot obtain prescription of that property over any length of time, even if he himself has accepted it and possessed it in good faith. Such is the most common opinion of Doctors, and it is clearly to be understood from many laws. Thus *Bartolus L. et ex diverso 36. in principio num. 12 ff. de rei vendicat. Abbas cap. gravis num. 10 de restit. spol. et ibi Beroius num. 38. et Menochius re recup. possess. remedio 15. num. 617. quos citat, et sequitur Sanchez in opere morali libro 2. cap. 23. num. 154. Covarruvias regula possessor §. 9. Molina tomo. 1. disp. 65, Lessius libro 2. cap. 6. dub. 13. Bonacina tomo 2. disp. de contractibus, quaestione ultima puncto 2. §. 2. num. 21.* There he cites Azorius, Sayrus, Fillucius,

Turrianus, and others. The opinion is proved from *L. cum haeres 11. ff. de diversis, et temporalibus praescriptionibus*, where the following is stated. *"Since the heir succeeds to the entire right of the defunct, he does not cancel out the defunct's wrongdoings by his own ignorance. For just as the defunct knowingly possessed what was another's, or possessed it by unsound title, so likewise the ignorant heir (for all that he is not responsible for the unsound title, nor may he rightly be subjected to interdict), cannot acquire the usucaption which the defunct could not acquire."* And in addition, *"The law is the same when a very lengthy possession is involved, where it is clear there was not good faith at its beginning."* And in *§. Diutina. Instit. de usucap.* it is said, *"If he* (the defunct) *did not have a just commencement* (i.e. if he began his possession through bad faith), *the possession does not stand to the heir and holder of his dignities, even though the latter is ignorant."* The same is in *L. ultima cap. communia de usucapione.* Finally, since the heir represents the person of the defunct, it is reasonable that in the law's disposition he is treated as being the same person as the defunct, and the possession of both is treated as one continuous possession. Hence, given that the commencement of the heir's possession in the person of the defunct was vitiated by bad faith, there is judged to be bad faith also in the heir to whom it extends. On the same legal principles the heir also is considered to possess in bad faith, and therefore not validly, according to the passage *"what was not valid from the beginning does not gain validity by passage of time"*. With bad faith prescription does not proceed in any way, as all admit: therefore just as the defunct was by no means able to prescribe that thing, neither is that possible for his heir. This standpoint is clearly to be gathered from the laws and Doctors cited and especially from the gloss in *L. citat. verbo Rei.* where it says, *"The beginning must be seen in the person of the testator, since the heir is understood to be the same person."*

Hence the kings of England have not been possessors but rather detainers of Ireland for many years. Detention for very many years, however, does not confer right but increases the sin. *Cap. Non debet de consanguinity. Et affinity. Bonacina citatus tomo 2. disp. 1. de restitutione q. 6. n. 9. Sousa citatus libro 3. cap. 5. num. 21,* and others.

71. The fifth condition necessary for prescription was active and passive capacity, as we said in No. 66 above, and the kings of England would not have been deficient in this for prescribing temporal goods and worldly wealth, if the other conditions had been present: but this condition was lacking for the possession of church properties and the judgement of ecclesiastical law, and consequently they lack all of the conditions necessary for prescription. Hence they never had any right in Ireland in times past, nor do they have any right *de facto* today.

SECTION SIX

Conclusion of the argument with our opponents

72. Already we have resolved and disabled our opponents' objections, and we have demonstrated our own justice against their injustice. But lest they should demur and come forward with new arguments to reinforce their case and undermine ours, we have thought it worth taking the trouble to close off all means of escape so that they cannot make further progress, unless perhaps by the age-old means of falsehood and deception, which has ever been familiar to heretics of all sorts.

73. Purely for the sake of argument, then, let us grant that the kings of England once were true and legitimate lords of Ireland (as some Englishmen baselessly maintain) – nevertheless the estates of that kingdom with the fullest right can and should deprive such kings of all dominion over Ireland, now that they have become heretics and tyrants. This right and power of deposing tyrant princes exists in every kingdom and commonwealth, whether the mode of government be monarchical, aristocratic or democratic. Now if the Apostolic authority concurs with the consensus of the kingdom or commonwealth on this issue, who but a heretic or a fool will dare deny what we are affirming here and what doctors of theology and experts in both laws say continually, establishing their reasons and providing examples?

74. So far as the doctors are concerned, Suarez teaches this in his *Defence of the Catholic Faith against the Errors of the English Sect*, bk. 3, ch. 2, 3, 23, and bk. 6 ch. 4. *Molina tom. 1. de iustitia disp. 23 et 26. et tom. 6. tract. 5. disp. 3. Azorius tom. 2. institutionum moralium. lib. 11. cap. 5. q. 9. Bellarminus tomo 1. controversarium libro 5. de Romano Pontifice*, and in reply to the *Apology* of King James of England, which is in tome 7 of the Cardinal's works pp. 701 ff.; and in the *Tractate on the Power of the Supreme Pontiff in Temporal Affairs, against William Barclay*, tome 7 pp. 830ff., where he cites over 70 illustrious authors, who in many cases were noted not only for great wisdom but also for sanctity, with miracles to their credit, and others who were adorned with great dignities and titles; for brevity's sake I omit their names here. But the Angelic Doctor, who is cited there with his disciples, may be selected as one representing all. Others have since come forward, such as Guilielmus Rossaeus in his book *On the Just Authority of the Christian Republic Against Impious Kings and Heretics*; Sebastianus Caesar in *A Review of Ecclesiastical Hierarchy 1. part disput. 1* on the Roman Pontiff *§. 5.*, where with high erudition, soundness and subtlety he demonstrates the point I am making. Francisco Valasco, already cited, 1. p. §. 1. 2. and 3. Franciscus de Mendoca tomo 2. on the 1st Book of Kings, *cap. 8. No. 5. in expositione literae §. 15.* Andreas, Eudaemon Ioannes in *An Admonitory Letter to John Barclay*, which is in tome 7 of Bellarmine's works, pp. 998-1027. Doctor Antonio de Sousa in his *Lusitania Liberata*, proemium 2. §. 2. No. 23. ff.; Franciscus Freyre in *Apology for Truth and Justice* No. 23. ff., citing laws and Doctors.

75. Coming therefore to the reasons, first of all I take it as being certain among Catholic doctors that political authority introduced in a due manner is just and legitimate; on the other hand, if introduced in an undue manner it is power usurped by tyranny, which however is wicked violence, not just power, since it is without a just and true title. This supposition, in both its parts, is drawn from various places in Sacred Scripture. Proverbs 29, 2: *"When just men increase, the people shall rejoice: when the wicked shall bear rule, the people shall mourn"*; and 4: *"A just king setteth up the land: a covetous man shall destroy it "* and 14: *"The king that judgeth the poor in truth, his throne shall be established for ever"*; and Wisdom 6, 26: *"A wise king is the upholding of the people. "* In these and other testimonies it is assumed that the temporal kings are true and legitimate princes or lords. And thus Saint Peter in the canonical letter 1. cap. 2. no. 13. commands the faithful to obey them. *"Be ye subject therefore to every human creature for God's sake: whether it be to the king as excelling; Or to governors as sent by him for the punishment of evildoers, and for the praise of the good: For so is the will of God."* And below no. 17, *"Fear God. Honour the King."* And Saint Paul to the Romans 13 no. 1. *"Let every soul be subject to* *higher powers."* And below no. 5, *"Not only for wrath, but also for conscience' sake."* Now no one is obliged to obey for conscience sake unless the person obeyed has legitimate power to command. In this sense we must understand the words of Saint Bernard in his tractate *On Precept and Dispensation*: *"When either God or man as the vicar of God has issued any command, certainly both must be obeyed with equal care and deferred to with equal reverence; assuming however that man's commands are not contrary to God's."* And Saint Clement the Roman in the *Constitutions, bk. 4, ch. 12*: *"Be subject to every king and those who exercise power in affairs that are pleasing to God, treating them as God's ministers, even the pagan judges."* And further on, *"Render them all due reverence, tax and tribute."* And he adds, *"For this is the law of God."* And Saint Jerome in *Epistle 4* affirms this truth, giving the brute animals as examples, saying, *"The dumb animals and wild species follow their own leaders: the bees have their lords, the cranes follow one leader in precise order, one is the emperor, one the judge of a province, etc."* It stands to reason, therefore, that political lordship is not only legitimate and just but even necessary for the conservation of the state. Hence *Proverbs 11, 14* says: *"Where there is no governor, the people shall fall."* And *Ecclesiast. 19, 16. "Woe to thee, O land, when thy king is a child."* Because it is not enough to have a lord, unless he is also good and fitted for governing. And God through *Isaiah ch. 3 no. 4.* threatens: *"And I will give children to be their princes, and the effeminate shall rule over them."* Hence it is clear that some head or prince or governor is necessary for the conservation of the Republic. We can elucidate this with the example of the human body, which cannot conserve itself without a head, or a ship which will perish without a helmsman, or an army without a general, and other such examples. See Suarez *op. cit. bk. 3 ch. 1.*

76. Secondly, I assume it as certain among Catholic doctors and a general axiom of theologians that no king or monarch holds or has held his political sovereignty directly from God or by divine institution, but rather by the mediation of human will and institution, that is to say by ordinary law. Thus Suarez in *Defence of the Catholic Faith* bk. 3. ch. 2, where he cites laws and doctors whom for brevity's sake I omit.This truth may be proved directly from the Church Fathers cited by Suarez, who frequently assert that man was created by God unsubjected and free, and that he received immediately from God only the power of domination over brute animals and inferior things. The dominion of men over men was introduced by human volition, whether because of sin or because of adversity of some kind. And what the Sacred Doctors say about the liberty of each individual man and, opposed to that, his servitude, applies equally to the mixed person of the given human community, commonwealth or state. Insofar as he is immediately ruled by God, he is free by the law of nature and by God's law. This liberty does not exclude, but rather includes the power of governing himself and commanding his limbs; it excludes, however, subjection to another man (insofar as it derives from the power of the natural law alone, since God did not give such power immediately to any man) until such time as it is transferred to someone by human institution or election. It is in this sense that we must understand the celebrated sentence from Saint Augustine's *Confessions, Bk. 3 ch. 8*: *"There is a general pact in human society to obey its kings."* By these words he means that the lordship of kings and the obedience which is due to them has its basis in a pact of human society, and consequently it is not immediately instituted by God, since a human pact is contracted by human will, as all must admit.

The second proof. For power over something is said to be immediately from God when it has come to that thing through God's will exclusively, or by the force of purely natural reason, or through some divine institution: but royal power is not given by any of those modes to kings by God speaking of the ordinary law: therefore, etc. Proof of the minor. It is not through the special will of God, since no such will has been revealed or made known to men. Nor does the natural law in itself dictate that kings must have this power. Nor, finally, is any divine institution or determination, or translation of this power from God, made immediately to kings, and this is clearly borne out in practice. Otherwise this institution would be immutable and all man-made mutation in it would be wicked. In fact, all kingdoms, commonwealths and states would be bound to maintain the self-same institution; it would as rational for any one as for any other, since no one commonwealth could be said to have accepted such a divinely ordained institution more than the next. We conclude, then, that this institution is human and immediately made by men: therefore power is given to kings immediately through men; their dignity is created by such institution; mediately, however, this power is said to be given by God to kings, since God gave it immediately to the people, who have transferred it to the king, and God himself consents to this translation made by the people, approves it, and wishes that it be preserved. Accordingly human law has immediate compelling force through the will of the human prince who embraces it; mediately, however, it is obligatory also through the will of God, who desires that legitimate princes should be obeyed.

The third proof. A clear indication of this truth is the fact that the royal power is not equal in all kingdoms, nor is it the same in terms of duration and succession, etc. For in some kingdoms power is monarchical, in others there is an admixture of aristocratic power or dependence on a senate to give its decisive or definitive votes, at least in some cases. Power is given to certain kings not only extending to their own persons, but even to their sons and heirs; hence they may transmit this dignity to their sons and grandsons, as is the case with the kings of Spain and France, etc. To others, however, power is given only for their own persons and not for their sons, hence when one king dies another may be elected who is not the son of the deceased: such is the case in the Holy Roman Empire and in the kingdom of Poland, etc. It is manifest therefore that this institution is immediately human, since it may admit such a variety. Therefore, since the royal dignity or power derives from men, those men when transferring it to kings can never transfer it in such a way that it ceases to remain with themselves, in their nature as it were, so that in certain circumstances they may revoke it and themselves exercise it. For if the king should turn his power into tyranny, abusing it to the manifest ruin of the commonwealth, then the kingdom or commonwealth may use that power to defend itself, for it has never deprived itself totally of this power. By natural law the commonwealth has power to defend itself against all unjust invaders and to choose another sovereign or means for its government and self-preservation. It would therefore be against natural reason to say that the commonwealth could not change the sovereign which it had chosen for its preservation, when rather than preserving it he was destroying the commonwealth by tyranny or heresy, etc. Many peoples, commonwealths and kingdoms have made use of that right, as I will soon demonstrate. See Suarez in *Defence of the Catholic Faith against the Errors of the English Sect*, bk. 2, ch. 2 and 3, where he propounds this doctrine at length in response to King James of England and other heretics, and bk. 6, ch. 4, No. 15, where he reasons as follows about a king who is a tyrant only in governing the kingdom, not in possessing it.

"This difficulty requires that the penalty of deposition may be imposed on a king even in his temporal capacity and that he may be sentenced to deprivation of his kingdom. The king of England refuses to hear this, but it is absolutely true and evidently follows from the arguments set out in bk. 3 and will be repeated in what follows, etc. For in the commonwealth power exists only in the mode of defence necessary for its conservation, as I said above in bk. 3 ch. 3. Therefore if the legitimate king governs tyrannically and the kingdom has no other means of defending itself except to expel and depose the king, the entire commonwealth by the public and general consent of its citizens and nobles may depose the king, both by virtue of the natural law, which allows force to be repelled by force, and because always this instance where it is necessary to preserve the commonwealth itself is understood to be excepted in that original treaty whereby the commonwealth transferred its power to the king."

– This is what Suarez says in so many words, and he cites St. Thomas, 2, 2, q. 42 art. 2 & 3, and other doctors.

The fourth proof. There is an explicit or tacit pact between sovereigns and their commonwealth that they will see to the preservation of the commonwealth in peace and war, to the best of their ability, and that the commonwealth will be required to obey them, give them tribute etc. It has chosen them as sovereigns under the legal condition that they shall do this; otherwise it may set itself at liberty and depose them, unless they keep the pact by which they are obliged to uphold the commonwealth under natural and divine law. There are various fundamental grounds which I might adduce to prove that this is so, but one may suffice: *Ezechiel* 17, 16 where God speaks as follows: *"And shall he escape that hath broken the covenant? As I live, saith the Lord God: In the place where the king dwelleth that made him king, whose oath he hath made void, and whose covenant he broke, even in the midst of Babylon shall he die."* On this passage St. Jerome speaks as follows: *"We learn from this that faith should be kept even among enemies, and the important question is not to whom but through whom you have sworn. The man who believed you on account of God's name and was deceived is much more faithful than you are, if you have made use of the Divine Majesty to lay traps for an enemy, then supposedly a friend."*

The fifth and final proof. In order to safeguard his own life every individual person can remove an unjust invader from his midst, at least when under the discipline of an unimpeached authority; therefore the entire commonwealth may kill or depose an unjust invader in like manner. The foregoing is assumed to be a certainty not only by Christians but even by pagans, and it may be found expressed in both laws. Thus St. Thomas, 2, 2, q. 64, art. 7, and almost all theologians and doctors of either law. Of the pagans take Marcus Tullius Cicero, the outstanding master of Roman eloquence, who reasons as follows in defence of Milo, the killer of Clodius: *"If there is ever a time when the killing of a man is not only just but necessary, it is when aggressive force is being forcibly resisted."* And in the same oration: *"Reason prescribes it to the educated, necessity to the barbarians, custom to the peoples, and nature even to the wild beasts, that they should repel all force which attacks their life and limb with whatever strength they possess."* Of the poets read Ovid at least, bk. 3 on Art, where he says:

To my mind, we may use deceit to repel deceit;
the laws permit taking up arms against armed men.

Here we find pagan writers brilliantly expressing the force of the law of nature.

77. Is it not a natural axiom of both civil and canon law, *"Force may be repelled with force"*? Indeed it is! *L. ut vim ff. de iustitia, et iure. L. 1. per tot. ff. de vi, et vi armata. L. scientiam § qui cum aliter ff. ad leg. Aquil L. is qui aggressorem, et L. si quis percussorem. C. ad leg Cornel. de Sicar. et Capit. Significasti 2. de homicidio, capit, si vero de sent, excommunicationis, et cap. delecto eodem titulo, libro 6.*, on which Doctors of both laws passim.

78. Following from this, the soul is more precious than the body and it is to be preferred to all things as being more precious. *"For what doth it profit a man, if he gain the whole world, and suffer the loss of his own soul?"* So Christ Our Lord says in Mat. 16, 26. *"Or what exchange shall a man give for his soul?"* (ibid.) So then, if men may repel force with force to defend their temporal goods, all the more may they do so for the spiritual life of the soul and for eternal bliss hereafter. The heretical princes attempt to deprive Catholics of these spiritual goods by compelling them to desert the Catholic faith and embrace heresies.

79. I move on to examples of the many kingdoms and commonwealths which have deposed or killed kings or sovereigns on account of tyranny in possession or in government, or other demerits. I omit those whom God manifestly spared in this life, reserving for them the eternal pains of Hell in another life; but I will say a little about them in passing. My examples are taken from divine and human writings, from pagans and from Christians, so as to make it clear that this occurs by the law of nature itself and is common to almost all nations, since all laws and systems of right allow force to be repelled with force.

80. Our first example may be taken from the *2nd Book of Chronicles*, ch. 26, where we read that King Oziah, when he usurped the office of the priests, was ejected from the temple by the priest and pontiff Azariah, and after God had afflicted him with leprosy on account of his sin, he was forced to withdraw from the city and surrender his kingdom to his son – although previously he had been a good and faithful king, as we read in the chapter referred to. This example might well suit King Henry VIII of England, who in 1535 tyrannically presumed to declare himself head of the church in temporal and spiritual affairs, usurping the office of the Pope and the other bishops. And therefore he was infected by leprosy, which is to say heresy, and he was a heretic until his death; for leprosy in Sacred Scripture signifies heresy, as St. Augustine and other scriptural exponents teach.

81. We have a second example in the *2nd Book of Chronicles*, ch. 23. When Queen Athalia tyrannically occupied the kingdom and promoted the cult of Baal, the High Priest Ioaida convoked the centurions and soldiers and ordered them to kill her, which they did. The cause of the deposition and killing of Athalia was double: tyranny and false religion or idolatry, as we find in the sacred text. This example of Athalia may justly be applied to Queen Elizabeth of England, who tyrannically occupied and governed the kingdom for 44 years, promoted heresies, and attacked the Catholic faith and religion; at length she died and went off to Hell on March 23, 1602, as some writers say, though others say she died on April 4, 1603.

82. I will briefly touch on some other examples given in Sacred Scripture. King Joas, being a tyrannical, sacrilegious ingrate, killed the priest Zacharias, son of the Pontiff Ioiades, and for that reason was killed by his servants and deprived of royal burial, since he had ruled not as a good king but as an evil tyrant. *2. Chronicles ch. 24.* Also Amafias, King of Judah, although at first he was a faithful and good prince, later on became an idolater and was killed by his people. *2. Chronicles. ch. 25.*

King Amon, who did evil before God and served and gave sacrifice to idols, was killed by his people. *2. Chronicles ch. 33*. Finally, the *Book of Judges, ch. 3*, praises Aod, the killer of Eglon, king of the Moabites, who had been the tyrannical ruler of Israel.

83. Let these examples from the sacred books suffice: for brevity's sake I omit others, and I move on to examples from the more refined literature, both pagan and Christian. It is certain that some of the Roman kings were violent, proud and criminal in their conduct (especially Tarquinius the Proud and his son Sextus Tarquinius, who raped Lucretia, a lady of the high nobility); the people of Rome, infuriated by this act and roused by the oratory of Lucius Brutus, responded by expelling their kings and vindicating their own liberty. By that time Rome had been ruled by kings for about 245 years, and then two consuls were created, to serve for a two-year term. This is what we are told by Titus Livius, Lucius Florus, Horatius Tursellinus, and other historians. Long afterwards, when the Roman commonwealth was ruled by emperors, many of them, both pagan and Christian, were deprived of imperial power and put to death on account of their faults. Julius Caesar, the first emperor, although previously his achievements had covered him in glory, because of his unjust occupation of imperial office was stabbed twenty three times by Brutus, Cassius and other conspirators in the Senate, by the Pompeian theatre. And not only Cicero but St Thomas also approves this deed (*lib. 2. sententiarum distinctione ultima, q. 2. art. 2. in corpore, et ad tertium, et libro 2. de regimine Principum capit. 6*), as do other Christian scholars.

At the beginning of his reign Tiberius Nero gave promising signs of being a good and moderate prince, and there is a celebrated saying of his to that effect, *"The good shepherd must shear his sheep, not skin them."* But after he had poisoned Germanicus, his fear undid him and he became dissolute and lapsed into cruelty of all kinds. He got rid of Drusus Caesar, his own son whom he had fathered, by poison, because he suspected him of having designs on the crown. He killed Nero and Drusus, the sons of Germanicus and his own nephews, by starvation. Finally he forgot about ruling and gave himself over to intemperate sexual indulgence. Completely exhausted by his lusts, he died at Misenum, not without suspicion of poisoning.

Caius Caligula was at first considered worthy of the office because of his father Germanicus and because he enjoyed support from the

Roman people. But in his brief tyranny he proved even more ferocious than Tiberius: totally given over to savagery and lust, he did not shrink from taking the wives of his friends or even his own sisters. That frightful saying of his shows well enough what a hatred he had for the Romans: *"If only the Roman people had a single neck!"* He went to such an extreme of madness that he had himself honoured as a god, with temples dedicated to him in Rome and elsewhere. But in the fourth year of his reign the new god was killed by his people with a sword thrust through his genitals, emphasising the cause of his fall.

Nero unquestionably was a cruel and most evil man. Heedless of his majesty, he appeared on stage not only in a tragic role but even as a minstrel with a lute. He never wore the same garment twice; he used to go fishing with a golden net. He never took any journey with less than a thousand wagons, the horses and mules being shod in silver. His greed was equal to his extravagance. That was a stupendous saying of his, *"Let's do this properly so that no one will have anything at all!"* Nero's cruelty has become proverbial. He killed his mother Agrippina, his wife Octavia and other near relations of his, his tutor Seneca, Lucan the poet, and other upright men besides. Having himself set fire to a large part of the city, he blamed the fire on the Christians, whom he was the first in Rome to persecute. He had Peter and Paul, the leaders of the Apostles, put to death. Not long after, when the Senate and people of Rome were searching for him to kill him, hateful alike to mortals and immortals he laid impious hands upon himself, performing the executioner's duty.

Sergius Galba, made emperor by the army, succeeded Nero. But his extreme severity and cruelty made his rule brief. In the very first month of his reign he was caught in an ambush by Otho Sylvius and slaughtered.

Otho Sylvius, after usurping supreme power, was emperor for scarcely any longer than the man he had deposed. He was easily defeated in battle near Cremona by Vitellius, who had accepted imperial office from the German legions, and he opted for a voluntary death, stabbing himself with his dagger.

Vitellius had spent his boyhood and adolescence among whores. In his later years he was stained with the guilt of other crimes. When he entered camp he denied nothing to anyone who asked him, and he let criminals deserving of death escape their punishment. Hence when scarcely a month had gone by, he was suddenly proclaimed emperor by the soldiers. When he discovered letters to Otho seeking for having taken part in the murder of Sergius Galba, he had one hundred and twenty of the authors rounded up and executed. On his travels he had himself carried in the style of conquerors. When he was approaching a battlefield that gave horrible evidence of decaying corpses, he dared to express approval in the detestable words, *"The enemy dead are stinking nicely, the Romans will stink even better!"*

Eventually he entered Rome, in full armour among the flags and standards, with mantled comrades round him and his armed soldiers guarding him. More and more he disregarded every human and divine law and himself took the office of high priest. He gave himself over completely to luxury, wine, gluttony and savagery. By a variety of treacherous arts he killed noblemen who had been his fellow-students and peers. Eventually he was seized by Vespasian's commanders and their soldiers and dragged in disgrace half-naked through the city with his hands tied behind his back and a rope round his neck, while the crowds shouted abuse. But he spoke out once with no mean spirit, defying the Tribune, *"I used to be your emperor!"* Finally, he was put to death at Gemonia with the most refined tortures, his throat was cut and he was thrown into the Tiber, in the eighth year of his reign.

Domitian, son of Vespasian and brother of Titus, as emperor had his various virtues and vices. He ended up more like Nero than Titus. Nonetheless, aiming to emulate his much-praised brother, he presented himself as a friend of the people and a believer in justice. He kept the urban magistrates and provincial presidents in such subjection that they could never have been more modest or more just. Denouncers were repressed with the severest punishments. Domitian is supposed to have said, *"If a ruler does not punish tale-bearers, he encourages them."* He had women of scandalous reputation deprived of the right to use litters and to obtain legacies. A senator who had a passion for dancing was removed from the Senate by the emperor's command.

Not content with human eminence, Domitian hurtled onwards to the last extreme. He gave orders that he was to be called Lord and god, the first emperor to do so. From then on, declining into rabid cruelty, he had many of the senators killed for the slightest of reasons, and he persecuted those who bore the name of Christians. In his time John the Evangelist was banished to the Isle of Patmos. Cletus and Anacletus, Supreme Pontiffs of the Catholic religion of Christ, were killed. But this emperor himself in the 15th year of his reign was himself killed by his followers on account of his faults. And he who had arrogated divine honours to himself was denied human honours.

Commodus, hated by his people for cruel behaviour unworthy of a Caesar, was strangled in the 13th year of his reign.

Julianus Didius lost his empire, making a bad end to a reign that was badly begun. The Senate deprived him of imperial power and transferred it to Septimus Severus, on whose orders Didius was killed. (Aelius Pertinax, a good emperor, had been killed unjustly by soldiers through the agency of this same Didius.)

Valerianus Augustus, named emperor by the senate, with Galienus his son conducted a slaughter of Christians. He adorned many of them with the glory of martyrdom, especially Archbishop Cyprian of Carthage and Pope Sixtus II, who by his example inspired the deacon Laurentius to die in the same manner. However, in the seventh year of his reign Valerian felt the vengeance of God. For in the Persian War he was defeated and captured by the Persian king Sapor. Paraded among the enemy as a miserable captive, his power shrank to nothing, to the point where the barbarian king, elated by the excess of fortune, used Valerius Augustus's back as a footstool when mounting his horse; so true is it that no human majesty is safe from the ultimate indignity. (Romanus Diogenes, the Greek emperor, is reported to have had a similar misfortune: after attacking the Turkish Sultan in Asia he was defeated and fell into the power of the enemy, who trod upon him with their feet.) In fact, Augustus served the barbarian king as a footstool whenever he was ascending or descending from his throne.

There is a similar story of Baiazetes, king of the Turks, who was defeated and captured by Tamerlane, king of the Tartars, and kept in an iron cage as a butt of ridicule. When Tamerlane was dining, Baiazetes with a golden chain on his neck would take his food among the dogs under the table: and he presented his prostrate back to Tamerlane when he was mounting his horse – so barbarously was one barbarous king treated by another royal barbarian. Galienus also came to a most miserable end.

These examples of Gentile or pagan emperors are sufficient: now I would like to say a few things about the Christian emperors also.

84. Philip senior, who had treacherously killed the emperor Gordianus, took imperial power and made his son Philip junior his co-regent. But about their sixth year in office the plotting of Decius brought about their deaths, and a reign that was born in crime was lost by a similar crime. According to many authors, these were the first Roman emperors who were Christians.

Julian, having taken imperial power, deserted the Catholic religion and thus received the name 'The Apostate'. In many wicked ways he persecuted the Christians. But in the second year of his reign, waging war against the Persians, he was betrayed by one of his commanders; he fell into an ambush and there was a great slaughter of his men. There are some who say he was transfixed by an arrow sent down from Heaven, and he exclaimed, *"You have won, Galilean!"* (his mocking name for Christ). This impious man, however, died impiously.

The emperor Valens, an Arian heretic, persecuted the Catholic creed sorely. A bitter enemy of Basil the Great, he abducted monks from their spiritual exercises and impressed them to do military service. But the penalties that he paid to Providence, even if long-delayed, were no light ones. For he lost his army in battle against the barbarians; wounded by an arrow, he fled and took refuge in a mean hut; but the barbarians discovered him there and burned him alive. A striking demonstration of God's anger against an impious ruler, after he had held the empire for fourteen years.

The emperor Anastasius Dicorus was an Eutychian heretic, an evil man who came to an evil end. It was said that before death a kind of horrible human figure appeared to him, holding a book in its hand and crying out, *"Because of your wickedness I am striking out fourteen years of life!"* Soon he was struck by lightning and died, his life cut short by a gesture of God's (as often seems to have happened to wicked men) – a memorable example of the wrath of Heaven.

Phocas, more tyrant than emperor, began his reign badly and continued worse. His cruelty, drunkenness and lust were notorious. He had unjustly killed the emperor Mauritius, having first butchered his wife and children before his eyes. Becoming afterwards a plague on the human race, Phocas lost many of the empire's provinces, but he disregarded the enemy and in his lunacy began tormenting the citizens of Rome as if they were actually enemies. Heraclius, however, came from Asia at the call of the nobility, waged war upon the tyrant, defeated him, captured him, and finally, stamping upon his neck, he killed him, in the eighth year of his tyranny.

The emperor Philippus Bardanes did all he could to dissolve the Sixth Orthodox Synod. But not with impunity, because in the third year of his reign he was overthrown by his subjects, blinded and sent into exile.

Nicephorus Logotheta, Emperor of the Greeks, was exceptionally wicked and treacherous and infamously greedy. Even after he had seized numerous fortunes by unjust means, he kept plotting new ways of amassing money. There were some people who had gone from slender means to huge riches: he accused them of coming by their wealth criminally and stripped them of their entire fortunes. While he was plundering the imperial capital in this manner, the Saracens began plundering on their own account in the rest of Asia and the Bulgarians in Thrace. Nicephorus used his gold to buy peace with the Saracens and then led an army against the Bulgarians, whom he defeated and drove from their strongholds. But over-confidence vanquished the victor. Puffed up with success, the emperor refused to offer his enemies terms of peace, and the Bulgarian leader Crumus, in desperation, was driven to take audacious risks. In a surprise attack by night on the Greek camp there was a great slaughter of Greeks; Nicephorus himself was cut down, and for long afterwards his head, fixed on a pole, was an amusing spectacle for the barbarians. A warning to posterity, to be prepared to leave the enemy some way out!

Those who have written about the emperors include Caius Suetonius, Cornelius Tacitus, Horatius Torsellinus, Ioannes Baptista Aegnatius, Franciscus Thamara and many others, from whom I have taken the above examples. Now to the kings.

85. The Italians have deposed many princes from their kingdom. For my purposes now it will suffice to take one example, a man whom God deprived of his kingdom and his life – Theodoric, king of Italy and an Arian heretic. He punished Symachus and Boethius, who were Catholics, consuls and men of a high reputation for wisdom, first with exile and afterwards with death. He caused the death of Pope John, debilitated by long imprisonment, and had many others unjustly executed. But the wrath of heavenly Providence came quickly and unmistakeably. While the impious king was dining, suddenly the head of an enormous fish was brought to the table. It seemed to him that it was the head of Symachus whom he had lately killed, with wild eyes and bared teeth threatening him with his end. This horrible apparition struck him so deeply with terror that he wandered about, extraordinarily disturbed and horror-stricken, deploring the reckless cruelty with which he had imposed summary executions. Tursellinus in *Epitome historiarum lib. 6. pag. 285*, and others.

86. The Germans deprived the incompetent Carolus Crassus of his royal name and empire and put him under the tutelage of his cousin Arnolph. On account of this conspicuous humiliation Crassus sank into such depression that a short time later he took his leave of life. *Ioannes Baptista Egnatius lib. 3 pag. 47. Tursellinus lib. 7. pag. 373* and others. The Emperor Wenceslas also, because of his lethargy and vice, was deposed by the German Electors and the other principal men of Frankfurt, with the consent of Pope Boniface IX. *Ioannes Azorius tomo 2. Institutionum moralium lib. 11 cap. 5. q. 14, pag. 1102. Tursellinus libro 9. pag. 550. Bobadilla in politica lib. 5. cap. 1. num. 136.* and others.

87. The French sought advice from Pope Zacharias: who should rule us, an ignorant and negligent prince or an energetic, hard-working and diligent one? The Pope answered, The one who is energetic and diligent! Immediately the French expelled Childeric from the kingship because he was lethargic, that is to say incompetent and unsuitable for governing, and made Pipin their king. *Ioannes Azorius op. cit. pag. 1102 et cap. alius 15 q. 6 ubi glossa.*

88. By general consensus of their nobility and people the Spanish expelled Pedro, known as the Cruel, king of Castille and Leon, from his kingdom, because he had been mistreating his subjects savagely. His brother Henry, although he was illegitimate, was chosen to replace him. *Ioannes Marian de Rebus Hispaniae lib. 27. cap. 8. et Ioannes Azorius tomo 2. lib. 11. cap. 5. q. 3. pag. 1101*, and other historians.

89. The Portuguese deposed King Sancho II for being remiss and neglectful in governing the realm, choosing instead his brother Alfonso, Count of Bononia. *Duardus Leonis in libro de vera Regum Portugalliae genealogia, pagina 10. Ioannes Azorius tom. 2. lib. 11. cap. 5. q. 14. pag. 1102. Antonius Vasconcellus in Actibus Regum Lusitaniae pag. 61 ff. in editione Antuerpiana,* and others.

90. The Scots have furnished example in this area not once but many times. For there were many kings of the Scottish realm (some Christian, others pagan) whom the nobility and people deprived of their lives and royal dignity on account of their crimes. (See John Leslie, Bishop of Ross, in his *Account of the History and Customs of the Scots*, George Buchanan, a Scot, in his *History of Scotland lib. 4. ff., Ioannes Azorius tomo 2. lib. 11. cap. 5.* and others.) I will choose a few examples, omitting many others for brevity's sake.

Nothatus, fifth in the line of the kings of Scotland, continually subjected citizens of both high and low rank to unjust treatment, depriving them of their goods and punishing them with exile, death, and other afflictions, until he had left no further extreme of savagery still to be reached. He was finally cut down by his subjects after twenty years of cruel and greedy administration. This man was a pagan. When Dardanus, 20th of the kings, began governing, there were higher expectations of him than of any king before him; and none more thoroughly betrayed the hopes that were placed in him. Before becoming sovereign he had indeed been an example of liberality, moderation and courage. But by the time he had completed three years in office he was already sinking headlong into vice of all kinds. He expelled from his hall the upright and prudent men who had been counsellors to his father, because they took a stand against his ruffianliness. By contrast, flatterers and people who could invent new pleasures were held in special esteem. Dardanus put to death his relative Cordonus, who had been principally responsible for the equitable administration of the law under the preceding king, because he raised irritating questions about his pleasures. Before long many others who were eminent in wealth or personal merit fell victim to his villainy and perished. When these and other crimes became publicly known there was a widely-supported conspiracy against the monarch; after reigning for four years he was arrested and killed, his head was used as a butt and his body was thrown in a sewer. This man also was a pagan.

Luctacus, the 22nd king, a pagan, was a most criminal individual. He spurned the advice of his seniors and abandoned himself to wine and whores. Neither close kinship nor reverence for law, nor respect for husbands, could secure any woman against his lust. To this he added inhuman cruelty and greed beyond explanation. In his youth he had shown proclivities towards vice, and it was easy for him to degenerate into the moral conduct of his time as king. When his rapes, plunders and murders had caused general degradation and no one dared to oppose his frenzy, eventually there was a convention of the principal nobles and an assembly of the people, and they killed Luctacus along with his ministers of crime; the third year of his reign had scarcely concluded. However, his father Corbredus, an excellent man, was shown honour: his remains were buried in the cemetery of the princes, while the others' corpses were thrown outside and left unburied.

Methodius (or Ethodius) the Second, the 28th king of Scotland, could almost be called stupid. Certainly he had a more limited intelligence than would suit for keeping the fierce Scottish people in restraint. Aware of this, the assembled elite showed respect for the race of the excellent King Fergus: while conceding the name of king to this man, however ignorant, they also appointed governors to assert the law in the individual regions. These latter were so just and so moderate that the affairs of Scotland were tranquil as never before. It was not so much that they punished crimes but rather that they restrained the king's avarice, thus relieving the people. The king was finally killed in the 21st year of his reign in a family brawl. This man was a Christian.

Athcirco was the 29th king of Scotland. At first he was a good prince, exceptionally beneficent, humane and courageous. But with the passing years he lapsed into vice, becoming deeply avaricious, prone to rage, luxury-loving and lethargic; he gave only a brief consideration to anything good before putting it aside. Finally he seduced the daughters of Nathalocus, a man of the high nobility, and beating the abused girls into submission, prostituted them to his servants. This provoked a conspiracy of the nobility; after a futile attempt to defend himself, deserted by his followers, he took his own life, in the 12th year of his reign. Such was the end of the Christian king Athcirco: and with that I will end the examples given here from the kings of Scotland. If anyone desires more, let him consult the above-cited Leslie, Buchanan and Azorius.

91. The English deprived their second Edward of his kingdom, because of his sloth in public administration and other faults besides. They sent him to prison where he was eventually killed, and they made his 14-year-old son, Edward III, king in his place. Polydore Virgil in *History of England lib. 18*. George Lily in *Epitome Chronices Regum Anglorum*. Nicholas Sanders *lib. 1 Rise and Growth of the English Schism*, pag. 222 in the Roman edition, and other historians. Indeed, in this very year of Christ 1645 when I am writing, the English heretic Puritans or Calvinist Parliamentarians are waging atrocious war with their King Charles, who is also a heretic, but a Lutheran or Protestant one. With what right or with what wrong? Let them work that out for themselves.

92. Here I would like to insert a brief record of the crimes of King Henry VIII of England, who was the cause of so many evils and heresies. His English subjects did not deprive him of his kingdom or his life, though he deserved it much more than Edward II; but alive or dead he was not able to escape the hand of Almighty God. For in this life he left an infamous name and the accursed memory of his crimes, and in the other life he was put in eternal bondage in the flames of Hell.

This Henry was at first a Catholic prince, endowed with an excellent physique and not wanting in mental acumen, ripeness of judgement or gravity. He fostered the liberal arts and increased the salaries of some of the professors. The bishops he nominated were learned and virtuous (with one or two exceptions); afterwards many of them, in the reigns of Edward and Elizabeth, were imprisoned in chains for professing their Catholic faith. Henry always held the Most Holy Sacrament of the Eucharist in the highest honour. When he was eighteen years old he married the Most Serene Princess Catherine, daughter of Ferdinand and Elizabeth, the Catholic monarchs of Spain. By her he had three sons and two daughters, of whom only Mary, born in 1515, later to be the wife of his Catholic Majesty Philip II, survived.

King Henry and Queen Catherine lived for 20 years in holy matrimony. When the fire of the Lutheran heresy began to spread, inspired by Catholic zeal Henry wrote, or had written for him, a truly learned and erudite book on the seven sacraments of the Catholic Church against Luther and other heretics who wanted to make the sacraments fewer or less efficacious. (It is believed, however, that the author or co-author of this book was John, bishop of Rochester, a man of high learning, imprisoned martyr and eminent cardinal.) For this pious Catholic service Pope Leo X awarded Henry the title of Defender of the Faith (Pope Leo's Bull on this matter, issued in 1521, is in Sanders, bk. 1 of *Rise and Growth of the English Schism*, p. 225). He and his royal successors might have preserved that distinction safely, if they had been willing to persevere in the Catholic faith. Since, however, they basely deserted the orthodox religion and embraced heresies, they proved themselves unworthy of such a title. From then on they have merited the name of offenders against the Faith, not its defenders.

But this man Henry, so highly gifted and of such fine character, afterwards fell into all the whirlpools of vice. He was addicted to three or four vices above all others, those being lust, avarice, drunkenness and cruelty, and the two first-mentioned vices commonly unhinge the minds of men who are otherwise sagacious, as the Word of God says in *Ecclesiasticus* ch. 19. *"Wine and women make wise men fall off, and shall rebuke the prudent. And he that joineth himself to harlots, will be wicked",* etc., as happened to this most unfortunate king. Many have spoken and written a great deal about Henry's vices; I will say just a little here.

So then, his lust was so unbridled that even while he was living amicably with his wife Catherine he had two or sometimes three of her maids as concubines. Where that particular sin was concerned, he was rarely able to see a pretty woman without lusting after her, or to lust after a woman without going on to violate her. One of those he laid eyes on was a noble lady, the wife of Sir Thomas Boleyn, and to enjoy her all the more comfortably and freely he did Thomas the seeming honour of sending him as ambassador to France. Before his departure Thomas had fathered one daughter by his wife, named Maria Boleyn. While he was away the king had intercourse with his wife and begot a daughter by her, who was given the name of Anne Boleyn. Returning after a two-year stay in France, Thomas discovered that his wife had borne a daughter, and he wanted to repudiate or kill her. His wife told this to the King, who commanded Thomas strictly to spare his wife and bring up Anna as his daughter; and he did so, motivated by fear and by his wife's meekness and tears. Falling on her knees before him, she begged him to spare her because she had not had the strength to resist the king (who was Anne's father).

What more? The king successively and incestuously had carnal knowledge of both the mother and Maria Boleyn, her daughter. Now Henry's house was full of the most dissolute men, including gamblers, adulterers, pimps, perjurers, blasphemers, felons and heretics, and there was one who was a prime rogue among them all, named Francis Brian, who was nicknamed the Vicar of Hell. The king asked this man how bad a sin he thought it was to have sex first with a mother and then with her daughter. The wastrel replied glibly, *"Your Majesty, it's as bad as eating a hen first and then eating her chicken!"* When he heard that the king laughed heartily, saying, *"It's not for nothing that you're my vicar of hell!"*

Shortly afterwards (as if that were not bad enough), led by his blind love for Anne Boleyn, the king resolved to repudiate his legitimate wife Catherine and marry Anne. And since Pope Clement VII refused to listen to the frivolous and insane grounds that Henry presented when applying for this divorce, he became a schismatic and heretical apostate. Immediately he repudiated his legitimate wife and installed in her place Anne Boleyn, with whom he had multiple ties of relationship: she was the sister of Maria Boleyn, who had previously been his concubine, and it was by her mother that he had begotten that same Anne, who was Henry's daughter and whore. But, *"Putting aside the name of whore, she'll be a wife."* Or, as the jocular verse puts it:

"Juno was sister and wife of Jove, but Anne Boleyn
was bastard daughter and wife of Henry."

Maybe someone would like to know what endowments of body and mind she had, this Anne Boleyn who made Henry burn with love and for whom he repudiated his genuine wife. Anne Boleyn was thin and tall in stature, with black hair, an oblong face, sallow complexion (as if she were suffering from jaundice), and one of her upper teeth protruded somewhat from the gum. On her right hand she was known to have a sixth finger. There was a swelling growth, I don't know what, under her chin; to hide this deformity she kept her throat and the upper part of her bosom covered. But she did have rather charming lips, and she was accomplished in witty banter, dancing, and playing the lute. Where her mind was concerned, she was full of pride, ambition, envy and sensuality.

When she was 15 years old she let herself be deflowered by two domestic servants or companions of Thomas Boleyn. Soon after that she was sent to France, where she was educated in a certain nobleman's house at the king's expense. She next made her way to the French king's palace, where she lived so shamelessly that the French had a vulgar name for her, 'The English Mare'. When she formed a familiar attachment with the French king they began to call her instead 'The Royal Mule'.

She was attached to the Lutheran heresy, but nonetheless she professed to be a Catholic. When she returned to England and was received into the royal household she pretended to be a chaste virgin. And when the news went round that King Henry wanted to marry her, all over France it was bandied about how the king of England was going to marry the king of France's mule. See what a monster Henry loved! – and he made her a Countess, thinking of her as a woman of high nobility.

When after some time Anne had not conceived a male heir by Henry, nor did she expect to do so in the future, she decided to explore whether there was some other way, besides being the king's wife, by which she might become a king's mother. She thought that it would be easier to conceal the crime of adultery if she committed it with her brother George Boleyn than with somebody else. But when even this wicked incest did not produce the result which she most desired, she began to apply her mind to promiscuous sex, inveigling many men (some of them nobles and others plebeians) into the royal bed and having carnal intercourse with them. Her lust was in such an overflow that it could not long remain concealed from the king. He ordered Anne to be arrested and beheaded, and this was done on May 17, 1536. Afterwards her brother George Boleyn, Henry Norris, William Bruerton, Francis Weston, a nobleman, and Mark Smeton, a musician, all of them attached to the royal chamber, were publicly tortured and executed, just three days after Anne's execution, as their just deserts for the incest and adultery they had committed with her.

On September 8, 1533 this Anne Boleyn gave birth to a daughter who was called Elizabeth. Although by common estimation she was considered the daughter of King Henry, nevertheless on account of Anne's notorious promiscuity there was always doubt about the identity of the father of Elizabeth, who would afterwards be a heretical and usurping queen.

Let us say a few words about Henry's drunkenness and gluttony. Every day he was drunk almost from breakfast time, and by filling his stomach too much it became deformed and so expanded that he could scarcely get through doors and could not by any means climb stairs (although in his youth he had been agile and physically handsome). So he remained at home among the women and domestics, like another Sardanapulus.

Henry was so avaricious that (besides the many tributes he imposed on his vassals, which provoked frequent rebellions) he seized the goods and livings of all the monasteries and other sacred buildings. So that it could never be reclaimed or restored to the Church, he made a general distribution of this wealth to the noblemen and other laymen, partly in return for services to be given, and partly by putting compulsion on many people to buy what he was selling, so that in this way he would oblige them to defend his crime. It is difficult to estimate the destruction this impious man, this other Nebuchadnezzar, wrought on monasteries, temples and sacred edifices. A learned writer of King Henry's time summed it up in two lines of verse:

One single year took away ten thousand temples:
for punishment, I fear, one thousand won't be enough.

Whatever the number may have been, whether it was ten thousand or more or less, the temples and monasteries were devastated. It is a well-established fact that many of the monasteries were splendidly adorned and opulent, and that impious fellow plundered and stripped them and levelled them to the ground. Not sparing libraries, nor the literary works of antiquity nor the saints' relics, he uttered these barbarous words, "The crows' nests must be destroyed completely, so that they will not come back to live in them again." Crows: that is what the sacrilegious fellow, the villainous thief, called the priests and monks whose goods he had pillaged. But his sacred booty left the sacrilegious bandit poorer, since (as commonly happens) things badly begun came to an evil end.

Henry's cruelty can be gathered from the large number of men of the high nobility and other citizens, both lay and clerical, whom he unjustly condemned to death. After forcing through his divorce from his legitimate wife and the break with the Catholic Church, it is almost indescribable what a ruin of his nobles and citizens this Nero made in the few years that remained to him. Two Cardinals, John of Rochester and Thomas Wolsey, are listed in the criminal register, and a third, Cardinal Reginald Pole, a near relative of Henry himself, was declared a public enemy in his absence (though he had done no wrong) and sentenced to death, with a bounty of fifty thousand gold sovereigns offered to anyone who would contrive his death. Dukes, earls and the children of earls, made up twelve victims; barons and knights ten and eight respectively; abbots and priors of monasteries, thirteen; priests, monks and members of religious orders seventy seven. From the remainder of the nobility and people they could scarcely be counted.

Henry did not spare even women. Of his six wives and many concubines he killed or repudiated almost all. His first legitimate wife was the Most Serene Queen Catherine whom he unjustly repudiated, and she died overcome by sorrow and grief. The second was Anne Boleyn, whom he killed with her paramours, as stated already. The third was Jane Seymour, whom the doctors and surgeons cut open on the king's orders so that she could give birth, which she did, and died immediately after; Henry remarked that he could easily find wives but not so easily sons. The fourth was Anne of Cleves, whom Henry also unjustly repudiated. The fifth was Catherine Howard, who was convicted of adultery (on the king's orders, the king himself being the accuser) with her paramours Thomas Culper and Francis Dinham and condemned to death. What a fitting example for posterity: just as Henry kept faith neither with God nor with his first wife, so also two wives violated the faith they had pledged to him! Henry's sixth and last wife was Catherine Parr, widow of Baron Latimer; she had better fortune than the others in this much at least, that king Henry was himself removed from life before he could remove hers, as he had intended. I omit many other women, both noble and plebeian, whom that murderer sent to their deaths.

Henry, with so many crimes committed, was often admonished and appealed to by many princes, by prominent and pious Catholics, and also by Pope Clement VII and Pope Paul III to put an end to his evildoing. When he obstinately refused, both of these Popes put him under anathema and deprived him of his right to the kingship. And even then the miscreant, not wishing to be corrected, chose rather to be condemned.

Finally the king was approaching his end, when he would have to render an account to God of all he had done during his life. He became ill, and as the disease worsened, warned by his friends that death was imminent, he asked for a cup of white wine, drank it down, and said, *"I have lost everything"*; and he spoke the truth, because he had lost both temporal and eternal life. Straightaway he died and descended to the underworld, to be fuel for eternal fire. Henry died in London on January 28, 1546 in his 56th year. At the same time Luther died in Germany and went to Hell to suffer eternal torments. The deaths of both of these heretics came as most welcome news to all good people. This brief account of Henry is sufficient for our purposes here. Whoever desires more should read the English historians, especially Nicholas Sanders bk. 1 *Rise and Growth of the English Schism* and Edmund Campion in his *Narrative of the Divorce of Henry VIII from his Wife Catherine and his Secession from the Church of Rome.*

93. I wish to present an example from the kingdom of Denmark. Christernus, king of Denmark, was the first king who followed the wicked apostate and heresiarch Martin Luther, deserting the Catholic faith. But not long afterwards he was deposed from his three kingdoms by his subjects, and his successors put him in chains and kept him behind bars in in a cage until his death. And justly, because it is scarcely possible to find a crime that more deserves the privation of office, dignity and life than heresy, which spreads like a cancer till it corrupts the whole body of the commonwealth. It is therefore normal that in every well-regulated Catholic kingdom and commonwealth heretics are burned at the stake, lest they should infect other men with their contagion and lead them to eternal damnation. Tursellinus lib. 10 pag. 598.

94. George of Podiebrad, King of Bohemia, was condemned for heresy and the kingdom of Bohemia was given to King Matthias of Hungary. The heretic Podiebrad thereby also lost Moravia, Silesia and other Catholic regions and towns, which preferred to follow a Hungarian Catholic rather than a Bohemian heretic. Tursellinus lib. 10 pag. 578.

95. And finally, our own countrymen the Irish can show some examples in this connection. Let them consult their histories, which I do not have to hand just now. But I can give one example which I found recently in Richard Stanihurst's *On the History of Ireland*, p. 106. Murchadh, king of Leinster and father of the criminal Dermot, inflicted manifold injuries on his province and above all on the citizens of Dublin. By this he aroused great hate and resentment, and the councillors of the city laid a plot to kill him. With the greatest pomp and ceremony they invited him to visit a magnificent building. Murchadh suspected nothing, because he had often been present in that hall before. After giving him various amusements to relax his mind and put him in a carefree humour, suddenly they sank their daggers into his throat, and they buried the corpse in the meanest grave together with a dog. For brevity's sake I omit many other examples from the Greeks, Assyrians etc., because those given here would appear to suffice.

96. We may end our examples with the reflection that not only in the secular commonwealth but also in the Church one may find the penalty of suspension and deposition or deprivation of office and dignity, so long as there are culpable sovereigns or culpable prelates of the Church. Certainly, in some religious orders the supreme prelates or generals may be deposed. The same is true of bishops in certain cases. And what is more, the supreme monarch of the Church, the Pope, can be deposed if he were to fall into heresy (which God forbid), as theologians and legal experts say with unanimous consent. All this being so, it is not surprising that Catholic vassals should resist heretical kings who command them to do what is unjust and that they should throw off the yoke of heretical government, as the Catholic Irish did with the fullest right in 1641, and are doing now as I write these lines. In other matters (which are not against God's law) they have hitherto obeyed King Charles, even if he is a heretic. They were nonetheless legitimately entitled to throw off his yoke completely, as may be gathered clearly from this argument. They have no less right to do so than the Catalans had when in 1638 they renounced their obedience to Philip IV, the Catholic king of Spain, (who had not observed their rights, privileges and agreements, as he and his forbears had promised, if what the Catalans have said in their published books is true), and they chose the Most Christian Louis XIII of France as their king. The Portuguese did likewise in 1640, choosing as their king John, the fourth of that name, formerly Duke of Braganza, a man clearly worthy of the sovereignty, and who had the highest hereditary right to that kingdom, as the Portuguese doctors and many others of different nations have demonstrated at length in their books. One may consult Doctor Francisco Velasco de Gouveia in his analytical tractate on the *Just Acclamation of King John IV*; Doctor Antonio de Sousa de Macedo in *Lusitania Liberata*; Master Francisco Freire in *Apologia Veritatis et Iustitiae*, and others.

97. It follows that the Catholic Irish, who are waging an entirely just war for the Catholic religion against the English and Scottish heretics (not against the Catholics of either nation) are not rebels or outlaws, nor are they guilty of the crime of *lése-majesté*, – as our heretical opponents say in their slanderous writings, impiously fabricating and impudently lying – since *"The highest reason is that which serves religion." L. sunt personae ff. de relig. et sumpt. fun.*

98. Somebody perhaps will put forward that vulgar and demagogic doubt or argument: if it is true that our opponents have acted against justice, piety and faith and are acting so still, why has the most just, pious and faithful God wished or permitted the English heretics to afflict and torment us, the innocent Irish Catholics, for so many years, killing great numbers of us and despoiling many of their goods? I reply, first of all, that we merited these torments and afflictions by our own sins and misdeeds and those of our forbears: *"We have sinned with our fathers: we have acted unjustly, we have wrought iniquity" (Psalm 105).* Also John, *Ep. 1* ch. 1, is true in the highest degree: *"If we say that we have no sin, we deceive ourselves, and the truth is not in us. If we confess our sins, he is faithful and just, to forgive us our sins, and to cleanse us from all iniquity."* And that is why the most just God wished or permitted us to be punished by our heretical opponents, just as he wished that Spain should be oppressed and chastised by infidels for 700 years and more. France also, Germany and many other Catholic kingdoms have been tormented by heretics and left almost desolate, on account of the inhabitants' sins.

I reply secondly. Even if we grant, purely for argument's sake, that we Irish were so blameless that no mortal crime could be found amongst us, nevertheless God might justly have permitted these afflictions, as he permitted the temptations and vexations of Job, Tobias and many other saintly men. In the words of the angel Raphael to Tobias, *"And because thou wast acceptable to God, it was necessary that temptation should prove thee". Tob. 12. n. 13.* Saint Augustine says very appositely in the *City of God,* bk. 4 ch. 13, *"A certain amount of suffering is imposed upon the just, not as a punishment for crime but as a test of their virtue."* It was therefore necessary that the outstanding constancy of our Catholics should be tested by affliction. For, as the philosopher Seneca says in a matchless sentence, *"The soul cannot be called constant if it has not battled with fortune".*

((99)) It may perhaps happen that someone who is concerned for religion will consider that the doctrine of this argument may harm or in some way prejudice English Catholics who are resident in Ireland or will reside there in the future, since it is proved that the English possession of Ireland, with its movable and immovable goods, has been unjust from the beginning. Responding to this scrupulously, I say, however, that there are no sufficient grounds for thinking so. For those English Catholics who possess goods of whatever kind in Ireland possess them with good title and in good faith, by title of donation, sale, exchange, gift, or other licit and honest contract. If afterwards they have been inhabitants for ten or twenty years, etc., they may be reputed native or indigenous Irishmen for all practical purposes, and they have the same right and title to possess their goods as the rest of the Irish have to possess theirs. If anyone from either of these groups, however, appears to have unjust possession of anything, justice will require that he be judged before one of the two legal fora. All this is confirmed in the laws established by the last General Assembly, where it is commanded that no distinction shall be made between the old and the new Irish, but all are to be secure. Which is indeed a just and prudent measure. Certainly in the general synod which was held in Ireland over a period of two months and a half (it began in the town of Kilkenny on October 24, 1642 and ended on January 9, 1643) 41 laws were established and proclaimed, of which No. 23 includes the following.

"So as to avoid civil discords and enmities, and so that all may devote themselves in thought and deed to furthering the common Catholic cause, no one who is included in this sacred union is to be molested or harmed or ejected from any of his possessions which he has held for three full years preceding."

And in law No 24 the following occurs:

"Since the distinction of nations among the subjects of the Most Serene Majesty is altogether odious: it is commanded that every Catholic, no matter whether he be English, Scots or Welsh, who professed the Catholic religion before the beginning of this war and has come into this kingdom and bound himself in this sacred union, shall possess his goods like any other Irish Catholic. And this privilege is granted to him, that a third part of the tributes which others pay as war subsidies shall be remitted in his case."

And in law No. 25 it is said:

"There shall be no difference between the ancient pure Irish and the new Irish descended from the old or modern English, nor among the families of nobles and magnates, nor among those residing within or outside the towns: all who are or who will be encompassed in this Holy Catholic union must be considered and treated with Christian equality, on pain of the highest penalty that can be inflicted on the authors of discords."

100. It is clear from all this that there could no basis for suspecting that any harm or damage could come to English Catholics, much less to the orthodox new Irish, from the doctrine in this argument of ours. Indeed there are good grounds for hoping it will be extremely useful if all understand the justice of our war and play their own part in it, obeying the laws of the Catholic kingdom of Ireland, dissociating themselves from the heretics' unjust war effort, and entirely rejecting the schismatic and heretical laws of England, which are, as we have said already, contrary to the law of Christ Our Lord, to whom praise and honour be given for ever and ever. Amen.

End of the argument.

DISPVTATIO APOLOGETICA, ET MANIFESTATIVA DE IVRE REGNI Hiberniæ pro Catholicis Hibernis aduersus hæreticos.

AVTHORE CONSTANTINO MARVLLO HIBERNO.

Accessit eiusdem authoris ad eosdem Catholicos exhortatio.

FRANCOFVRTI Superiorum permissu typis BERNARDI GOVRANI.

Anno Domini 1645.

A slightly different wording in this title page

Call To Action
To The Irish Catholics

by the author C. M.,
from IRELAND

In the Argument above I have demonstrated that the right to entire dominion of the kingdom of Ireland belongs to the Irish Catholics and in no way to the English heretics. In the following call to action I aim to persuade the Irish that having once shaken off the heretical yoke they should never again submit to it or tolerate it, rather they should elect a Catholic king, an indigenous or native-born Irishman who will be able to govern them as Catholics.

1. Long ago God foresaw that a time would come when his Israelite people, having broken free from the power of the Egyptians (not without miracles and prodigies) would want and demand a king. He therefore imposed on them this law and command, as contained in the sacred text of *Deuteronomy* ch. 17: *"When thou art come into the land, which the Lord thy God will give thee, and possessest it, and shalt say: I will set a king over me, as all nations have that are round about: Thou shalt set him whom the Lord thy God shall choose out of the number of thy brethren. Thou mayst not make a man of another nation king, that is not thy brother. "* – Such are the words of God. This condition, that the King should be a brother, that is, of the same nation and not an alien, was expressly laid down by God on account of the danger of idolatry, perversion, false doctrine and false worship of God, as the commentators on this passage observe.

2. The Hebrews demanded a king from the judge Samuel, saying: *"Make us a king, to judge us, as all nations have."*(1 Kings 8, and 11). This occasion arose because Samuel had grown old and his sons Joel and Abia, whom Israel appointed as judges, did not follow in their father's footsteps but accepted bribes and perverted judgment, degenerating on account of their greed. Furthermore, King Naas of the Ammonites had come to attack the Israelites; and besides, they wished to imitate all other nations which had kings of their own.

3. Now listen to me, my fellow Irishmen. You have entered what is truly your own land, and which the Lord your God has given you to possess, expelling the unjust and heretical possessors: you possess it, you live in it, in almost the same manner as befell the Jews who had come from Egypt to Palestine, killing and expelling the pagan Gentiles who were unjustly in possession there. Many of those kings of England who sat in judgement over you grew old and died, whether well or badly; their sons and successors did not follow in their fathers' footsteps, at any rate not in Catholic paths, but became still worse than their forbears. They degenerated due to greed, they accepted bribes; they perverted human and divine judgments, became schismatics and heretics who frequently betrayed the faith of God and man, accepting heresies and intolerable errors and coercing their subjects and vassals to commit similar sins. And therefore you have just cause to demand and accept a Catholic king, one of your Irish brothers, as the Hebrews did (and at that time God ordered Samuel to hear their request and give them a king, and he did so).

4. Naas, king of the sons of Ammon (whom the Hebrews feared extremely, and this was why they demanded their own indigenous or native king to defend them) came to Iabes, which was the principal town of half of the tribe of Manasses, beyond the Jordan, in the region of Galaad. He laid siege and began to attack the town, intending to take it. The men of Iabes, in the grip of terror, sent messengers to King Naas to say to him, *"Make a covenant with us, and we will serve thee. "* (1 Kings, 11). That was certainly a very humble condition of peace, and hard on themselves, since they were delivering their whole population into servitude to avoid losing their lives. It was an exceptionally honourable proposal and distinction for the king and his Ammonites, whose great praise should have been, *"To spare his subjects and wage conquering war on the proud."* This is the praise that Marcus Tullius gives to Pompey in his speech on the Law of Manilius: *"Such is his humanity",* he says, *"that it is difficult to say which is the greater, the fear that his enemies feel when they fight him, or the clemency they enjoy when they are conquered."* But how do we suppose that that proud and tyrannical king responded to the humble petition of the men of Jabes and their terms of peace? *"On this condition will I make a covenant with you, "* he said, *" that I may pluck out all your right eyes, and make you a reproach in all Israel. "* O immortal God, what a harsh and bitter condition of peace! That cruel king wanted to tear out the right eyes of all; but with good reason you will ask, why?

5. Three literal reasons are usually given, and several mystical or spiritual reasons. Of the literal reasons, the first is so that the Hebrew soldiers or Israelites would be incapacitated for war, because while their left eye was unsighted by the shield as they dealt with the threat of being wounded from that side, if they lacked the right they would be no better than blind men at warding off enemy blows or striking blows of their own, and therefore they would be useless as warriors. Secondly, so that the Jabesites, men as well as women, when deprived of one eye would be reviled and in eternal disgrace, being held in general contempt throughout Israel. Thirdly, Naas and his Ammonites wished by inflicting mutilation on the Jabesites to infect the other Israelites with a terror of their power: those other Hebrews, seeing how harshly Jabes had been treated, would be intimidated and would abstain entirely from rebellion against the Ammonites after that.

These constitute the literal reasons, which I will now apply. The kings of England, especially those who were heretics, and their heretical ministers have often tried to render your leaders and Catholic soldiers incapable of war by depriving them of their eyes and of life itself. They forbade the living to practise the use of arms or the soldier's profession, as we learn from the illustrious Lord Peter Lombard, Archbishop of Armagh and Primate of All Ireland, in his *Commentary on the Kingdom of Ireland* ch. 18. *"Although the Irish are very well suited to the military life and deeply devoted to it, the English are at pains not to let them learn military discipline or have the use of arms in any form. Or if any of them have pursued the use and discipline of arms somewhere else, they are not to be given high military rank, even if they come of the most respectable families and are outstandingly proficient in military science."* – Those are his words. The English wished to bring your noble men and women into lasting disgrace, making them deserters from the true Catholic religion. But the divine goodness did not permit this. They have often wished to inflict slaughter and to bring incurable plagues upon you Catholics, and sometimes indeed they have done so, in order to spread terror among others and make them afraid in future to resort to arms in their own defence.

6. So as to be able to give some mystical or spiritual reasons, we assume with the exponents of Scripture that the word Naas may be taken to mean "serpent" and signifies the Devil. With this assumption we can draw a multiplicity of mystical reasons from the multiple significance of the right eye, which the Devil wants to pluck out of human beings.

7. Firstly, the right eye signifies the virginal state of the Church, the left eye the conjugal state, as interpreted by St. Jerome, *Against Jovinian*, bk. 1. However much the Church finds to praise in the married state, the virginal state is more praiseworthy still; the right eye is compared with the latter, the left eye is compared with the former. The first mystical reason stems from the fact that the Devil makes this right eye his particular target of attack and has armed countless battle formations against the virginal state – all of them, being limbs of the Devil, preach that the virginal state is either impossible or contemptible or damnable for the human race. Their aim is to eradicate it completely from the earth. They do not wish either priests or nuns to be chaste, rather they want them all to be married or have concubines in imitation of the criminal apostate and heresiarch Martin Luther, who broke his vows as a monk by seducing the nun Catherine Boria or Borra and keeping her as his lifelong concubine. There was also John Calvin, who though he was a priest and quite nobly born became a heresiarch and a most infamous fornicator; the reader may find his portrait, painted in a hundred criminal colours, in the book by Nicolaus Romaeus, *Effigy of Calvin,* etc. As limbs of the Devil, the English heretics (and always it is those only whom we speak of here, not the Catholics, whom we love and honour), have again and again tried to dissolve the virginity and chastity of our men, especially our clerics, by word, deed, example, threats and prizes. They took away their monasteries and covents from the priests and nuns. And consequently some few Irish churchmen, motivated by worldly greed, temptations of the Devil, fleshly lures, fear of punishment or love of gain, have crossed over from the Catholic faith to perfidious heresy and have taken wives, or concubines rather, in sacrilegious marriages and begotten sons and daughters. Those miserable beings did not fear the eternal torments to which they exposed themselves, nor did they appreciate the eternal rewards which they were renouncing: they had vowed to be continent and chaste, but they practised incontinence and lust. Such is the blindness of heresy, which cannot see the evil that it ought to flee and the good which it ought to embrace.

8. Secondly, the right eye signifies wisdom of the spirit, the left eye wisdom of the flesh. Thus Saint Thomas on the Apocalypse, cap. 9 No.

2, where he expounds the word "sun" as meaning the human intellect: this is partly obscured, he points out, by the Devil, but is not darkened completely, because the Devil is robbed of his prey by spiritual wisdom, which is the right eye, not by the carnal variety, which is the left. *"For the wisdom of the flesh is death; but the wisdom of the spirit is life and peace."* According to the testimony of the Apostle to the Romans, 8, 6, the aim of the the Devil's stratagem is that men will be carnally sighted but spiritually blinded, and so they will see what should not be seen, and they will fail to see what they ought to see and embrace.

The English heretics have often desired to extinguish your spiritual wisdom, leaving the carnal wisdom alone. Have they not extinguished the study of literature, which they had never wished to establish? They have killed some of the Catholic masters and sent others to prison and to exile. Again I quote the Archbishop of Armagh: *"Although the Irish were eager for the study of literature and the liberal arts and highly talented, being very often gifted with acute and sound minds, to this day they have never managed to make the English authorities consent to the erection of a university in Ireland."* In earlier times the country had abounded with excellent academies, as for example in Armagh, Cashel, Dublin, Lismore, Ross etc. On these see Sullivan, *Life of St. Patrick*, bk. 2 fol. 137 and *Relation of Ireland*, p. 4 No. 8, citing others.

9. Thirdly, the right eye signifies contemplation of celestial things, the left eye the action of sublunary things. The third reason is derived from this. For the Devil does not try to impede the latter as much as the former. Thus Venerable Bede lib. 2. on Samuel cap. 4, St. Peter Damian, St. Nilus, and others. For action without contemplation, i. e. without grace, is neither good nor meritorious. If you doubt that, why does the Devil not crave to extract both eyes, the right eye of contemplation and the left eye of action? Certainly it is so that he can instil in sinners a vain hope and confidence of salvation, leaving them the lesser part of their strength. Let me clarify this with examples. The Devil allows the man who carries out robberies to utter some prayers; the man who is swelling with pride to live abstemiously; the reckless rake to give alms, and so on: so that each one will set too much store by the good works that he does, and will not bother about reforming his evil ways.

The English heretics strove mightily to deprive you of the contemplation of heavenly things and to divert you to wicked actions, therefore they removed temples, oratories, crosses, images, rosaries and pious books which could be motives for contemplation, and they introduced heretical dogmas and sacrilegious ceremonies.

10. Fourthly, the right eye signifies spiritual goods, the left eye corporal goods. From this we have the fourth reason. When men have either kind of goods they come under attack from the Devil, but he targets spiritual goods principally. Thus Saint Bernard in *Cantica, Sermon 7,* referring to the right and left sides of the human body and explaining those words in Psalm 90, *"Two thousand shall fall at thy side, and ten thousand at thy right hand."* And he asks why more demons attack from the right side than from the left, when more are said to have fallen from the right than from the left? And he resolves the question as follows: what it means is that spiritual happiness is combated more by the Devil than temporal. *"The enemy"*, he says, *"are busily trying to wound you, but they take more pains and are much more cunning in attacking the right side than the left; it is the stuff of the heart, more than the limbs, that they seek to carry off; they strive to remove happiness of whatever kind, whether heavenly or earthly, but they prize far more the dew of the heavens than the fat of the earth."* These are the words of the saintly and sweet-voiced Abbot of Clairvaux. And here we should bear in mind that a thousand demons are armed to tear out the left eye of terrestrial happiness; but ten thousand are armed to tear out the right eye of supernatural happiness – so then, many more are opposed to the latter than to the former. But just as the Devil more bitterly assaults the right side, that is the spiritual goods; so God defends that part more assiduously, as David says from personal experience, Psalm 15, 8, *"For he is at my right hand, that I be not moved."* And for this reason, in so far as the Devil's gaping jaws are greedier to devour spiritual goods than corporal, what the king of the Sodomites said to Abraham is the same thing the Devil says to Christ, *"Give me the persons, and the rest take to thyself"* (Genesis 14, 21).

Thus God commits himself much more to defend spiritual goods than corporal, in accordance with His own words to Satan about Holy Job (ch. 2, v. 6): *"Behold be is in thy hand, but yet save his life."* Hence Bernard appeals to God to protect his soul rather than his body. *"May you be always at my right side, good Jesus; may you always hold my right hand; for I know and am certain that no adversity will harm where no wickedness takes control. Let the left side be beaten, let it be injured and lashed, let it be overwhelmed with reproaches; I happily expose it so long as I am guarded by you; so long as you are my protection, on guard over my right hand."* This is what Bernard says, and immediately he gives a severe warning to anyone who commits himself more to the protection of his left side than his right, that is to say, more to corporal goods than spiritual. *"Watch out for yourself, you who neglect the right side and cultivate the left, lest you receive a place with the goats in the left hand which you have chosen. Does the thought appal you? One needs to take care and not simply to be appalled."*

The English heretics have tried to destroy completely your spiritual goods, namely the sacraments, priests, monks and monasteries, and they have not hesitated to seize your temporal goods also: though they have concentrated more on the former than the later, so as to do you more injury and greater harm.

11. Fifthly, the right eye signifies perfect men, the left eye imperfect ones. For Saint Bernard, cited above, interprets the two sides of the Church, right and left, as meaning the spiritual and carnal men respectively. Now those who are most perfect are called ambidextrous in Sacred Scripture. An example is Aod, whom God inspired to save Israel, and who used either hand as a right hand, as told in the Book of Judges, ch. 3 v. 15, on which place Origen, Homily 3, speaks as follows: *"See what kind of man he is, he who is called to save Israel; he has no left hand, but has each hand as a right hand; it is precisely he who is worthy to be prince of the people and judge of the Church, a man who does nothing left-handed but is right-handed on either side, right in the faith and right in deeds; there is nothing of his that has been accomplished by left hands."* And further on in the same homily, *"I think that in a spiritual sense all the saints are called ambidextrous; the Devil, on the contrary, and his princes are called ambilaevous; for all that they do is left-handed, all is perverse, all is for eternal fire with those who are steered by the left hands."* So Origen says. The fifth reason is taken from the fact that the Devil sustains a bitterer fight against the holier men, and a less intense fight or none at all against the imperfect men: this is the plain teaching of many saints, whose testimony I will now cite. The prophet-king in his 36th Psalm says (with the Devil being understood by the word "sinner"), *"The wicked watcheth the just man, and seeketh to put him to death."* On this St. Ambrose says, *"The more just a particular man is, the more he is assailed by the enemy."* St. Gregory Nazianzenus in Oration 18 illustrates this with many examples. *"From the beginning* *the Devil stealthily made his way into Paradise to attack him who was first created, and he stood among the Angels demanding Job for torture, and ultimately he did not hesitate to attack the Lord himself, who is not vulnerable to any temptation: the Devil tempted him as if he might overcome him too."* With these words that great theologian adequately expresses the Devil's ferocious attempt to overthrow and ruin all of the best. Hence St. Jerome says in his letter on *Guarding Virginity* to Eustochius, *"The devil is not seeking unbelievers, it is not those who are outside that he busies himself trying to seize from the Church of Christ. He wanted to subvert Job; and having devoured Judas, he exerted his power to catch the Apostles in his sieve."* For just as wheat is separated from chaff with a sieve and the former is retained, while the latter is despised, likewise the Devil separates the bad from the good, attacking the latter and omitting and despising the former. On this let us hear St. Cyprian of Carthage, Bishop Primate of all Africa and most glorious martyr, bk. 3 of his letters, epistle 1 to Lucius. *"Christ's adversary attacks only Christ's strongholds and persecutes only Christ's soldiers; he despises the heretics, who are once and for all prostrate, and all their works, and passes them by; he wants to knock down those whom he sees standing."* And the same author in his book on *The Singularity of Clerics* (though others say this was written by Origen). *"The devil's poisons are always skilfully contrived. Using his intelligence and cunning, he offers those committed to the life of holiness deceptive pleasures and comforts, so as to ruin them."* Thus he clearly says that whenever the Devil despairs of subverting a just man by threats and force, he will attack him with treachery and deception. This battle formation of saints may be completed by St. Peter Chrisologus, the most learned and eloquent Archbishop of Ravenna; see his Sermon 96. *"The enemy desires the commander more than the private soldier; he does not lay siege to the dead but invests the living. Thus the devil does not wish to capture sinners, whom he already has, rather he labours to seize the just. For this reason those who are more perfect are in need of more divine aid, lest they succumb to the Devil's temptations."* King David, rightly understanding this, prayed to God in Psalm 85, *"Preserve my soul, for I am holy."*

The English heretics have killed many of your perfect men, your spiritual monks and secular priests, and driven others into exile; and they have left the imperfect ones, wickedly striving to destroy those who are ambidextrous and leave the 'left-sided' ones. For after the English deserted the Catholic religion and the orthodox faith and embraced heresy and impiety, one can scarcely imagine how many evils our Irish Catholics suffered. Many of our bishops have been killed by English heretics, and the others have often been hunted with murderous intent; likewise secular priests and monks, noblemen and plebeians and countless women, and that is leaving out of account confiscation of goods, banishment, prison and the like other evils, the extent of which God knows best. I am not unaware of these things, because I have seen some of them personally, others I have heard about from trustworthy people, and others still I have read in books.

I will give some examples of those Irish prelates who, because of defending the Catholic faith, or because of the English heretics' hatred of it, were killed or driven into exile. Let me acquaint Catholic readers with a few of their names. Richard Creagh, Archbishop of Armagh and Primate of All Ireland, died in prison in London, England, for professing his faith under the heretic Queen Elizabeth. His biography is given briefly by Philip O'Sullivan in the *Compendium of the History of Catholic Ireland*, tom. 2, bk. 4 ch. 10. Archbishop Edmund Magauran, also Archbishop of Armagh and Primate, who was making his way through Ireland on horseback with two companion riders, met with a crowd of English heretic horsemen who recognised him and killed him along with his companions. (O'Sullivan op. cit. tom. 3, bk. 2 ch. 6.) Dermot Hurley, Archbishop of Cashel, an indomitable martyr, after many kinds of torture was hanged on the gallows at Dublin and died on January 7, 1584. O'Sullivan among others has written of him, op. cit. tom. 2, bk. 4 ch. 19. Patrick Hely, bishop of Moy, had his arms and legs broken with a hammer and finally was hanged and departed to Heaven in Kilmallock under William Drury, the heretical English viceroy in Ireland, with his companion Fr. Conn O'Rourke. It is worthy of being remembered that when that prelate, in the last hour of his life, already hanging on the gallows, was exhibited to the people, he summoned the heretical viceroy to the divine tribunal and ordered him to show cause, within the fifteen days following, for the unjust sentence pronounced against him as bishop and his companion the priest. This Drury did, because he died miserably on the 14th day after these two illustrious men departed together to Heaven. (O'Sullivan, tom. 2, bk. 4 ch. 11 p. 90, with references to other miracles.) Thomas Herlihy, bishop of Ross, wasted physically after a long imprisonment in London, by the Lord's bounty escaped the heretics' hands and fell asleep in the Lord in his own country. (O'Sullivan tom. 2 bk. 4 ch. 13.) Cornelius Duane, Bishop of Down and Connor, was hanged and quartered by the English heretics with his companion Fr. Patrick Luoran at Dublin on February 1, 1611, during the reign of King James, under the most impious judge Dominic Sarsfield. His biography, full of miracles and piety, has been diligently written by O'Sullivan tom. 4, bk. 1 ch. 18. Cornelius Mulryan, bishop of Killaloe, died in exile in Lisbon, Portugal, in 1617. (O'Sullivan, tom. 2, bk. 4 ch. 16.) David Kearney, Archbishop of Cashel, ended his days in exile in Bourdeaux in 1622; earlier the English heretics had put a price of 500 pounds on his head. They promised that price also for the head of Eugene Mahony, Archbishop of Dublin, but they did not obtain it. Raymond Gallagher, Bishop of Derry, at the age of eighty was struck down with the double-edged axe and had his head cut off by the English heretics. (O'Sullivan tom. 2, bk. 2 ch. 4.) Peter Lombard, Archbishop of Armagh and Primate, a noble, pious man and wise theologian, died in exile in Rome in 1624. Hugh McCaughwell, Archbishop of Armagh and Primate, Lombard's immediate successor and a Scotist theologian of great wisdom who produced learned studies on Scotus, died in exile from his country in 1626. Flaithrí Ó Maolchonaire, Archbishop of Tuam, a deeply learned and pious man, whom I once had friendly dealings with in Spain, died in exile in Flanders in 1627. Malachy Queally, Archbishop of Tuam, in this very year of 1645 was killed in Ireland by the English Parliamentarian heretics with two companions, of whom one was a Franciscan friar. These examples of our prelates, including eight archbishops and five bishops, will be sufficient.

12. Sixthly, then, and lastly, the right eye signifies faith in Christ's divinity. And this brings us to our sixth and final mystical, spiritual reason. The Seraphic Doctor Saint Bonaventure, in tom. 3 on Quinquagesima Sunday, speaks as follows. "The Devil", he says, "takes most delight in blinding the right eye, that is faith in Christ's divinity &c." And he gives as an example Naas, who sought to pluck out the right eyes of those men. And so the Devil through his heretical ministers uses mightier engines to try to wipe out the faith of Christ, knowing well that if this were removed, the other mysteries of the Catholic religion might be got rid of easily.

Ultimately the English heretics have attempted to destroy your faith, the orthodox faith of Christ (which is the foundation of the whole spiritual edifice), so that with this foundation removed the whole building would collapse and they could oppress you and keep you down.

So then, what should you do now? Certainly you should do the same as the men of Jabes: they sent envoys to all parts of Israel, built a most powerful army and elected a native of their own as king, and then vigorously took the war to their enemies, routed and scattered them and killed a great number of them (1 Kings 11). You too made a sound beginning in 1641, when you began doing likewise; continue and complete your task, because *A good start is half the work*. You have sent envoys not only into all parts of Ireland but even into other lands, where you have acquired reinforcements and large quantities of arms. You have routed, scattered and killed many of your heretical opponents in a just war for the Catholic faith, for your beloved country, for your lives and fortunes. Elect, therefore, some native-born *brother of yours*, a Catholic Irishman, as your king. Let no heretic so much as come into consideration: you should not allow that by any means, you should not permit such a monstrosity! And in this you should imitate the other nations which have their own kings, each from the given nation. Your neighbour England has had 45 of its own kings from Egbert, its first king, to Charles who is now reigning. See George Lily, *Epitome of the Kings of England*. Scotland, a still closer neighbour, had 108 kings from Fergus, its first king, to James VI who also took the throne of England, according to George Buchanan in *Catalogue of the Kings of Scotland*. Why, therefore, should Ireland (which had had 190 kings before the coming of the English, and besides is a much more distinguished kingdom and in temperateness of climate, fertility of the soil, fruitfulness and abundance leaves England and Scotland far behind) – why should Ireland be without a king of its own? Especially since one may find there many Catholic princes, nobles from many illustrious kingly families, from among whom you will easily be able to choose someone as king. And indeed, even if none of those families survived, you should choose as king some Catholic even from the plebeian population, rather than accept a foreign heretic; for the world has often seen men of inferior rank and condition rise to the purple – to crowns, sceptres, mitres, tiaras and other high dignities.

13. Among the many sins of the Jews, two in particular are noted by the Doctors and justly condemned. The first is that they demanded the most wicked robber Barabbas be let off with his life, but for Christ Our Lord, their most innocent Saviour and King, they demanded death.

"Away with this man, and release unto us Barabbas." (Luke 23, 16): they were gentle towards the miscreant of death, while being most cruel to the Lord of life. That is to say, they spurned Christ, their indigenous or native king, and demanded the foreign, pagan Caesar. *"We have no king"*, they said, *"but Caesar"*.

In both these sins the Jews violated the natural and positive law; the degree of their wickedness and perversity is sufficiently clear. I say that they broke the natural law, since they deprived Christ the Lord of his right and conferred it improperly on Caesar. They also broke the positive law which commanded that no alien be accepted as king. *"You are not to give yourselves a foreign king who is no brother of yours"* (Deuteronomy 17, 15). But those very people who professed to be the most faithful upholders of the law chose a foreigner as their king. Why did they do this? Certainly their crime brought its own punishment. They sinned by demanding a foreign king and rejecting their own: for this they were chastised by being given over to the tyranny of foreign kings, Greeks, Romans, etc. Under those they were beaten, crucified, tortured, and they have neither king nor law now.

14. Here the question arises: why did the Jewish leaders, who had the right of the sword over their own citizens, prefer to take no cognizance of the case of Christ and hand it over to a foreign judge, the pagan Pilate, rather than reserve it for themselves? The solution given by many interpreters is that those exceedingly cruel men were afraid of the power of nature in themselves, which might compel them to be more lenient towards their fellow-citizen and brother: because foreign judges are normally crueller towards those who are subjected to them. Let us hear with reverence the works of Pope St. Leo in Sermon 3 on the Passion. *"As though fearing that your savage fury would have abated if the president of your province had given judgment on your behalf, you led Jesus in chains to Pilate, and with evil yells overwhelming the timid procurator, you chose a murderer and you demanded the death penalty for the Saviour of the world."* Pope St. Leo assumes that the Jews had judges of their own race who presided in capital cases, as they previously had under Babylonian rule (Daniel 13), but not wanting to rely on the judgment of their own judges, they resorted to a foreign judge, believing that even in rabid Jewish hearts nature could inspire some leniency and clemency towards their own fellow-citizen. Accordingly they feared their ferocious resolve might be blunted and reduced by a judge of their own, and therefore, abandoning their own native judge, they proceeded to a foreigner, from whom they might expect nothing but ferocity and cruelty towards his subject.

Ah, my Irish countrymen, what bestial cruelties you have experienced from foreign judges, from English heretics! What extreme evils and slaughter your Catholic kingdom has suffered under alien heretical kings, which you would certainly not have suffered if your kings and judges had been natives and Catholics, which they properly ought to be! Dear countrymen, do not imitate the Jews by asking for a heretic and foreigner as king, but rather elect a native and a Catholic, who will be naturally clement towards you and will judge your cases rightly!

15. Saint John Chrysostom, Sermon 86, pondering the words, *"There was in the days of Herod, the king of Judea, a certain priest..."* &c. (Luke 2), continues as follows. *"Until the time of Herod the sanctity of the priesthood, the gravity of elders, held sway over the Jewish people; their code was the divine law. But Herod, coming from an alien people, invaded the kingdom, violated the priesthood, confounded order, altered customs, mixed tribes, destroyed the lines of regular descent, corrupted the people, removed all divine and human discipline."* Those are his words. That is what alien, foreign judges and kings typically do when they have power in the commonwealth. Any Irishman, as soon as he he has read and understood these words of Chrysostom's, must clearly see how aptly they may be applied to our own kingdom and commonwealth of Ireland and its people living under foreign English rule; or experience itself, the teacher of mortals, will give them its testimony.

16. The argument which I am advocating was expressed with a well-chosen example by Saint Synesius in his book *On the Kingdom*, where he warns his sovereign: *"We must not put wolves among the dogs* (guarding the flock), *because whenever they sense any foolishness or ignorance among the dogs they will immediately turn savagely upon dogs, sheep and shepherd. Nor should the Legislator give arms to those who were not born and raised under his laws and institutions, because the laws have no guarantee of goodwill from men like that."* Such are the words of that saint and learned bishop. The English heretics, like wolves, have often attacked and still continually attack our flocks and our shepherds the Catholic priests, of whom they have killed many; I have given some examples above, and O'Sullivan offers more extensive knowledge in his *Catholic History*. Those English were born and raised not under our laws, which are Catholic, but under their own, which are heretical. Let us not give them arms, rather let us seize from them those they already have; we must not suppose that there can be any guarantee of their goodwill, mercy or fidelity. They have broken their faith to you and to Jesus Christ so many times; are they going to keep faith in future, however much they promise? By no manner of means! For given that *"once bad, presumed bad always"*, at least in this type of crime (*L. filius sec. 1 et cap. semel malus de Regulis iuris in 6*., on which doctors passim), how could you not presume the English to be bad when not once but many times you have found them perfidious faith-breakers?

To this day you retain the memory of past wrongs, unless you have become weak-minded. How many times do you think Britain, or England, and its inhabitants have defected in great numbers from the Faith of Christ, from the time of its first reception until this present day when I am writing? I ask you to read Venerable Bede, priest and monk, undeniably a Catholic Englishman, of venerable antiquity, revered in religion, outstanding in wisdom, a witness superior to all exception (see the examples cited below). He does not want to defame his English fellow-countrymen by lying, nor does he wish to leave a false narrative to posterity. Read your own Philip O'Sullivan in the *Compendium of Catholic History*, tom. 2, bk. 2 ch. 1, and the *Life of Saint Patrick*, bk. 10 ch. 5, and other writers too, and you will find that eight or nine times most of the English, or a great many of them, were deserters from the Catholic faith, since they first accepted it from Joseph of Arimathea in 50 AD, as Polydore, Sanders and others relate, drawing on the ancient writer Gildas. About seven deviations of prime importance may be found in Bede's works tom. 3, *Ecclesiastical History of the English People* bk. 1 ch. 4, 6, 8, 10, 17, 21 and 22, also bk. 2 ch. 5, and bk. 3 ch. 1, 3 and 19. Bede finished his history in 731 AD, according to his own testimony in bk. 5 ch. 24. Regarding the two further defections or rebellions of the English against the Catholic faith, see O'Sullivan, Sanders and other Catholic writers. I do not deny, in fact I staunchly affirm, that in all former ages there were many Englishmen who were exemplary martyrs and holy confessors, famous for their wisdom and prudence, who defended the faith and the Catholic religion to the death. Here I am concerned only with heretics.

17. Irishmen, my countrymen, you should not expect that either now or in the future they will keep human or divine faith with you! – that people which is so fickle, so changeable and inconstant, virtually barbarian, bestial, lawless and blind, which prefers the wicked sects of Luther and Calvin and other heretics to the Catholic faith of Christ and the Apostles and the entire Catholic Church, and persuades itself and seeks to persuade others that heretics, unordained boys, and women, have been and can be Supreme Pontiffs of God's Church in temporal and spiritual affairs and defenders of the Catholic faith. In reality they were evil-doers and aggressors against that faith, who promoted and spread heresies, absurd errors and wicked sects. I speak of those who have gone to a criminal extreme of flattery by conferring on heretic kings the titles of heads of the Church and defenders of the faith.

18. St. Bernard gives thanks to the immortal God that the Angel did not receive the rule of mankind, *"Thanks to you, father of orphans and judge of foundlings."* In the opinion of many of the Fathers, the Angel had ambitions to be the ruler of men, but God did not wish to subject human beings to this most proud alien, who had said (Isaiah 14, 13): *"I will ascend into heaven, I will exalt my throne above the stars of God, I will sit in the mountain of the covenant, in the sides of the north. I will ascend above the height of the clouds, I will be like the most High. But yet thou shalt be brought down to hell, into the depth of the pit."*

O most proud Lucifer, you will be cast down into the depths of the lake of Hell, you will not be the lord of good men nor angels; for God as nature's Lord chose to take the kingship of his creatures and give it to Christ His Son rather than to the proud Angel! Bernard continues, *"I will ascend, he said, over the highest mountain and I will sit on the slopes of the north: by this he would achieve some similitude of the Highest, and just as, seated above the Cherubim, he governed all the angelic creatures, so also he would sit in the heights and govern the human race. Away with him, for he has meditated iniquity in his den. Iniquity has deceived itself. For we do not recognise any other judge but the Creator. Not the Devil but the Lord shall judge the orb of earth."* These are Bernard's words in Sermon 17 in the *Cantica,* implying that he excluded every alien and extraneous judge, and therefore considered that the affairs of men were well-conducted only if they were under the rule of a native or indigenous judge.

To apply this – we Catholics of Ireland do not want, not should we ever want or allow ourselves to be governed by a vainglorious heretic king who declares himself head of the Church in spiritual and temporal affairs and defender of the Catholic faith, when in reality he is an evil-doer and aggressor against the faith and its mysteries. What then? Let us have a Catholic king, a brother of ours, and native-born Catholic judges in temporal affairs; and in spiritual affairs the Vicar of Jesus Christ and successor of Peter, the Supreme Pontiff of Rome, and under him our Catholic ministers and priests, anathematising now and forever all heretical ministers of whatever sect as limbs of the Devil.

19. My Irish countrymen, you have excellent commanders who are versed in military affairs and extremely brave soldiers who surpass the enemy in numbers and fortitude by a large margin. Our Ireland is a highly fertile and fruitful region, with abundant resources for times of war and peace. From the yearly tributes which you have previously paid to the English heretics you will be able to make the necessary contributions to your Catholic commanders and soldiers, with a generous subsidy for the Church besides. You have many good towns surrounded by strong walls, deep trenches and powerful towers, where you will find it easy to defend yourselves and attack the enemy. You have, for example, Wexford, Waterford, Galway, Limerick, and other ports, not to mention those towns and well-equipped fortresses which are inland, some miles or leagues distant from the sea. The entire kingdom, being an island, is surrounded by the sea, so that your opponents have no means of access except through some of your ports, which you can immediately close off by constructing the necessary castles and fortifications, using your resources and your soldiers' strong hands. What remains, then? You yourselves should draw the conclusion from the premises I have laid out, while I continue my argument. There are only four or five towns, more or less, which still remain in the enemies' hands, and you can deprive them of these with the same ease and despatch with which you have seized the others.

20. Irishmen of mine, continue and complete the work already begun of defending yourselves and your liberty, and kill your heretical opponents, and drive their supporters and collaborators from your midst. Already you have killed 150,000 of the enemy during these four or five years from 1641 to 1645, when I am writing these words. Your bellowing opponents admit this openly in their writings and you do not deny it; and I believe that even greater numbers of the heretical enemy have been killed, and if only they had all been! It remains for you to kill the remaining heretics or expel them from the territory of Ireland, lest the infection of their heretical errors should spread more widely in our Catholic country. You should know that the English heretics have never obtained a victory against you without being helped by some of the Irish, so that it may truly be said: *"The English did not conquer the Irish, it was the Irish who conquered the Irish."* And so Ireland was desolated because of dissension among the Irish themselves, as in Christ Our Lord's infallible saying, *"Every kingdom divided against itself, shall be brought to desolation."* (Luke 11, 17). And in Matthew 12, 25: *"Every kingdom divided against itself shall be made desolate: and every city or house divided against itself shall not stand."*

21. Do not be afraid of the English heretics, Christ's opponents, even if at some time or other their soldiers may seem to be more numerous than yours. Consider the justice and piety of your cause and the injustice and impiety of theirs. You are fighting for the defence of the Catholic faith and of your country; they are fighting to introduce heresies and impieties. Since it is diversity of causes that produces diversity of effects, it has never happened, when Catholic sovereigns and peoples were loyal to God with all their hearts, that they failed to triumph easily over their enemies. First of all, there are the well-known victories in the Old Testament of Abraham, Moses, Joshua, Gideon, Samuel, David, Ezechiel, Hosiah, and the Maccabees. In the New Testament period Constantine the Great, who was the first of the Roman Emperors to defend the Catholic Church, defeated the tyrant Maxentius almost in the same manner as Moses did Pharaoh.

St. Augustine writes about this in Bk. 5 of the *City of God*. *"The Emperor Constantine, who did not pray to demons but worshipped the true God, was endowed with a great many worldly gifts, more than any one would dare to hope for; this single Augustus held and defended the universal Roman orb; in administration and war he achieved great results and triumphs; he was successful everywhere in suppressing tyrants. When greatly advanced in years he became ill and died of old age, and he left the empire to his sons."* In the same work, ch. 26, Augustine writes that the emperor Theodosius, because he was a Catholic, had such success in all things that even the enemy's javelins, by divine agency, were hurled back at them in battles; and Theodoretus, *lib. 5 historiae cap. 24*, adds that Saints John and Philip the Apostles, riding white horses, appeared in one of those battles and fought on the emperor's side. St. Augustine also writes of the Catholic emperor Honorius (in op. cit. bk. 5 ch. 23), that in one battle, because God was fighting on his side, 100,000 of the enemy were cut down; the enemy king and his sons were captured and killed, while the Romans did not have even a single man wounded, let alone killed.

Socrates, lib. 5 hist. cap. 18, writing of Theodosius Junior, says that when Saracen reinforcements came to support the Persians, whom his army was fighting, the Saracens were disorientated by the angels and around 100,000 of them were drowned in the Euphrates. Justinian, who had an outstanding reputation for success and wisdom, reigned most prosperously as long as he remained a Catholic. For he restored Italy, Africa and many other regions to the Roman Empire, as is clear from Evagris, lib. 4 hist. cap. 16ff. But when he became a Eutychian heretic and was planning to issue an edict decreeing that his heresy be adopted, he was promptly carried off by sudden death, and a great fear was removed from the Catholic Church. Heraclius likewise, while he was a Catholic, was victorious in war, killing Phocas, the most cruel tyrant in the Roman empire; afterwards he gained a most splendid victory over the Persians, and he took hold of the Cross of Christ when the Roman position seemed desperate. But afterwards when he became a Monothelite heretic everything turned out disastrously, and he himself died of a new disease, till then unheard of.

The Eastern emperors in general, from the time when they quarreled with Rome over sacred images and became schismatic separatists, grew steadily weaker and weaker, until eventually they lost their empire entirely. In the west, on the other hand, what is clear from history is that the emperors have had more or less success according as they have been more or less true sons and protectors of the Holy Roman Church.

Later on, in the time of Pope Innocent III, in a single battle in France a total of one hundred thousand, consisting partly of Albigensian heretics and partly of their supporters, fell at the hands of eight thousand Catholics, as Emilius writes in book 6 of the *History of the Franks*. In 1531 the Swiss fought five battles; and the Catholics always won, though in numbers and arms they were far inferior. See Cochlaeus in the *Acts of Luther* for that year. Charles V, Roman Emperor and Catholic king of the Spanish territories, claimed victory in 1547 over the Lutherans, one might say by a divine miracle. At that time almost all of Germany had defected both from the emperor and from the orthodox religion. The leaders of the breakaway were Landgrave Philip and Frederick, Duke of Saxony. But the Emperor Charles, though inferior to them in force, proved superior in strategy; he overcame the Germans' ferocious onslaughts by a policy of evasion. Then he attacked the enemy when they least suspected it and destroyed them, equally by force and good fortune, and had both the leaders put in chains, though afterwards he mercifully released them and reduced all Germany to peace and obedience.

22. In France and Belgium too the Catholics have reported many victories over the heretics, not without miraculous intervention. Indeed, the heretics scarcely ever emerged victorious when the battle was fought fairly, as the Catholic authors say in numerous places, especially Antonius Possevinus in his dispute with Niccolo Machiavelli and other atheistic politicians. Both in ancient times and during these recent years our Catholics have recorded many victories over the heretics, which is equally a misfortune for the English and a cause of jubilation for the Irish. This being so, why should the English heretics abuse our patience any longer? How long shall we be the playthings of their fury? Where will their unrestrained audacity end? And how long are we going to serve the English, whose ancestors served our own forefathers as slaves; for many Englishmen whom our ancestors captured in battle or seized from others were sold by dealers at slave-marts all over Ireland, like animals on market-day, so that there was scarcely any Irishman of moderate means who did not have one or more English slaves. Eventually all of the Irish freed their English slaves by command of the bishops at the Council of Armagh, for those venerable prelates judged that it was unworthy of Christians to keep Christian captives. From 1169 to this year 1645 when I am writing, we do not see or read that there were any Christian captives remaining in Ireland, and we hope there will be none in future. See Richard Stanihurst in *On the History of Ireland,* p. 109; Lord Peter Lombard in his *Commentary on Ireland* ch. 17 p. 252; O'Sullivan, and others.

Go into action, then, Catholic Irishmen, and bring the work you have begun to a happy end, and do not fear your heretical opponents. Fear and love God, keep his commandments and defend the faith, and he will reward you with an unfading crown of glory. May he be pleased to confer it upon me and upon you.

PERORATION

I have presented the case for the justice of the Irish Catholics against the injustice of the English heretics. And (unless I am deceived in my opinion) I have demonstrated this clearly and fully, as I intended. Finally, I have called on the Catholic Irish to choose for themselves a Catholic king who will be able to govern them in a Catholic manner in truth and justice. In doing so I had no wish whatever to offend the Most Serene King Charles of Great Britain, whose person I love and honour; however, I loathe and condemn his heretical sect. Nevertheless I ask and entreat His Royal Majesty in God's name to abjure heresy, to abandon false opinion, and to banish from his presence those flatterers and heretical ministers who propound pernicious teachings and wicked dogmas, deceiving the peoples and thrusting them into the pit of eternal perdition. If he will do so, henceforward he will hold this and other Catholic kingdoms in peace and quiet, and he will gloriously obtain an eternal kingdom hereafter. We have hopes of this from the Most Serene King's benignity, his greatness of mind, the honesty of his morals and the maturity and prudence of his judgment: were it not for the fact that error, having become imbued in him, obscured and perverted his mind, it would be easier for the King to acknowledge the plain truth than to campaign against it, in the manner of the impious heretics who sin against the Holy Spirit. Let the Most Serene King know that no one can have God as his father who is unwilling to recognise the Catholic Church as his mother – that Church which is the pillar and firmament of truth, and outside which no one can be saved, just as in the general deluge no one outside the ark was able to avoid death.

End of the Call to Action.

****

Errata principaliora corrigenda.

In paucis folijs, quæ in hoc opusculo inueniuntur, non pauci errores irrepserunt, defectu præsentiæ Authoris, & diligentiæ Impressoris. Catholicus lector inter legendum calamo corrigere poterit quos hic notamus, & alios, quos fortasse inueniet.

Pagina. 1. linea 6. alciendum, lege, alliciendum. Pag. 3. lin. 22. mudata, nudata. Pag. 5. lin. 7. scibicet, scilicet. Ibidē lin. 28. alos, alios. Pag. 14. lin. 9. accepitis, acceptis. Ibidem lin. 11. O tinam, O vtinam. Pag. 15. lin. 25. Duuedaldo, Duuenaldo. Pag. 16. lin. 8. legibus, legimus. Pag. 18. lin. 2. li b2. lib. 2. Pag. 19. lin. 11. Gracia, Garcia. Ibidem lin. 22. ab, ob. Pag. 20. lin. 10. valore, valére. Pag. 21. lin. 30. Iurestæ, Iuristæ. Pag. 23. lin. Oxomensi, Oxonensi. Pag. 24. lin. 30. vt, & Pag. 27. lin. antepenult. explicarunt, expilarunt. Pag. 31. lin. 20. voxati, vexati. Pag. 36. lin. 16. constrictu, constrictum. Ibid. lin. 22. ad asylam, ad asylum. Pag. 40. lin. 3. forsitam, forsitan. Pag. 41. lin. 16. Sūmo, Summus. Pag. 42. lin. 27. iustia, iustitia. Pag. 43. l. 11. dia, die. Pag. 45. lin. 25. precipit, præcepit. Pag. 48. lin. vlt. contractuit, contractui. Pag. 49. lin. 24. Iudicium, Iudicum. Pag. 51. lin. 23. Matinus Martinus. Pag. 53. lin. 8. interpetres, interpretes. Pagin. 59. lin. 7. in quibus causis integrum necessaria non est. Corrige. In quibus causis in integrum restitutio necessaria non est. Pag. 62. lin. 12. regulam iuris, regulam 2. iuris. Pag. 63. lin. 2. accipirit, acceperit. Pag. 65. lin. 8. diximus, duximus. Pag. 67. lin. 11. destruit, destruet. Pag. 80. lin. antep. maistas, maiestas. Pag. 86. lin. 10. æquati, æquitati. Ibid. lin. vlt. proicta, proiecta. Pag. 87. lin. vlt. Angelica, Anglica. Pag. 89. lin. 27. solene, solent. Pag. 91. lin. 22. repudiaui, repudiauit. Pag. 92. lin. 26. carnalem, carnale. Pag. 93. lin. 7. putatur, putabatur. Ibid. lin. 13. ventrē, ventris. Ibid. lin. 22. Monasterium, Monasteriorum. Pag. 94. l. 29. cōsangulneo, consanguineo. Ibid. l. 30. filios, filij. Pag. 95. l. 9. pararet, pareret. Pag. 97. l. 3. hæreicus hæreticus. Pag. 98. l. 8. vassalij, vassalli. Ib. l. 18. abedientia, ab obedientia. Ib. l. 26. anteo, antea. Pag. 99. l. 5. Angelis, Anglis. Pag. 100. l. 18. monantur, morantur. Pag. 101. l. 1. stalbitæ, stabilitæ. Ib. l. 9. ege, lege. Pag. 103. l. 12. Hibernarum, Hibernum. Ib. lin. 26. natiodis, nationis. Pag. 104. lin. 11. siuos, suos.

Original Errata Page

EXHORTATIO
AD CATHOLICOS
Hybernos Authore C. M.
HIBERNO.

IN Apoligia ſupra demonſtraui ius, totaleque dominium Regni Hiberniæ eſſe penes Catholicos, Hibernos, & nullum omnino apud hæreticos Anglos. In ſequenti exhortatione opto perſuadere Hibernis, vt hęreticorum iugum ſemel excuſſum nunquam iterum admittant, nec permittant, ſed potius eligant ſibi Regem Catholicum, & vernaculum ſeu naturalem Hibernarũ, qui eos Catholicè gubernare poſſit.

1 Præuidens olim Deus quòd populus ſuus Iſraeliticus à poteſtate Ægyptiorum ereptus (non ſine miraculis, & prodigijs) fore vt aliquando deſideraret, ac poſtularet ſibi Regem, hanc ei poſuit legem, & præceptum, in Deutoronomio capite 17. vbi ſic habet ſacer textus. *Cum ingreſſus fueris terram, quam Dominus Deus tuus dabit tibi, & poſsideris eam, habitariſque in illa, & dixeris: conſtituam ſuper me Regem, ſicut habent omnes per circuitum nationes: eum conſtitues, quem Dominus Deus tuus elegerit de numero fratrum tuorum. Non poteris alterius gentis hominem Regem facere, qui nõ ſit frater tuus.* Huc vſque verba Dei. Hęc conditio, vt Rex ſit frater, hoc eſt, eiuſdẽ natiodis, & non alienigena, pręcipuè à Deo poſita eſt, ob periculũ Idolatrię, peruerſionis, falſæque de Deo doctrinæ, & cul-

O tus,

Page from the original

Additional Details

Complete translation

The first thing to be said is that this translation is complete. For a lazy translator it was tempting to cut the extended discussions of property rights, just possession, prescription etc., and King Naas's threat to pluck out the right eyes of the Jabesites. Even the biographies of the rogue monarchs, though they had plenty of human interest, made for a lot of work. (I was grateful that O'Mahony hadn't had the *Annals of Ulster* at his elbow in Lisbon, or his catalogue of deposed kings would have been longer still.)

However, as the publisher pointed out to me, with a book as controversial as this you need to do all or nothing. What you personally find tedious may be full of insights for somebody else. And of course, if you cut the book you will be accused of trimming it to suit the way you are interpreting it. So then, critics take note: the entire book is here, complete and unexpurgated!

O'Mahony's sources

O'Mahony's sources are precisely referenced, making the task easy for anyone who might wish to follow them up. The books he refers to are overwhelmingly in Latin, but he also cites published works in Spanish (*Breve relación de la presente persecucción en Irlanda*, Seville 1619 – referred to as 'The Relation of Ireland', Call to Action, Sec. 8), Portuguese (Francisco Velasco de Gouveia, *Justa acclamação do serenissimo Rey de Portugal: D. João o IV*, Lisbon 1644 – Argument 64, 74, 98) and English (John Davies, *A Discovery of the True Causes why Ireland was Never Entirely Subdued*, London 1612 – Argument 47). Moreover, he refers the reader to histories in Irish which he personally does not have access to at the present time (Argument 95).

What to do with those long lists of Latin book titles? Mostly I decided not to translate them, with a few exceptions: some, like the *City of God*, are famous, others, like O'Sullivan Beare's *Catholic History*, are of special interest. Where I do translate a title, this does not necessarily mean that a published English version exists. On the other hand, it is likely that some of the relevant passages from Suarez, Molina etc. have appeared in English translation, but tracking those down is a job for another editor.

Though he gives as much in the way of reference as a reasonable reader can demand, O'Mahony does not have a rigorous procedure. For Bible citations he mostly gives chapter and verse, occasionally just the chapter. Editions and page numbers of certain books are specified, chapter number for others. When condensing longer accounts he may just give the book's title or the author's name – "Suetonius" will do if he's writing about Roman emperors. He gives no source at all for some of his poetic quotations, and I have identified those below ("Poetic Sources Used in the *Argument*") to the best of my ability.

If one compresses a book of, say, sixty chapters, e.g. Suetonius on Caligula, down to one paragraph, naturally much will be lost. Taking that into account, one can say that O'Mahony does his summaries competently. Almost all of his materials for the first eight emperors selected, Julius to Domitian, will be found in Suetonius (but see below, *Errors in the Text*). His scandalous account of Henry VIII is taken from *Rise and Growth of the English Schism* by Nicholas Sanders (though since I haven't seen the original but only the English translation, I'm in some doubt about whether Henry was supposed to be drunk from breakfast time or only from dinner time). I would expect that elsewhere too O'Mahony's accounts will prove to be more or less accurately taken from the sources given.

Canon Law and Civil Law When citing canon law O'Mahony only gives abbreviated references to the relevant books, because all who were interested would have known his source. It was the *Corpus Iuris Canonici*, issued in three enormous volumes by Pope Gregory XIII in Rome in 1582: (1) *Decretum Gratiani*; (2) *Decretales D. Gregorii Papae IX* (also called *Liber Extra*); and (3) *Liber Sextus Decretalium*. These three volumes have been put on the internet by the University of California, Los Angeles (UCLA). Anyone who wants to explore O'Mahony's use of his legal sources will be able to negotiate this territory better than I am and will not require my help.

But let's take, for example, the principle which is cited in Sections 56 and 68 of the Argument: that someone who gains possession in bad faith cannot acquire prescriptive rights, whatever the time elapsed (*Possessor malae fidei ullo tempore non prescribit*). For this he refers the reader to *regula secunda iuris in 6.*, "the second rule of law in 6.", – "6." being his way of referring to the *Liber Sextus*. On page 781 of the *Liber Sextus* we find the passage referred to: *Num malae fidei possessor ullo tempore, id est, qui in aliquo tempore possessionis habet malam fidem, non praescribit.* – It will be seen that O'Mahony does not quote slavishly, but shears off the quibbling definition and gives the substance.

O'Mahony draws on the Roman Civil Law in the same fashion. The catchphrase cited in the Foreword to Catholic Readers, "he who avails of his own right does no one any injury" (*nulli facit iniuriam, qui iure suo utitur*), is from the Digest of the Emperor Justinian. (*Digest* 50. 17; 55; 155.1).

Errors in the text In the hurry of compiling his book the author made a number of slips. Some of these are trivial, e.g. the passage in *Breve relación* (about the ancient schools in Cashel, Lismore, Armagh, etc.)

which is relevant to the point he is making in Call to Action, Section 8, is in the body of the text on page 4 running on to page 5 – not in side-note 8 on page 4, which is about Irish saints in Europe. A few of the other errors may be worth noting.

In Section 1 of the Argument, calculating the length of time since the Milesians came to Ireland, he mixes up the Year of the World with the year B.C., making the period much longer than it was meant to be. O'Mahony maintains that ''most computists'' believed the world was created in 3949 B.C. This was the estimate given by the great Protestant chronologer Joseph Scaliger (Anthony T. Grafton, 'Joseph Scaliger and Historical Chronology: the Rise and Fall of a Discipline', *History and Theory* 1975 p. 171). I cannot say whether some of the Catholic chronologers accepted his reckoning (the most famous of them, the Jesuit Denis Pétau, apparently did not).

Matthew 18, 70 (Argument 46) should be *Matthew 18, 17. Ecclesiastes 19, 16* (Argument 75) should be *Ecclesiastes 10, 16. Luke 2* (Call to Action 15) should be *Luke 1, 5.* Flaithrí Ó Maolchonaire died in Madrid in 1629 (cf. Hazard p. 153), not in Flanders in 1627 (Call to Action 11).

O'Mahony also says that the Roman emperor Tiberius poisoned his son Drusus (Argument 83). Here he seems to have confused Tiberius with Sejanus, the commander of his Pretorian Guard and Drusus's rival to succeed him as emperor, who committed this poisoning, according to Suetonius (II, p. 49) and other Roman sources. The statement that in the Milesian Conquest Eremon took the southern half of Ireland, while Eber got the northern half (Argument 1), is copied from Cambrensis; O'Mahony wouldn't have wanted to court controversy on this, but it was supposed to be the other way round (cf. Keating Vol. 2 p. 96). The reader may come upon other things of this kind.

Douai-Rheims Bible Except in one case, I have not tried to standardise quotations with existing English translations, although there are many published versions e.g. of Augustine's *Confessions* and *City of God.* The exception is the Bible. It would be unfair to associate the author with English translations of the Bible which he would have rejected, and there is only one such translation which we can be certain he would have accepted: the Douai-Rheims Catholic version of 1588-1610.

I have used this for all Biblical quotations. The language is old-fashioned, but it is clear and directly corresponds to O'Mahony's Latin Vulgate version, whereas modern Catholic translations do not. For example, take the Argument's first quotation from the Psalms, *Narraverunt mihi iniqui fabulationes* (Section 7). Douai-Rheims translates: *"The wicked have told me fables".* The Jerusalem Bible's equivalent is: *"The arrogant have told foul lies about me".* Whatever the merits or demerits of this version, it is out of touch with Conor O'Mahony's Latin and what he wants to convey.

The Douai-Rheims Bible is identical with the Latin Bible which O'Mahony used as regards the numbering of Psalms and naming of books. However, both of them differ from the King James Bible and from modern Catholic Bibles. For most of the Psalms the King James version has the Douai-Rheims number plus one, e.g. Psalm 105 in Douai-Rheims is Psalm 106 in King James. Also the *1st Book of Kings*, mentioned several times in the Call to Action in connection with the Jabesites, is the *1st Book of Samuel* in the King James and modern Catholic Bibles.

Theory of Royal Legitimacy Much could be said on this subject, but I leave that to the next editor. It is clear that O'Mahony and his Spanish and Portuguese mentors were at odds with prevailing political doctrine not only in Protestant England but also in Catholic France. Peter Brooke has pointed out that O'Mahony's long lists of authorities do not include Jean Bodin. This is because Bodin held incompatible views on kingship.

Francisco Velasco de Gouveia (*Justa acclamação,* p. 57) cites Bodin as holding an opinion opposite to his own, namely that *"vassals can do nothing against their natural kings, even if those are evil, cruel and tyrannical"* (citing *de Republica lib. 5 cap. 5*). This is the doctrine of absolute monarchy plainly stated, and in France other doctrines were considered subversive. It was not for nothing that Suarez's *Defense of the Catholic Faith* was burned in Paris in 1614. If O'Mahony by any chance had published his book on French territory, he might not have been treated as gently as he was by the Portuguese.

Suarez, O'Sullivan Beare and de Sousa In mainstream academic literature, e.g. university law textbooks, Francisco Suarez is often referred to as one of the fathers of modern international law. Philip O'Sullivan Beare is probably heavily indebted to him for his ideas of international right and wrong, though it's not so easy to prove. One can show this conclusively in Conor O'Mahony's case because he gives his sources. But O'Sullivan Beare doesn't bother with the scholarly apparatus, so the very probable influence of Suarez on him also, or whoever originally formulated the arguments that he uses, is not explicitly acknowledged. This question (opened up by Clare Carroll) could profitably be explored further. Also, since many of the arguments used by Antonio de Sousa, etc. had been applied to Ireland 20 years earlier by O'Sullivan Beare, the question arises whether Portugal's independence literature is in some way indebted to the Irish.

Poetic Sources Used in the *Argument*

1. (Foreword to Catholic Readers) "What breaks or sustains..."
   Frangit, et attollit vires in milite causa,
   Quae nisi iusta subest, excutit arma pudor.
   Propertius, *Elegies* IV vi. 51-2.
2. (Argument 13) "Oh, if only then..."
   O utinam tunc, cum Regna Anglica classe petebat,
   Obrutus insanis esset adulter aquis.
   Ovid, *Heroides* Ep. I, 5-6 – slightly modified, since in the original the adulterer Paris is heading for Lacadaemon (Sparta).
3. (Argument 76) "To my mind, we may use deceit..."
   Iudice me fraus est concessa repellere fraudem;
   Armaque in armatos sumere iure sinunt.
   Ovid, *Art of Love* III, 491-2.
4 (Argument 92) "Putting aside the name whore, ..."
   Nomine deposito pellicis, uxor erit.
   Ovid, *Heroides* Ep. IX, 132.
5. (Argument 92) "Juno was Jove's sister and wife ..."
   Iuno Iovis soror, atque uxor, verum Anna Bolena,
   et spuria Henrici filia, et uxor erat.
   Based on Ovid, *Metamorphoses* III, 266.
6. (Argument 92) "One single year..."
   Millia dena unus templorum sustulit annus;
   quam timeo in poenas, vix satis unus erat.
   Jacques Marchant's *Hortus Pastorum*, published in the 1620s, has these lines in a later edition, Lyons 1668, on page 187. *Quidam*, "someone", is said to have written them about the seizure and destruction of Catholic churches in 16th century England.

Editions of O'Mahony's book

There are two editions of O'Mahony's work, the original 'Frankfurt' edition of 1645 and the Dublin edition of 1827. The first edition has a page of errata, all of them corrected within the text of the second edition, which otherwise seems to reproduce everything faithfully, including obvious typos. It is easier to get copies of the second edition, so I have used it (comparing it with the original) for the purposes of my own work.

Finally, any Latinists who want the amusement of finding errors in my translation have their task made easy, thanks to the New York City Library and the firm of Google. The 1827 edition of O'Mahony's original has been put on the internet. It will be found at Google Books under the title *Disputatio Apologetica de Iure Regni Hiberniae.*

BIBLIOGRAPHY

(A = Aubane, D = Dublin, L = London, O = Oxford)

Aiazza, G:*The Embassy in Ireland of Monsignor G. B. Rinuccini*, tr. Annie Hutton (D 1873).
Breve Historia: *Breve Historia de el Origen y Progressos de el Collegio de los Irlandeses de Sevilla.* NLI MS 16,236.
Breve Relación: *Breve Relación de la Presente Perseccución en Irlanda* (Seville 1619).
Byrne, Matthew: *Ireland Under Elizabeth* (D 1903). – Translation of the Elizabethan chapters of Philip O'Sullivan Beare's *Historiae Catholicae Hiberniae Compendium.*
Callaghan, John:*Philopatri Irenaei Vindiciae Catholicorum Hiberniae* (Paris 1650).
Canny, Nicholas: "What Really Happened in Ireland in 1641?" – Included in *Ireland from Independence to Occupation* ed. Jane Ohlmeyer (Cambridge 1995).
Canny, Nicholas: *Making Ireland British* (O 2005).
Carroll, Clare: *Circe's Cup. Cultural Transformations in Early Modern Ireland* (Cork 2001).
Carte, Thomas: *Life of the Duke of Ormond* (O 1851).
Castlehaven, Earl of (James Touchet): *Memoirs of the Earl of Castlehaven* (D 1815).
Casway, Jerrold L.: *Owen Roe O'Neill and the Struggle for Catholic Ireland* (Philadelphia 1984).
Comm. Rin.: *Commentarius Rinuccinianus* ed. Joannes Kavanagh (D 1932 -)
Conlon, J. P.: *Some Notes on the Disputatio Apologetica.* Bibliographical Society of Ireland Vol. VI No. 5 (D 1955).
Cruz, Antonio: *Papéis da Restauraçao* Vol. 1 (Porto 1967).
Curtin, Benvenuta: 'Dominic O'Daly: An Irish Diplomat'. *Studia Hibernica* 5 (1965).
da Costa, Manuel Gonçalves: *Fontes Inéditas Portuguesas para a História de Irlanda* (Braga 1981).
de Gouveia, Francisco Velasco: *Justa acclamação do serenissimo Rey de Portugal: D. João o IV* (Lisbon 1644, repr. Lisbon 1846).
de Sousa de Macedo, Antonio: *Juan Caramuel Lobkowitz* (L 1642). Included in: Cruz, Antonio.
de Sousa de Macedo, Antonio: *Lusitania Liberata* (L 1645).
Feiritéar, Piaras: *Dánta Phiarais Feiritéir* tr. Pat Muldowney (A 1999).
Finegan, Francis: *Conor O'Mahony (1594-1656), Separatist* (D 1991?) = Ó Fionnagáin, Proinnsias.
Franco, Antonio: *Synopsis Annalium Societatis Jesu in Lusitania* (Lisbon ? 1726)
Gerald of Wales, see Giraldus Cambrensis.

Gilbert, John T.: *A Contemporary History of Affairs in Ireland* (D 1879-1881).
Gilbert, John T.: *History of the Confederation and the War in Ireland* (D 1882-91).
Giraldus Cambrensis: *Expugnatio Hiberniae* (The Conquest of Ireland) ed. & tr. A. B. Scott and F. X. Martin (D 1978).
Giraldus Cambrensis: *The History and Topography of Ireland* tr. John J. O'Meara (L 1982).
Haicéad, Pádraigín: *Filíocht Phádraigín Haicéad* eag. Máire Ní Cheallacháin (D 1962).
Hardiman, James: *History of Galway* (D 1820).
Hazard, Benjamin: *Faith and Patronage. The Political Career of Flaithrí Ó Maolchonaire* (D 2010)
Hogan, Edmund: *Chronological Catalogue of the Irish Members of the Society of Jesus from the year 1550 to 1814* (D n.d.)
James I, King of England: *A Premonition to All Most Mighty Monarchs, Free Princes and States in Christendom* (L 1609).
Keating, Geoffrey: *Foras Feasa ar Éirinn* ed. David Comyn, P. S. Dinneen (L 1901-1914).
Lombard, Peter: *De Regno Hiberniae Sanctorum Insula Commentarius* (D 1868).
Lynch, John: *Cambrensis Eversus* ed. & tr. Matthew Kelly (D 1851-2).
Mac Aingil, Aodh: *Scáthán Shacramuinte na h-Aithridhe* eag. Cainneach Ó Maonaigh (D 1952).
Mac an Bhaird, Gofraidh Óg: *Do dhusgadh gaisgeadh Gaoidheal*, NLI MS G167 p. 325 (unpublished).
Mac an Bhaird, Gofraidh Óg: *Deireadh flaithis ag féin Gall*, NLI MS G167 p. 340 (unpublished)
Mac an Bhaird, Gofraidh Óg: *Cia ler múineadh Maol Mhuire*, A II 20 (Stoneyhurst), p. 144; RIA 23 G 24, p. 414, etc. (unpublished)
Mac an Bhaird, Gofraidh Óg: *Treoin an cheannais clann Dálaigh,* ed. Owen McKernan, Éigse Vol. 5 (1945).
Mac an Bhaird, Somhairle: *Neart gach tíre ar Thír Chonaill*, eag. Eoin Mac Cárthaigh, Ériú 1999.
Mac an Bhaird, Uilliam Óg: *Dia libh, a uaisle Éireann*, ed. Eoin Mac Cárthaigh, Ériú 2002.
Mac Curtain, Margaret:' Dominic O'Daly, an Irish Agent of the Counter-Reformation'. *Irish Historical Studies* 1966-7.
MacGeoghagan, Abbé: *The History of Ireland* tr. Patrick O'Kelly (D 1844).
MacKenna, Lambert (ed.): *iomarbháigh na bhFileadh* (L 1920).
MacNeill, Charles: *Publications of Irish Interest Published by Irish Authors on the Continent of Europe prior to the Eighteenth Century* (D 1930).
Minahane, John: *The Christian Druids: on the filid or philosopher-poets of Ireland* (D 1993, repr. D 2008).

Minahane, John: *The Contention of the Poets* (Bratislava 2000).
Minahane, John: 'Ireland's War Poets 1641-1653'. In *The Poems of Geoffrey O'Donoghue/Dánta Shéafraidh Uí Dhonnchadha an Ghleanna* ed. J. Minahane (A 2008).
Minahane, John: 'Conor O'Mahony and his Argument for Irish Independence', *O'Mahony Journal* Vol. 33 (2010).
Moore, Séamus P.: 'Ever MacMahon, Soldier Bishop of the Confederation of Kilkenny', *Studies* 1951, 1952.
Moran, D. F.: (ed.) *Spicilegium Ossoriense* (D 1874).
Nicholls, Kenneth: 'Kinelmeaky and the Munster Plantation', *O'Mahony Journal* Vol. 10 (1980).
Ó hAnnracháin, Tadhg: "Though Hereticks and Politicians should misinterpret their goode zeal". Included in: *Political Thought in Ireland in the 17th Century* ed. Jane Ohlmeyer (Cambridge 2000).
Ó hAnnracháin, Tadhg: *Catholic Reformation in Ireland: the Mission of Rinuccini* (O 2002)
Ó Buachalla, Breandán: 'James Our True King': the ideology of Irish royalism in the 17th century'. Included in:*Political Thought in Ireland since the Seventeenth Century* ed. D. George Boyce et al. (L 1993).
Ó Buachalla, Breandán: *Aisling Ghéar* (D 1996).
Ó Conchubhair, Toirdhealbhach: A *óga do ghlac na h-airm*. In 'Toirdhealbhach Ó Conchubhair' eag. Cuthbert Mhág Craith, *Father Luke Wadding* ed. Franciscan Fathers, Killiney (D 1957).
Ó Criagáin, Seán: *A Mhurchadh Uí Bhriain tá fiadhach ar Ghaodhaluibh*. In: Minahane 2000.
O'Daly, Dominic: *The Rise, Increase and Exit of the Geraldines* tr. C. P. Meehan (D 1878, Latin orig. Lisbon 1655).
Ó Fiaich, Tomás:' Republicanism and Separatism in the 17th Century'. *Léachtaí Choluim Chille* II, 1971 (Maynooth 1971).
Ó Fionnagáin, Proinnsias: 'Conor O'Mahony (1594-1656), Separatist', *O'Mahony Journal* Vol. 16 (1993). = Finegan, Francis.
Ó Gallchóir, P.: 'Tirconaill in 1641'. In: *Father John Colgan*, ed. Terence O'Donnell (D 1959).
O'Mahony, Conor:*Disputatio Apologetica de Iure Regni Hiberniae, pro Catholicis Hibernis adversus haereticos Anglos* (Lisbon 1645, repr. D 1827.RIA MS 24 O 8 is a manuscript copy made in Lisbon in 1845 for R. A. Madden, with introduction and some documents).
O'Mahony, Edward: 'West Cork and the Elizabethan Wars 1565-1603', *The Irish Sword* 2004.
O'Mahony, John: 'A History of the O'Mahony Septs of Kinelmeky and Ivagha'. *Journal of the Cork Historical and Archaeological Society* 1907/8/9.
Ó Maolchonaire, Flaithrí: *Desiderius* ed. T. F. O'Rahilly (D 1942).

Ó Mealláin, Toirdhealbhach: 'Cinn Lae Ó Mealláin' eag. Tadhg Ó Donnchadha, *Analecta Hibernica* 3 (1931).
Ó Murchadha, Diarmaid Óg: F*uasgail solas-ghort Chonaire, a rí Chárthaigh*. In: Minahane A 2008.
O'Sullivan Beare, Philip: *Historiae Catholicae Hiberniae Compendium* (Lisbon 1621).
Prestage, Edgar: *The Diplomatic Relations of Portugal with France, England and Holland from 1640 to 1688* (Watford 1925)
Prestage, Edgar: *Frei Domingos do Rosário, Diplomata e Político {1595-1662}*(Coimbra 1926)
Sander, Nicholas: *Rise and Growth of the English Schism* tr. David Lewis (L 1877).
Schüller, Karin, *Die Beziehungen zwischen Spanien und Irland im XVI und XVII Jahrhundert* (Münster 1999)
Stanihurst, Richard: *De Rebus In Hibernia Gestis* (Brussels 1584).
Suarez, Francisco:*R. P. Francisci Suarez Opera Omnia* t. 24 (Paris 1859). = *Defensio Fidei Contra Errores Sectae Anglicanae* (Coimbra 1613).
Suetonius, Gaius:Suétone, *Vie des Douze Césars* I-III, texte ét. et tr. par Henri Ailloud (Paris 1989-1993).
Walsh, Peter: *The History and Vindication of the Loyal Formulary or Irish Remonstrance* (L 1674).

NOTES

PAGE 6

"The tired and inaccurate gibe": *Contested Island: Ireland 1460-1630* (O 2009) p. vii.

"Deliberate changes of focus": ibid. p. 3.

Macaulay on the Gaels: Thomas Babington Macaulay, *History of England from the Accession of James II* (New York 2009) pp. 100-3. ('The Hostility of Races: The Aboriginal Peasantry')

PAGE 7

Diarmaid Óg... Gofraidh Óg: Cf. bibliography, 'Ó Murchadha, Diarmaid Óg'; 'Mac an Bhaird, Gofraidh Óg'.

PAGE 8

O'Mahony's first language Irish: cf. Argument Sec. 9, *Omelachlen Hibernice dicimus* ("Ó Maoilsheachlainn, as we say in Irish").

PAGE 9

Ever MacMahon as rebel strategist: Moore 1951 pp. 327-8.

Éire arís d'fhilleadh orthaibh : NLI MS G167 p. 326.

Aithbheódhadh glóire Gaoidheal:Haicéad p. 34 (l. 30).

Do chongmháil cháigh na gcreideamh...: NLI MS G167 p. 325.

PAGE 10

Diarmaid Óg... defeat the Puritans: Minahane A 2008 p. 82.

"In all of the documents...": Paul Walsh, *Irish Leaders and Men of Learning through the Ages* (D 2003) p. 433.

Uilliam Óg... Ireland's martyrdom: NLI MS G167 p. 321 (v. 8); ed. Eoin Mac Cárthaigh, *Ériú* 2002 p. 96.

PAGE 12

King John ordered suppression: J.T. Gilbert CHA I pp. 739.

English ambassador's complaint to Pope: Comm. Rin. III pp. 37-8, 41. Book burned in Kilkenny: Walsh p. 739.

Eoghan Ruadh accused: Aiazza p. 322.

Nine sermons preached: Walsh p. 739.

Mayor/burgesses' of Galway: Hardiman pp. 123-4.

Rinuccini accused: Walsh p. 739.

"Barbarous and bloodthirsty": Comm. Rin. III p. 37.

PAGE 13

Born 1594: Hogan p. 29; Finegan p. 1.

Born Muskerry: Walsh p. 736 (information from Bishop Patrick Plunkett, who had met O'Mahony in Lisbon). Jesuit sources say he was from Desmond, or Munster: Finegan p. 1.

Geoffrey O'Donoghue... O'Mahony genealogy:RIA MS 24 P 8 p. 252.

O'Mahonys' history: Mainly taken from O'Mahony J. 1907/8/9, plus articles in the *O'Mahony Journal*.

Conor from one of three septs: O'Mahony J. 1909 p.17.

PAGE 14

Geraldines' rebellion: cf. O'Daly and Byrne.

O'Mahonys' lands forfeited: O'Mahony J. 1908 p.140.

O'Neill's staunch allies: O'Mahony J. 1909 pp.7-12.

Still holding out in 1603: Edward O'Mahony, "West Cork and the Elizabethan Wars 1565-1603", *The Irish Sword* 2004, p. 157.

Muskerry O'Mahonys received pardons: See *The Fiants of Elizabeth* e.g. Nos. 6467, 6485, 6539, 6764.

"Let them consult their own histories...": Argument Sec. 95.

PAGE 15

F. Ón Cháinte at Curravurdy: T.F. O'Rahilly, 'Irish Poets, Historians and Judges in English Documents 1538-1615", Proceedings of the Royal Irish Academy Vol 35C (1921-4) p. 109.

Ovid, Virgil taught in poetic schools: Apart from the evidence in poetry, there is e.g. the testimony of an informed outsider, Matthew de Renzi: Brian Mac Cuarta, 'Matthew de Renzi's letters on Irish affairs', *Analecta Hibernica* 34 (1987) p. 147.

Poetic passages mainly by Ovid: cf. *Additional Details,* 'Poetic Sources Used in the *Argument'.*

PAGE 16

O'Mahony in Seville about 1614: Finegan p. 1.

O'Rourke incited to attack Saxons: *The Poems of Tadhg Dall Ó hUigín* ed. Eleanor Knott (L 1922) pp. 108ff., esp. p. 111.

Fearann cloidhimh críoch Banbha: ibid. pp. 120ff.

Kings God's viceregents: A *Premonition to All Most Mighty Monarchs,* opening paragraph.

King a little god on earth: B*asilikon Doron* (L 1603). *On a King's Christian Duetie towards God. The First Booke*, first paragraph.

PAGE 17

Kingship given by people: Suarez lib. 3 cap. 2,3.

"If the king turns...": ibid. lib. 3 cap. 3 s. 3 (p. 213).

James: "licence for sedition": cited ibid. lib. 3 cap. 3 s. 1 (p.213). James's exact words were:

> "And as for the setting up of the people above their own natural king: he (Bellarmine) bringeth in that principle of sedition, that he may thereby prove, that kings have not their power and authoritie immediately from God, as the Pope hath his; for every king (saith he) is made and chosen by his people; nay, they do but transferre their power in the king's person as they do notwithstanding retain their habitual power in their own hands, which upon certain occasions they may actually take to themselves again. This I am sure is an excellent ground in divinity for all rebels and rebellious people, who are hereby allowed to rebel against their princes; and assume liberty unto themselves, when in their discretions they shall find it convenient."
>
> (A Premonition to All Most Mighty Monarchs)

Suarez says, not so: ibid. s. 2 (p. 213).

Pope might depose kings: ibid. lib. 3 cap. 23.
Heretical king endangered subjects: ibid. lib. 3 cap. 23 s. 21 (p. 321).
Tyrant king legitimately killed: ibid. lib. 6 cap. 4.

PAGE 18

Killing of Caesar: ibid. lib. 6 cap. 4 s. 7 (p. 677).
Legitimate king killed by due process: ibid. lib. 6 cap. 4 s. 2,3,4 (p. 675-6).
"Suarez specifically argues...": Carroll p. 130.
"Though in the beginning...": Suarez lib. 6 cap. 12 s. 15 (p. 735).
Pope congratulated James: Moran pp. 109-111.

PAGE 19

Suarez says James legitimate: Suarez lib. 6 cap. 4 s. 2 (p. 675).
Heretic king not immediately deposed: ibid. lib. 6 cap. 4 s. 14 (p. 680).
"King James, who denies...": ibid. lib. 3 cap. 23 s. 1 (pp. 314-5).
"*As deimhin...*": Ó Maolchonaire p.128.

PAGE 20

Mac Aingil on King James:Mac Aingil pp. 166, 167-8, 170.
Irish learning famed... Druids, Bards: B*reve Relación* p. 5.
Irish saints in Europe: ibid. pp. 7-8.
Conditions of Adrian's Bull broken: ibid. pp. 20-21.
O'Sullivan Beare: Adrian's grant void: c.f. O'Sullivan Beare tom. 2 bk. 1 ch. 7.
On the Laws/O'Sullivan: Carroll pp. 127-8.

PAGE 21

Irish College at Seville:Details in *Breve Historia.*
Seville hit by plague in 1616: Fernand Braudel, *The Structures of Everyday Life* (L 1985) Vol. 1 p. 84.
"Sweet harmony was disturbed": B*reve Historia* p. 10.
Ordained 1619: Finegan p. 2.
"Fr. Conor O'Mahony...":*Breve Historia* p. 10; cf. Finegan p. 2.
"Of choleric temperament": Finegan p. 8.
Suggested O'Mahony resented Jesuit takeover: ibid. p. 2.
O'Mahony's association with Ó Maolchonaire:Call to Action, Sec. 11.
Ó Maolchonaire's conflicts with Jesuits:Hazard p. 39, and elsewhere.
"Such student trouble was endemic": Finegan p. 2.

PAGE 22

"With this cruel edict...":*Breve Relación* p. 36.

PAGE 23

O'Mahony cites Breve Relación:Call to Action, Sec. 8 ("*Cum antea optimis abundaret Academiis, ut fuerunt Armachana, Casselensis, Dublinensis, Lismorensis, Rossensis…*"; compare *Breve Relación* pp. 4-5, "*demas de las universidades domesticas que en Ibernia mesma florecian, como la Casselense, Lismorense, Armacana...")*
Breve Relación circulated widely:Enrique Garcia Hernán in: *Irish Communities in Early-Modern Europe* ed. Thomas O'Connor & Mary Ann Lyons (D 2006) p. 267.
Conway's History of Ireland: 'Conway, Richard', *Oxford DNB*, article by Thomas

O'Connor.
Conall MacGeoghagan cites *Compendium*: *Annals of Clonmacnoise* ed. D. Murphy (D 1896) p. 25.

PAGE 24
"A valuable corrective...":c.f. 'O'Sullivan Beare, Philip' in *Oxford DNB*.
"In my three...": O'Sullivan Beare tom. 4 intro. and lib. 1 cap. 1, pp. 266-7.
"When originally...": ibid. p. 267.

PAGE 25
"to invite...": ibid. p. 270-1.

PAGE 26
"Parliament –the word...": ibid. pp. 306-7.
"The viceroy therefore...": ibid. p. 308.

PAGE 27
"Whenever the viceroy...": ibid. pp.308-9.
"Our parliamentarians decided...": ibid. p.313.
"One of three...": ibid. p. 315.

PAGE 28
"Nevertheless, the heretics...": ibid. p. 317.
"Neither by force...": ibid. p. 318.
"to give all...": ibid.
"Men of different...": ibid. p. 319.

PAGE 29
"You delegates...": ibid. p. 323. An English version of the speech, broadly the same, is in *Calendar of Carew MSS* Vol. 6 (L 1873) pp. 288-292.

PAGE 30
"What reason...": ibid.

PAGE 31
"Astonished by their response...": ibid. p. 327.

PAGE 34
Letter translated in full: C.P. Meehan, *The Fate and Fortunes of Hugh O'Neill* (D 1886) pp.395-7.
Ó Buachalla's picture of Irish attitudes: In Ó Buachalla 1993.

PAGE 35
"Flaithrí Ó Maolchonaire...": O'Mahony C. (Call to Action, Sec. 11)
"Although he was a Franciscan...": *Archivium Hibernicum* 3 (1914) p. 297.
Ó Maolchonaire... 1627 invasion plan: Ó Fiaich pp. 74-81; Hazard pp. 144-6.
Lombard's faction unable to block rivals: Ó hAnnracháin 2002 p.61; Hazard p. 139.

PAGE 36
Ó Maolchonaire associated with O'Sullivan Beare:Hazard p. 140; Carroll p. 116.
Iomarbhágh na bhFileadh: cf. MacKenna, and Minahane 2000.

O'Sullivan Beare admired Mac Bruaideadha: Philip O'Sullivan Beare, *Zoilomastix* ed. Thomas O'Donnell (D 1960) p. 94.

PAGE 37

"Taken as a whole...": *Contested Island 1460-1630* (O 2009) p. 388.
"The kings of England...": O'Sullivan Beare pp. 339.
"I will not list...": ibid. pp. 333-4.

PAGE 38

O'Mahony's Jesuit profession: Finegan p. 2.
Cornelio de São Patricio: Walsh p. 736; da Costa p. 57.
Studied at Coimbra, Evora: da Costa p. 57.
1623 in Lisbon: Finegan p.2.
O'Mahony wanted for Ireland: ibid.

PAGE 39

Sent to Azores about 1626: ibid. p. 3.
"A professorship in the Azores...": ibid.
Taught moral theology... islands: Franco p. 316.
"A river of burning sulphur...": da Costa p. 57.
"A great solace...": Franco p. 316.
Tractatus Theologici...: da Costa p. 58.
Irish College 1636-1641: da Costa p. 57.
Asked to give opinions: ibid. p. 58.

PAGE 40

"The greatest seventeenth century exponent...":Jane H. Ohlmeyer, *The Origins of Empire* ed. Nicholas Canny (O 1998) p. 137, citing *The Earl of Strafford's Letters* Vol. 1 ed. V. Knowler p. 450.
Síorchumhdach reacht gan riaghail: Attrib. Flann Mac Craith in 23 F 16 p. 156. Printed in *Dánta do chum Aonghus Fionn Ó Dálaigh*, ed. Lambert MacKenna p. 74.
Irish-language testimony under James, Charles:Ó Buachalla's views on this are in *Aisling Ghéar* pp. 50-4.
Rebel MacSwineys in 1641:Ó Gallchóir pp. 79-81.

PAGE 41

Atáid, gá truaighe pudhar: A II 20 (Stoneyhurst) p. 144; RIA 23 G 24 p. 414.
Plot against King John IV:Details from Mac Curtain pp. 393ff.

PAGE 42

Antonio de Sousa: 'Sousa de Macedo, Antonio de', *Dicionário Histórico*; Cruz, Introduction, passim.
De Sousa cited: Argument 64, 70, 74, 96.
"With his accustomed erudition": Argument 64.
Local Catholics... Mass at his home:Prestage 1925 p. 106.

PAGE 43

"Even if the king...": de Sousa 1642 p. 254.
Settlement 143 years after Flood: de Sousa 1645 p. 53.
First settlement of Ireland: Argument 1; Keating Vol. 1 p. 156.

PAGE 44

"Ridiculus Homunculus": de Sousa 1645 p. 459.
English Catholics pro-Spanish: ibid. pp. 621-2.

PAGE 45

Army diverted from Ireland: ibid. p. 622.
"For five years...":Prestage 1925 p. 107.
"The old English histories": ibid. p. 108.
Suarez quoted repeatedly: e.g. de Gouveia pp. 45, 46, 47, 48, 53, 54, 55, 56, 57, 58, 59 (on some of those pages twice).

PAGE 46

"You will hardly find...": de Sousa 1645 p. 366.
Damaging attack on O'Mahony: Ó hAnnracháin 2000 p. 161.
O'Sullivan on Surrender and Regrant: O'Sullivan Beare pp. 75-6 (tom. 2 lib. 2 cap. 3).

PAGE 47

Get rid of obligation... confession: de Sousa 1642 p. 252.
O'Daly recruiting in Ireland for Spain: Prestage 1926 pp. 2-3.

PAGE 48

King wanted a palace coup:MacGeoghagan p. 563, and many recent writers.
Rebels allegedly claimed royal commission:e.g. TCD Depositions 839:3b; 828:208b, cited by Ó Buachalla 1996 p. 104. Thomas FitzPatrick, *Waterford in the Civil War* (Waterford 1910) p. xviii argues that this was merely puritan propaganda, without a factual basis.

PAGE 49

"In the year 1641...": Callaghan Vol. 1 pp. 1-2.
"Throughout the rest...": ibid. pp. 3-4.

PAGE 50

Walsh... essentially Gaelic movement: Walsh p. 739.
Rebellion part of three kingdoms' strife: Ó Buachalla 1996 p. 104.
Quotes agitational poets: ibid. pp. 108-110.

PAGE 51

Do dhuisgeadh gaisgeadh Gaoidheal...: NLI MS G167 pp. 325-6.

PAGE 52

Defensive, preventive uprising:Ó Buachalla 1996 p. 106.
Slipped out of leaders' control: ibid. p. 107.
Rabble with unbridled millennial aims: ibid.
Maguire, McDermott, Nugent, MacMahon: in depositions cited ibid. pp. 113-4.

PAGE 53

War being turned into religious war: ibid. p. 108.
MacCarthy explained why he joined rebellion: Patrick MacCarthy, 'The 1641 Rebellion in Cork to the Battle of Liscarroll, 3 September 1642', *The Irish Sword* Vol. 22 (2001) p. 377.
Rabble wanted own king: Ó Buachalla 1996 pp. 113-4.

O'Donnell, MacCarthy king of Ireland: See bibliography, first two poems listed for Gofraidh Óg Mac an Bhaird (to Seán Mac Aodha and an Calbhach Ruadh respectively) and Diarmaid Óg Ó Murchadha's poem (to Donough MacCarthy).
Leaders/rabble distinction over-simplified: Ó Buachalla 1996 pp. 114-5.
Distinction identifies two large groups: ibid. p. 115.

PAGE 54

Diarmaid Óg implies support for king: Minahane A 2008 p. 82.
Aithbheodhadh glóire Gaoidheal:Haicéad p. 34 (l. 30).
Deireadh flaithis ag féin Gall: NLI MS G167 p. 340.

PAGE 55

Confederate Oath: Callaghan Vol. 1 p. 6.
Ó Buachalla omits third principle: Ó Buachalla 1996 p. 111.
Catholics' 1644 demands: Gilbert 1882-91 Vol. III p. 128.

PAGE 56

(James) "treated the Catholics...": Aiazza p. xxx.
"And on the marriage...": ibid. pp. xxx-xxxi.

PAGE 57

"Wise and far-seeing" Strafford: ibid. p. xxxii.
"The rising, at first...": ibid. p. xxxv.

PAGE 58

"I must observe...": ibid. p. xl.
"You will endeavour...": ibid. p. xl-xli.
"This may be done...": ibid. p. lix.
"A second way...": ibid.

PAGE 59

"That the Irish army...": ibid. p. lix-lx.
Italian original the same: "*...senza paura d'esser tagliati in pezzi dei medesimi Inglesi che servono il Re.*" G. Aiazza, *Nunziatura in Irlanda di Monsignor Gio. Battista Rinuccini* (Firenze 1844) p. lix.
"That permission and authority...": Aiazza p. lx.

PAGE 60

Irish troops in Britain outside laws of war: Micheál Ó Siochrú, 'Atrocity, Codes of Conduct and the Irish in the British Civil Wars 1641-1653', Section II, *Past and Present* 2007.
"His Holiness, sending...": Aiazza p. lxi.
"It may be that at present...": ibid. p. lxi-lxii.
"Let him promote...": ibid. p. liv.

PAGE 61

De Sousa... Ireland to Philip: da Costa pp. 291-2.
Rinuccini welcomed: Callaghan Vol.1 p. 14.

PAGE 62

"But the two less apparent...": Aiazza pp.133-4.

PAGE 63

Tadhg Mac Dáire's victory poem:MacKenna Poem 29.

PAGE 64

Sean-Éireannach: Ó Mealláin p. 44.
Ever MacMahon too politicised: Aiazza p. 141.
"It is evident that...": ibid. p.138.

PAGE 66

"Freed from the thought...": ibid. p.145.
"As there is no human force...": ibid. pp.145-6.

PAGE 67

King rejected emancipation... politically impossible: Callaghan Vol. 1 p. 10.
Callaghan on separation/transferring: Callaghan Vol. 2 pp. 39-40.
"Besides his illustrious...": ibid. pp. 22-3.
Ormond has never expelled Catholics etc.: ibid. pp. 64-67.

PAGE 68

"After deliberating...": Aiazza p. 135.
"He has therefore heaped": ibid. pp. 136-7.

PAGE 69

O'Mahony in good health: Finegan p. 3.
"We know simply...": ibid.
O'Sullivan omits pre-Milesians: O'Sullivan Beare p. 32.
Portugal settled 143 years after Flood: de Sousa 1645 p. 53.
Keating on Gerald's pre-Milesian history:Keating Vol. 1 p. 75, pp. 146-152.
Scurrilous biography by Sanders: cf. bibliography, Sander, Nicholas..
Most Milesian kings killed their predecessors:Keating Vol. 3 p. 264.

PAGE 72

Lord Justices... 150,000 killed: Actually 154,000; cited in Ó hAnnracháin 2000 p. 163. This figure had been around since 1642: Brian Mac Cuarta in B. Mac Cuarta (ed.), *Ulster 1641. Aspects of the Catholic Rising* (Belfast 1993) p. 7.
"(O'Neill) had done many things...": Callaghan Vol. 1 p. 2.
"It is very certain...":Castlehaven p. 23.
"It is clear from the depositions...": Domhnall Mac an Ghalloglaigh, 'The 1641 Rebellion in Leitrim', Breifne Vol. 2 No. 8 p. 454.
Massacres and counter-massacres: Ó Gallchóir pp. 85-88; Canny 1993 pp. 33-35.
Estimates by cooler heads: W. E. H. Lecky, *A History of Ireland in the Eighteenth Century* Vol. 1 (L 1913) pp. 78-82.
"This passage has been unfairly...": O'Mahony J. 1909 p. 18.

PAGE 73

Comment taken from Suetonius: Suetonius III p. 38.
Spenser, OK to create famine: A *View of the Present State of Ireland*, ed. Andrew Hadfield and Willy Maley (O 2003) pp. 100-104.
Nothing against Catholic Englishmen: Argument 99.
Quotes Supreme Council: ibid.
No animus against King Charles: Peroration.

No malice against King of Spain: de Sousa 1645 "To the Reader", 3rd/4th pages.

PAGE 74

"Who financed the production...?": Finegan p. 8.
Examen Juridicum: MacNeill p. 19.
King's statement... printed in Portugal: Gilbert CHA I p. 739.
No information in German sources:The most extensive sources of information on German printers of the 17th century (Christoph Reske, *Die Buchdrucker des 16. und 17. Jahrhunderts im deutschen Sprachgebiet* (Wiesbaden 2007); the internet source www.vd17.de) have no mention of a Frankfurt printer called Bernardus Govranus or anything similar. Dr Claudia Bubenik of the Abteilung für Handschriften und Alte Drucke, Bayerische Staatsbibliothek, has informed me that there is no independent information on the *Argument* from German sources: E-mail, March 31, 2009.
"From the typography...": RIA MS 24 O 8, Intro.
Argument's watermark: Conlon p.72.

PAGE 75

"The pages of this book...":1645 edition, *errata principaliora corrigenda.*
"In some copies...": MacNeill p. 28.
"Certainly he selected...": O'Mahony J. 1909 p. 17.

PAGE 76

Ursulanus:MacNeill p. 19.
Dermot O'Mahony of Farnanes: O'Mahony J. 1909 p. 15.
Condemned April 6, 1647: Gilbert CHA I p. 739.
List of quotations from Argument: ibid. pp. 667-9.
"Many copies in the Nuncio's time...":Walsh p. 739.

PAGE 77

"Chester, a maritime town...": Callaghan Vol.1 pp. 22-3.

PAGE 78

"The most eminent...": ibid. p. 19.
"Any kind of war...": ibid. pp. 19-20.
"The whole province of Ulster...": Aiazza p. 196.
"And if they had a leader...": ibid.

PAGE 79

M'úidh leat...: Feiritéir p. 14.
Bádar Comhairli Cilli Cainnigh...: Ó Mealláin p. 44.

PAGE 81

Spiritual terror and Spanish gold: Callaghan Vol. 1 p. 34.
"That O'Neill's march...": Aiazza p. 226.
Preston's intrigue with Ormond: *Clanricarde Letter-Book 1643-1647* ed. John Lowe (D 1982) pp. 332 ff.
"Hatred of these Ulster troops...": Aiazza p. 309.

PAGE 82

"O'Neill had given proof...": ibid. p. 282.
Más é an leoghan... : Feiritéar p. 54; Minahane A 2008 pp. 119-122.

Intended Glanmorgan would be viceroy: Aiazza p. 206.
"Only meagre forces...": Callaghan Vol.1 p. 41.

PAGE 83

Agitation in Munster army: I reviewed this in Minahane A 2008 pp. 181-4, believing there was no other account in English. However, there is a fairly full account in Carte Vol. 3 pp. 312-5.
"Seeking to render...": Comm. Rin. II p. 611.
Complaint about pro-Butler agitation: ibid. p. 612.
"Within the space...": Callaghan Vol.1 p. 43.
"That most mild man...": ibid.
"The forces which support...": Comm. Rin. II pp. 617-9.

PAGE 86

Kilkenny Council's complaint: pp. 620-1.
"The Nuncio acceded...": ibid. p. 621.
"Suspicions and quarrels...": ibid.

PAGE 87

"Enthusiasm for O'Mahony":Thomas O'Connor, *Irish Jansenists 1600-1670* (D 2008) p. 272.
Strenuissimus dux: Argument 44.
Obthar libh...: Haicéad p. 42, l. 131.
Um chogadh do dhéanamh...: ibid. p. 38.
Gan chosg don chogadh...: ibid. p. 55, ll. 167-8.

PAGE 88

"The Ormond faction...": Aiazza p. 258.
"The clergy, by rejecting...": ibid. p. 265.
"It seems as if...": ibid.
"The Viceroy, informed...":Callaghan Vol. 1 pp. 44-6.

PAGE 89

"That the Irish, having perfidiously...":Richard Cox, *Hibernia Anglicana* Vol. 2 (L 1690) p. 172. (Reign of Charles I)

PAGE 90

"The Conde de Oñate...":Schüller p. 70, citing AGS, E. leg. 3017, 18.4.1647 and 16.7.1647.
"In the space...": Callaghan Vol. 1 p. 51.
"(Eoghan Ruadh) had been summoned...": ibid.

PAGE 91

Eoghan Ruadh played Fabius:Casway pp. 198 ff.
Gidh nár dheachas...: Ó Conchubhair p. 425. See also Minahane A 2008 pp. 187-91.
"The ill-willed...": Aiazza pp. 321-2.

PAGE 92

"In order to bring round...": ibid. p. 322.
Rinuccini denied Eoghan Ruadh sought kingship: ibid. p. 354.
Rinuccini... secret mandate for separation: Comm. Rin. III pp. pp. 37-8.

Protecting John Bane: Walsh p. 739.
"We do utterly detest...": Hardiman p. 124.
"He hath by manifold arguments...": Walsh p. 738.

PAGE 93

O'Mahony denies implications: Argument 99-100.
"Made the Confederates...": Carte Vol. 2 p. 17.
"(If) the heretical King...": Aiazza p. 322.

PAGE 94

"After I had shewn...": Walsh p. 739.

PAGE 95

"I, N.N., swear...": Callaghan Vol. 1 p. 6.
Eoghan Ruadh insisted he meant loyalty: Cited by Aidan Clarke in *Plantation to Partition* ed. Peter Roebuck (Belfast 1981) p. 29.

PAGE 96

What happened to Wallenstein: Golo Mann, *Wallenstein* Vol. 2 (Berlin 1989) pp. 409 ff.
Sanders... Pope's suggested motive: MacGeoghagan p. 240.
"Did the Pope make...": O'Sullivan Beare p. 66.
"The Kings of England...": ibid. p. 339.
Attempt to entrap Eoghan Ruadh: CR III p. 525.

PAGE 97

"That did not trouble...": Callaghan Vol.1 pp. 51-2.
A Mhurchadh Uí Bhriain...: Minahane 2000 p. 64.

PAGE 98

Ná bí meallta...: ibid. pp. 64-6.
Féach id dheoidh...: ibid. p.64.

PAGE 99

Inchiquin's settlements with South Munster septs: Minahane A 2008 pp. 191-2.
All O'Donnells made bargain:Ó Gallchóir p. 103.
Do shénsat Pádraig ar mhír: *Studies* 1949 p. 342, ed. Lambert MacKenna.

PAGE 100

Another poem to an Calbhach Ruadh: *Deireadh flaithis ag féin Gall.*
Dearna chorcra... : Mac an Bhaird, Gofraidh Óg 1945 p. 12.
Sluagh longlíonmhar Lonndan: ibid. p. 20.
Ionann breathnughadh... : ibid. p. 18.

PAGE 101

Tirconaill regiment assigned to New Ross:Herbert P. Hore, *History of the Town and County of Wexford* Vol. 5 (L 1906) pp. 280, 292-3.
Fighting all over Ireland for Tirconaill:Mac an Bhaird, Somhairle p. 49 (vv. 20, 21, 23).
"During 1648-9 Eoghan Ruadh...": Ó Fiaich p. 85.

PAGE 102

Ó Mealláin denounces massacres: Ó Mealláin p. 34.

Recent study of conduct of war: Micheál Ó Siochrú, 'Atrocity, Codes of Conduct and the Irish in the British Civil Wars 1641-1653', *Past and Present* 2007.
Charles wanted Ormond to deal (1644): Callaghan Vol. 1 p. 10.
King's promise to cheat Catholics (1648): C.V. Wedgwood, *The Trial of King Charles* (L 1965) p. 19, citing *Clarendon State Papers* II p. 442.

PAGE 103

"A more zealous Protestant": MacGeoghagan p. 569.
If Ormond remained Catholic one year: Moran p. 371.
"Your excellency's speedy arrival...": ibid. p. 369.
"Will not only call...": ibid. p. 370.

PAGE 104

O'Daly writing to King John: da Costa pp. 306-7.
'The government and settlement...": Curtin p. 101, citing Carte papers xxix 506, addend. 642, new pagin.

PAGE 105

Ormond was indignant: ibid., citing Carte papers ibid.
"Far be it from me...":O'Daly pp. 7-8.
"It is manifest...": ibid. p. 11.
"After the English...": ibid. p. 15.
"I have not the heart...": ibid. p. 21.

PAGE 106

De Sousa: O'Daly's greatest achievement: Curtin pp. 111-2.
"...greater care than is expected": Gilbert CHA I p. 738.
King to Jesuit head: da Costa pp. 59-60.
"Excellent intelligence...": Finegan p. 8.
During 1650s... expert opinions: da Costa p. 58.
Plunkett given copy: Walsh p. 736.
O'Mahony's 'second tractate': da Costa pp. 59-60, citing *Cartes d'El Rei João IV* p. 276.

PAGE 107

"Portuguese translation" of *Argument*:Prestage 1925 p. 100; da Costa pp. 59-60.
O'Mahony died 1656: Finegan p. 8.
Associated opponents with O'Mahony: Callaghan Vol. II p. 39.
Worried about being associated: John Lynch, *Cambrensis Eversus* Vol III (D 1853) pp. 67-69.
"This book, so barbarous...": Earl of Clarendon, *The History of the Rebellion and Civil War in Ireland* (L 1756) p. 91.
Burning book... 1666: Walsh pp. 740-2.
Reprinted by Mullen: Conlon p. 76.

PAGE 108

"a fitting example...":RIA MS 24 O 8, Intro.
Madden found *Argument* reprehensible: ibid.
Finegan... core in O'Mahony's work: Finegan p. 9.
"Why should Ireland... ?": Call to Action 12.

INDEX

Distributed by Athol Books

On-line sales of books,
pamphlets and magazines:

https://www.atholbooks-sales.org

Illustration from original edition

D

and
Morag Styles

Illustrated by
Sue Martin

PUBLISHED BY THE PRESS SYNDICATE OF THE UNIVERSITY OF CAMBRIDGE
The Pitt Building, Trumpington Street, Cambridge, United Kingdom

CAMBRIDGE UNIVERSITY PRESS
The Edinburgh Building, Cambridge CB2 2RU, UK
40 West 20th Street, New York, NY 10011-4211, USA
10 Stamford Road, Oakleigh, Melbourne 3166, Australia
Ruiz de Alarcón 13, 28014 Madrid, Spain

www.cup.cam.ac.uk
www.cup.org

Project editor: Claire Llewellyn

First published 1991

Reprinted 1998, 1999

Printed in the United Kingdom at the University Press, Cambridge

Typeset in concorde

A catalogue record for this book is available from the British Library.

Library of Congress Cataloguing in Publication data applied for

ISBN 0 521 39954 8 paperback

Acknowledgements

'Since He Weighs Nothing' from *About the House* by W. H. Auden, reprinted by permission of Faber & Faber Ltd and Random House Inc. copyright © 1965, 1964, 1963, 1962, 1959; 'I Wake Up' from *Quick Let's Get Out of Here* by Michael Rosen, André Deutsch 1983, reproduced by permission of Scholastic Ltd; 'Lines' from *Magic Mirror* by Judith Nicholls, reprinted by permission of Faber & Faber Ltd; 'Some Days' from *Rabbitting On* by Kit Wright. William Collins & Sons Ltd, 1978 reprinted by permission of the author; 'The Hawk' from *Bunch Grass* by Robert Sund, reproduced by permission of the University of Washington Press; 'Shapes and Actions' from *When I Dance* by James Berry, London 1988, copyright © James Berry 1988, reproduced by permission of Hamish Hamilton Ltd; 'Dream Variations' copyright © 1926 by Alfred A. Knopf Inc. and renewed 1954 by Langston Hughes, reprinted from *Selected Poems of Langston Hughes*, by permission of Alfred A. Knopf Inc. and David Higham Associates Limited; 'Listen' from *Two by Two* by John Cotton and Fred Sedgwick, Mary Glasgow Publications Ltd, reprinted by permission of the author; 'Where Winter Begins' from *The Poet Reclining: Selected Poems 1962–1980* by Ken Smith, Bloodaxe Books 1982; 'Wind and Silver' from *The Complete Poetical Works of Amy Lowell* by Amy Lowell, copyright © 1955 by Houghton Mifflin Co., copyright © 1983 renewed by Houghton Mifflin Co., Brinton P. Roberts and G. d'Andelot Belin, Esquire, reprinted by permission of Houghton Mifflin Co. All rights reserved; 'The Dream of the Cabbage Caterpillars' copyright © Libby Houston 1993 from *All Change*, Oxford University Press, reprinted by permission of the author; The Literary Trustees of Walter de la Mare and The Society of Authors as their representatives for 'Dream Song' from *Peacock Pie* by Walter de la Mare; 'Bully Night' from *Sky in the Pie* by Roger McGough, reprinted by permission of The Peters Fraser & Dunlop Group Ltd on behalf of Roger McGough; 'Falling Asleep' from *Open the Door* by Siegfried Sassoon copyright 1918, 1920 by E. P. Dutton. Copyright 1936, 1946, 1947, 1948 by Siegfried Sassoon. Used by permission of Viking Penguin, a division of Penguin Putnam Inc. Reprinted by permission of George Sassoon; 'On Not Counting Sheep' from *Collected Poems* by Helen B. Cruickshank, Gordon Wright Publishing, reprinted by permission of Alfred C. Hunter; 'Shepherd's Night Count' from *Dragon Night* by Jane Yolen, Metheun Children's Books. Reprinted by permission of Curtis Brown Ltd. Copyright © 1980 by Jane Yolen.

Every effort has been made to reach copyright holders; the publishers would be glad to hear from anyone whose rights they have unknowingly infringed.

Contents

Since He Weighs Nothing

Since he weighs nothing,
Even the stoutest dreamer
Can fly without wings.

W H Auden

Phansie

And Phansie, I tell you, has dreams that have wings,
And dreams that have honey, and dreams that have stings,
Dreams of the maker, and dreams of the teller,
Dreams of the kitchen, and dreams of the cellar.

Ben Jonson

EXTRACT FROM **Alice in Wonderland**

'Come and look at him!' the brothers
cried, and they took one of Alice's hands,
and led her up to where the king
was sleeping . . .
'He's dreaming now,' said
Tweedledee: 'and what do you think
he's dreaming about?'
Alice said, 'Nobody can guess that.'
'What about *you*!' Tweedledee exclaimed,
clapping his hands triumphantly. 'And
if he left off dreaming about you,
where do you suppose you'd be?'

Lewis Carroll

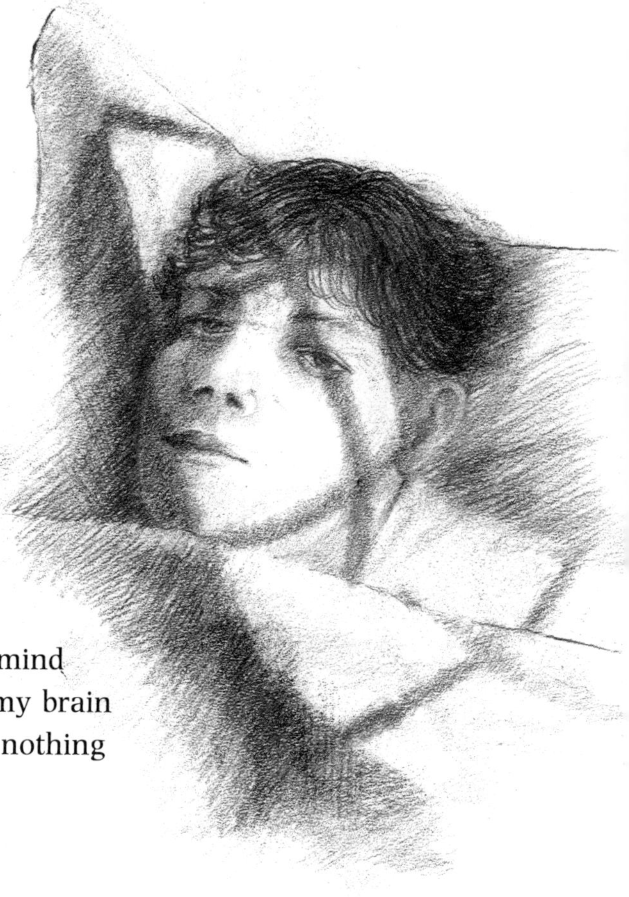

I Wake Up

I wake up
I am not me
I am bodyless
I am weightless
I am legless
I am armless
I am in the sea of my mind
I am in the middle of my brain
I am afloat in a sea of nothing

It lasts for one flicker
of one eyelash

and then
once again
I am my full heaviness
I am my full headedness
I am my full bodyness
Here.
Hallo.

Michael Rosen

Lines

I must never daydream in schooltime.
I just love a daydream in Mayshine.
I must ever greydream in timeschool.
Why must others paydream in schoolway?
Just over highschool dismay lay.
Thrust over skydreams in cryschool.
Cry dust over drydreams in screamtime.
Dreamschool thirst first in dismayday.
Why lie for greyday in crimedream?
My time for dreamday is soontime.
In soontime must I daydream ever.
Never must I say dream in strifetime.
Cry dust over daydreams of lifetimes.
I must never daydream in schooltime.
In time I must daydream never.

Judith Nicholls

Some Days

I didn't find it interesting,
Listening,
I didn't find it interesting,
Talking,
So I left the house – I went miles and miles –
And I didn't find it interesting,
Walking.

I didn't find it interesting,
Reading,
I didn't find it interesting,
Writing,
So I left the house – I went miles and miles –
And that wasn't terribly
Exciting.

I watched my sister playing
Patience,
But I didn't find it interesting,
Scoring,
So I left the house – I went miles and miles –
And that was *extremely*
Boring.

I didn't find it interesting,
Telly,
There wasn't much on
That night,
So I sat in a chair and I went to sleep,
A dull old day
All right.

Kit Wright

The Hawk

Afternoon,
with just enough of a breeze
                    for him to ride it
lazily, a hawk
sails still-winged
up the slope of a stubble-covered hill,
so low
he nearly
touches his shadow.

Robert Sund

Shapes and Actions

Like roundness or the rotating globe
head and wheel and ball make me think and sigh

Like gliding swim of a small or giant fish
drifting moon makes me think and sigh

Like a tramp's hunt in a waiting dustbin
a fox's city-search for food makes me think and sigh

Like a sloth's slow-motion climb
creeping-in sea-tide makes me think and sigh

Like humans and animals everywhere asleep
inner work of winter trees makes me think and sigh

Like unknown red wings taking off in flight
flame-leaps in open space make me think and sigh

James Berry

Dream Variations

To fling my arms wide,
In some place of the sun,
To whirl and to dance
Till the white day is done,
Then rest at cool evening
Beneath a tall tree
While night comes on gently,
  Dark like me, –
That is my dream!

To fling my arms wide,
In the face of the sun,
Dance! whirl! whirl!
Till the quick day is done,
Rest at pale evening . . .
A tall, slim tree . . .
Night coming tenderly,
  Black like me.

Langston Hughes

Listen

Silence is when you can hear things.
Listen:
The breathing of bees,
A moth's footfall,
Or the mist easing its way
Across the field,
The light shifting at dawn
Or the stars clicking into place
At evening.

John Cotton

Where Winter Begins

Birds fly south, a saw
yells through the woods.
Night is coming, water
chirrs in the stream.

I want to be an animal
between one sound
and another. At evening
I come to a river, the reeds
like the dark in my own skull.
I want to sleep, to be still
away from the villages,
night is coming.

Image of bird in the sky,
image of leaf, shadow on shadow.
Darkness begins in the trees
and the tight maize heads.

Burrowed out of the owl's look
I dream the shush of grass
in the night fields, sleeping.

Ken Smith

Wind and Silver

Greatly shining,
The Autumn moon floats in the thin sky;
And the fish-ponds shake their backs and
  flash their dragon scales
As she passes over them.

Amy Lowell

The Dream of the Cabbage Caterpillars

There was no magic spell:
  all of us, sleeping,
dreamt the same dream – a dream
  that's ours for the keeping.

In sunbeam or dripping rain,
  sister by brother
we once roamed with glee
  the leaves that our mother

laid us and left us on,
  browsing our fill
of green cabbage, fresh cabbage,
  thick cabbage, until

in the hammocks we hung
from the garden wall
came sleep, and the dream
that changed us all –

we had left our soft bodies,
the munching, the crawling,
to skim through the clear air
like white petals falling!

Just so, so we woke –
so to skip high as towers,
and dip now to sweet fuel
from trembling bright flowers.

Libby Houston

Les Silhouettes

The sea is flecked with bars of grey,
The dull dead wind is out of tune,
And like a withered leaf the moon
Is blown across the stormy bay.

Etched clear upon the pallid sand
The black boat lies: a sailor boy
Clambers aboard in careless joy
With laughing face and gleaming hand.

And overhead the curlews cry,
Where through the dusky upland grass
The young brown-throated reapers pass,
Like silhouettes against the sky.

Oscar Wilde

Dream Song

Sunlight, moonlight,
Twilight, starlight –
Gloaming at the close of day,
And an owl calling,
Cool dews falling
In a wood of oak and may.

Lantern-light, taper-light,
Torchlight, no-light:
Darkness at the shut of day,
And lions roaring,
Their wrath pouring
In wild waste places far away.

Elf-light, bat-light,
Touchwood-light and toad-light,
And the sea a shimmering gloom of grey,
And a small face smiling
In a dream's beguiling
In a world of wonders far away.

Walter de la Mare

Dreams

Here we are all, by day; by night we are hurled
By dreams, each one into a several world.

Robert Herrick

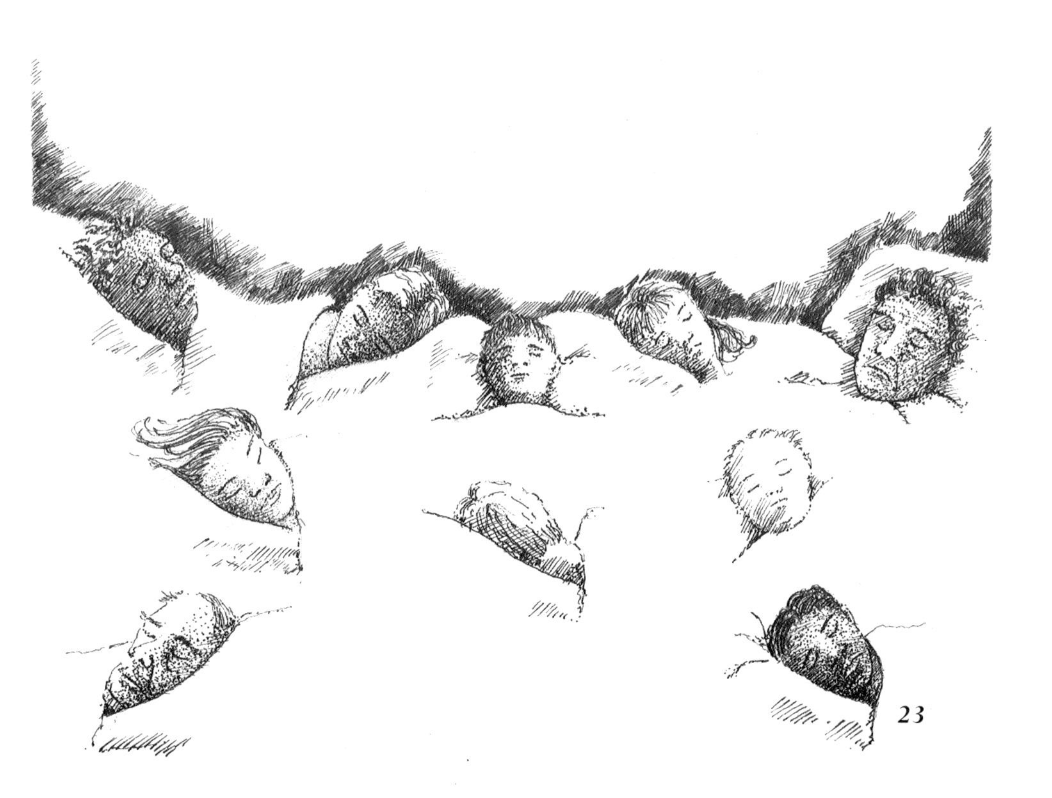

Escape at Bedtime

The lights from the parlour and kitchen shone out
  Through the blinds and the windows and bars;
And high overhead and all moving about,
  There were thousands of millions of stars.
There ne'er were such thousands of leaves on a tree,
  Nor of people in church or the Park,
As the crowds of the stars that looked down upon me,
  And that glittered and winked in the dark.

The Dog, and the Plough, and the Hunter, and all,
And the star of the sailor, and Mars,
These shone in the sky, and the pail by the wall
Would be half full of water and stars.
They saw me at last, and they chased me with cries,
And they soon had me packed into bed;
But the glory kept shining and bright in my eyes,
And the stars going round in my head.

Robert Louis Stevenson

Bully Night

Bully night
I do not like
the company you keep
The burglars and the bogeymen
who slink
while others sleep

Bully night
I do not like
the noises that you make
The creaking and the shrieking
that keep me
fast awake.

Bully night
I do not like
the loneliness you bring
the loneliness you bring
The loneliness, the loneliness
the loneliness you bring,
the loneliness you bring
the loneliness, the

Roger McGough

EXTRACT FROM **The Tempest**

Be not afeard: the isle is full of noises,
Sounds and sweet airs that give delight and hurt not.
Sometimes a thousand twangling instruments
Will hum about mine ears; and sometimes voices
That, if I then had waked after long sleep,
Will make me sleep again; and then, in dreaming,
The clouds methought would open and show riches
Ready to drop upon me, that, when I waked,
I cried to dream again.

William Shakespeare

Castles in the Air

My thoughts by night are often filled
With visions false as fair:
For in the Past alone I build
My castles in the air.

I dwell not now on what may be.
Night shadows o'er the scene.
But still my fancy wanders free
Through that which might have been.

Thomas Love Peacock

Falling Asleep

Voices moving about in the quiet house:
Thud of feet and a muffled shutting of doors:
Everyone yawning. Only the clocks are alert.
Out in the night there's autumn-smelling gloom
Crowded with whispering trees; across the park
A hollow cry of hounds like lonely bells:
And I know that the clouds are moving across the moon;
The low, red, rising moon. Now herons call
And wrangle by their pool; and hooting owls
Sail from the wood above pale stooks of oats.
Falling asleep . . . the herons, and the hounds . . .
September in the darkness; and the world
I've known; all fading past me into peace.

Siegfried Sassoon

On Not Counting Sheep

Seven apple trees, a willow and a pine
At the top of the garden, that makes nine.
A privet and a cypress, a winter flowering cherry,
A birch and a rowan, green tassel, crimson berry.
A juniper, a hazel, a laurel and a gean.
A yellow rose, a plum tree, with no plums to glean.
I'm counting my trees; no, I'm not counting sheep –

A rowan at the gateway,

I'm ____ falling ____ asleep

Helen B Cruickshank

Shepherd's Night Count

One ewe,
One ram,
Two sheep,
One lamb,
Three sheep,
One flock,
Four gates,
One lock,
Five folds,
One light,
Good dog,
Good night.

Jane Yolen